ARTS LIBRARY

SERGEI OBRAZTSOV

My Profession

Fredonia Books
Amsterdam, The Netherlands

My Profession

by
Sergei Obraztsov

ISBN: 1-58963-456-X

Copyright © 2001 by Fredonia Books

Reprinted from the 1950 edition

Fredonia Books
Amsterdam, the Netherlands
http://www.fredoniabooks.com

All rights reserved, including the right to reproduce this book, or portions thereof, in any form.

CONTENTS

	Page
WHY AND FOR WHOM I WROTE THIS BOOK	9

Chapter One
    FIRST CONTACTS WITH ART 13

Chapter Two
    PENCIL AND BRUSH . . . 19

Chapter Three
    THE PATH TO THE STAGE . . . 27

Chapter Four
    ON THE EVE OF A ROLE 38

Chapter Five
    A ROLE 48

Chapter Six
    LESSONS OF THE HUMAN THEATRE . 57

Chapter Seven
    COUNTERPOINT . . . 86

Chapter Eight
    PLAGIARY 99

Chapter Nine
    HOME THEATRICALS 114

Chapter Ten
    IN FOREIGN LANDS 136

Chapter Eleven
    POSITIVES AND NEGATIVES . . . 148

Chapter Twelve
    PARODY . . . 164

Chapter Thirteen
    THEME AND FORM . 176

Chapter Fourteen
    CONTACT WITH MY AUDIENCES 210

Chapter Fifteen
    ON REREADING THE BOOK 243

*To the Memory of My Father,
Academician Vladimir Obraztsov*

WHY AND FOR WHOM I WROTE THIS BOOK

I am accustomed to facing the public.

I have been producing in the theatre for eighteen years and I have been performing at concerts for over twenty-five.

My contacts with my audiences are to be numbered not in tens or hundreds, but in thousands; all the same whenever I arrive for a concert the first thing I do is to peep through a chink in the curtain and try to make out what sort of audience, what sort of judge, I have to face that evening.

A book is not a play or a concert, but from the first day of its appearance on the shelves of the book-shops I, as its author, have submitted myself to the judgement of the public—but with this difference, that I shall not hear the manifold reaction to my performance at once as I do in the concert hall.

The stir of discontent or applause, the bored coughs or the merry laughter will reach me only many days after the publication of the book. By then I can't correct anything, I can do nothing but curse myself for having written unconvincingly here, boringly there and simply wrong elsewhere.

The curtain of time hangs between me and my readers.

It is very difficult to find a chink in that curtain. Still more to see anybody through it. These very lines I am now writing, sitting at home in Nemirovich-Danchenko Street in Moscow, may be read in other cities and at other times thousands of miles away, many years later.

Nevertheless, I must form some opinion about whom I am writing for: a book is not a monologue, not a conversation with oneself. It is part of a dialogue. It is a conversation with readers. And you cannot converse with someone unless you can see or sense whom you are talking to.

Well, whom am I talking to now? Whom do I imagine is holding this book in his hands?

My profession is the puppet theatre but I do not want my readers to be confined to my fellow-puppeteers, I want there to be actors and producers in other genres of the theatre, cinema workers, dramatists, artists, all who are interested in art, though art may not be their main profession.

For me puppets were never an end in themselves.

Unless it were possible to lay on the frail shoulders of a puppet that honourable task, that obligation to be of some real service to society that lies on the shoulders of the "major arts" I should not want to write about puppets. I should not be interested in them, for then they would have turned either into casual "childish fun" or into extravagant grown-up pranks.

My profession did not take shape all at once. I was educated to be an artist and before running a puppet theatre spent fourteen years as an actor, first in opera and then at a legitimate theatre. I shall write about that too, because I have a feeling for art as a whole and the similarities in the creative process of different branches of art seem to me no less important than their differences. And it is precisely of creative processes, of the "kitchen" of art that I wish to write in this book, of my personal experience, and of the general conclusions that every producer, actor or artist inevitably draws from his experience, which gradually become laws applicable, maybe, only to himself.

The validity of these laws, moreover, has a time limit and much that seemed clear begins to grow doubtful and to give way to something new.

Ten years have passed since my *Actor with Puppets* was published.

In an open letter to my readers written at that time, I said:

"... It is possible that in some years' time I shall be in the place of those readers to whom this letter is addressed, I shall reread my book as a stranger, and it may very well be that I shall have my complaints about it—for being incomplete and, perhaps, insufficiently concrete."

And that is what has happened.

During those years I have staged many new numbers and my work on them has made me re-examine and review many of my ideas.

Those years include the war which made particular demands on me and on the theatre I run, and in the fulfilment of those demands new ideas and new forms were born.

During those years I have seen many new countries, cities and people, and this could not but influence my work and my ideas about art and life.

During those years I have read books, written articles, listened to lectures, watched plays and films, taken part in discussions, argued with many and agreed with not a few.

Moreover, during those years I have become ten years older. That is why I have accumulated a fair number of complaints to make about my last book, and if any of you, dear readers, know it I would be very much obliged if you would not catch me out and not reproach me for having said one thing then and another thing now. To some extent that is unavoidable for anyone who lives and works.

And please do not reproach me for repeating myself here and there or for using the same example to prove some point that I used in the other book.

Those things too are possible.

What it means is that I consider the formulation I made in the past still valid, and that I have not in the meantime found a better example to prove that point.

That is why I decided not to be afraid of repeating or refuting myself.

What I want to avoid more than anything else is any didacticism, any forcing of my own opinions and laws on others. Heaven forbid that this book seem like a text-book on the theory of creative work!

If I succeed in writing about my profession, about my personal experience, concealing nothing and inventing nothing, I shall consider my task fulfilled, because only then can my personal experience be at all useful or at least interesting to others.

CHAPTER ONE

First Contacts with Art

I have no intention of writing my memoirs, I want to write only about my profession, but I think I am justified in saying that something of that profession originated in my childhood sensations. So, willy-nilly, I shall have to begin with reminiscences

Fairy-tales and Songs

I was born in Moscow, in 1901. My parents had no connection whatsoever with art. My mother was a Russian teacher, my father a railway engineer. They were always busy, always working. Art occupied just that amount of room in their lives as was left free by their professional work which both of them found enthralling. They were an ordinary hard-working couple whose favourites were Tolstoi, Chaikovsky, Shalyapin and the Moscow Art Theatre.

These loves of theirs did not disturb the calm and even tenor of family life. The family did not talk let alone argue about the acting of Stanislavsky, Stepan Kuznetsov, Yermolova or Komissarzhevskaya. It did not become involved in literary and theatrical events; and although my parents had friends in the world of art the environment in which I grew up could by no stretch of imagination be described as artistic.

Nevertheless, my first contacts with art took place within the family circle, which, strange as it may seem, in no way contradicts what I have just said.

I remember my brother and I, both quite small, sitting on my father's knees in a cab that bumped along over the cobble-stones.

Father's jacket had shiny silver buttons with anchors and hatchets on them and he was telling us a fairy-tale about little mites who used those hatchets to fight against horrid monsters.

The tale was interesting and funny. Father made it up himself to distract us from a long and rather uncomfortable journey.

Of course he had no idea that he was "creating a work of art" and had no intention of "educating" us, but, all the same, our childish imaginations conjured up the characters and we became engrossed in the plot; we were frightened and amazed, we felt sad and merry and joyful; in short we went through everything that people go through when they are affected by art. We fell in love with those nice little mites and we loathed those wicked monsters. In other words the fairy-tale taught us a lesson, in just the way that a good work of art does.

Father had a remarkable memory. I think he remembered everything he had ever read; so, besides the tales he made up, he told us the fairy-tales of Afanasyev, the Grimms and Hans Andersen. He described various scenes from the history of Russia and the rest of the world—about Vladimir Monomakh, Alexander the Great, the Fall of Carthage and the Trojan Wars. Long before I read Homer I knew the *Iliad* and the *Odyssey* in Father's version.

Both Father and Mother had very good ears for music. They passed this gift on to us and often in the evenings the whole family would sing together in the lamplight. We knew very many songs. We sang them quietly. It was the songs themselves, not our performance of them, that we liked. We liked them for their gay or touching words, for their melodies. We liked the way the tunes intermingled and chased each other in the duet "Do not tempt me needlessly." In the old romance "Nights of Passion" we liked the way the lower voice climbs up the scale while the upper one, starting an octave higher, slips down to meet it, the way they blend and then, after a few bars, separate again. We did not impart any special "expression" to our singing, we never sang "with feeling" because we did not associate the mood of the song with our own moods. Of course the song sounded sad if we were singing "Alone I came to the road," or merry if it was the Ukrainian song "A peasant once came to the mill" with its comic refrain, but the sadness or merriment sprang from the song itself, from the melody, the words and rhythm. And that was the pleasantest thing of all.

And probably because we nearly always sang without any audience, just the four of us, this singing turned into a real contact with art.

Pigeons and Fish

This glee-singing was not done for any special educative reasons. It just entered our lives among other pastimes during the hours that were free from study.

There were many such pastimes.

During nearly all our childhood years we lived in Sokolniki, near the park. Today Sokolniki is only seven minutes by underground railway from the centre of Moscow, but in those days it was a long way off and on weekdays the vast park was quiet and deserted. We knew every inch of it. All the avenues, every path, each pond. We knew every pine-tree. The one with the hawk's nest in it, and that special one in whose sturdy boughs the hurricane of 1904 had deposited an enormous sheet of iron roofing. The rusty metal sheet rocked and rattled in the wind and we would look at it trying to imagine from just what roof it had been torn and how high it had been carried up to the sky.

We chased squirrels, trailed little grey nuthatches and, heads tilted, stood for hours watching orange-plumaged crossbills shelling pine-cones.

We would put a female bullfinch in a cage and lure plump red-breasted male birds into the trap, and our tame female tomtit would attract merry little male birds into the same cage.

We covered all Sokolniki on our bikes, we skied everywhere, we walked every inch of it. In winter we skated on the Sokolniki ponds until dusk drove us home. And in summer we caught wriggly red worms in those ponds to feed our fish. The fish lived in jam jars and aquarium tanks. We had very many. Goggle-eyed telescope fish, green and red striped macropods, moustached "cats." We warmed the water, aerated the tanks with special atomizers, segregated male and female and transferred the fry. On Sundays we walked to Trubnaya Square where in those days tropical fish and pet birds, dogs and pigeons were on sale.

Sometimes we brought back in a jar from the pet market a pink and white axolotl resembling at once both lizard and sucking-pig. The axolotl had soft red gills which looked like coral branches and was so phlegmatic by disposition that it would maintain the same pose for an hour. We used to say it was calculating π which we had to learn to only four places of decimals but which the axolotl evidently had to know to many more.

Sometimes in a special wicker basket we brought home pigeons: "sheer" ones, or "hooded monks," or the spotted Chigrash variety. At home we carefully bound their wings so that they should not fly farther than the roof of the shed until they grew used to their own cote.

Then we would release them and watch them circle high in the sky and see how the "monk" clapping its wings together first sat on its tail and then somersaulting down almost to ground level caught up the "sheer" ones, who did not deign to take such liberties but kept strictly in the lead of the flight making a succession of tight turns. If a "monk" somersaulted very well and made the loop we called it Utochkin after our favourite pilot.

My fondness of nature drew me to books of a particular character. Of course I knew Brehm's *Life of the Animals* from cover to cover, but Brehm led on to Kipling, Jules Verne, Seton-Thompson. Baloo the Bear and Rikki-tikki-tavi, and the wolf with the astonishing name of Lobo-King-Korumbo, and Chekhov's Kashtanka and Turgenev's Mumu I loved as I did my own pets, and I hated the hawk which killed the heroic faithful carrier-pigeon in the story "Arno" as much as I hated the live hawks which high up in the sky chased our pigeons and seized them in their grasping claws.

I would not have written about pigeons, fish and tomtits in this book did I not consider that my contacts with them in those days had a direct bearing on art in general and on my profession in particular.

It is not only that my fondness of nature and animals stored away in my subconscious memory images and emotions that later found expression in performances on the stage or the concert platform.

There is more to it than that.

Observation of nature and animals trains one to think associatively, in concrete images, that is, to think in a way which is essential if one is to occupy oneself with art, a way without which art cannot exist.

The pleasure that one gets from observing nature and animal-behaviour is very similar to the pleasure one gets from a work of art, whether it be literature, painting or drama. In any case, it prepares one's receptiveness to art. For involuntarily one always compares the behaviour and character of animals with those of human beings. These comparisons never cease to be surprising. One is surprised to see how carefully the female macropod builds a nest for its young out of bubbles of saliva; it is a surprise to find out how jealous the male dove is of its mate, how cunning is the tomtit, how devoted to you is your dog and how trustingly he gives you his hurt paw to bandage. You recall the self-important way the crow struts, the human look a fly has when it is rubbing its head, the dignified way in which the camel turns its head, the attentiveness with which a monkey examines a piece of toffy. You recognize in animals separate features of human beings, though they are disjointed and selected as it were. And he who can see man in another living creature will the more easily see him in sculpture, in painting, in a book, because the processes of perception are similar. In both instances it is a question of "recognition"—that is, of associative thought.

The Most Important Thing

But of all the most passionate enthusiasms of my childhood there was one I always considered my future profession.

If anyone asked me in those days what I wanted to be when I grew up I would always answer the same way: "I am going in for art."

And I "went in for art" not only in my dreams but in a straightforward practical way. I drew much and persevered at it—in coloured crayons, water-colours and oils. From the age of ten I took regular lessons with an art teacher.

And so the family took it for granted that I was going to be an artist. But probably, just because the family's attitude towards art was free from anything highfalutin, my future profession was not considered to be anything special or in any way different from other professions.

Which then ought I to consider the most important of my contacts with art in my childhood? Which of them had the greatest influence on my present profession?

Fairy-tales and songs set my fantasy to work and made the world appear full of enchantment and imagery.

My fondness for observing nature and animal life taught me to love that world concretely and to see imagery in the living process itself.

Painting taught me to take delight in the fact that a picture of the world around could be fixed on canvas or paper, "caught" and made one's own.

But, after all, the main thing was not these contacts with art but that something which united them all. And this was my parents' attitude to the phenomena of art and life. I suppose it might be called their "style" of looking at the world.

My father was a scientist, an academician, the founder of a whole school of engineers. He had the capacity for looking far ahead and for seeing the life of his country in deep perspective, but he never spoke of science in grandiloquent terms. He loved literature and art, would speak with enthusiasm about a book he had read, or of a play or film he had seen, but he would never resort to high-flown language or give rein to his emotions. In his version everything seemed to be both highly interesting and quite natural, everything, beginning from the railway track in a marshalling yard and ending with the most fantastic fairytales.

When we talked together about art we never used words like "self-illuminating" or "high calling" or "service to the public."

To this day I consider it an insult to use about an artist those reverential and flowery phrases that are generally applied to the Sistine Madonna or the "enigmatic" smile of the Gioconda.

In my childhood I felt art in a clear straightforward way, as an organic part of human life.

And this perception of art is for me the most important thing I received from the family I grew up in. The most important thing for my profession.

CHAPTER TWO

Pencil and Brush

The dreams of my childhood almost came true.

After finishing high school I entered the School of Painting, Sculpture and Architecture which after the Revolution was renamed the Higher Technical Art Studios. At first I studied in the painting department, in Arkhipov's studio, but later I transferred to graphic art and studied engraving under Favorsky.

Had I not gone on the stage I would have presented my diploma work and graduated.

Many years have passed since then. I have long ago given up considering myself an artist but I have never regretted those years I spent studying painting and engraving.

Before I started to write this chapter I looked in my drawers and cupboards and pulled out dusty albums, rolls of drawing-paper and canvas.

I have them before me now: pencil and charcoal drawings, sketches in water-colours and oils, portraits, landscapes, still lifes.

It was very difficult to unroll the stiff canvas. The thick layers of paint had cracked. The cracks were full of dust. I had to use soap and water.

I arranged all my work in date order, starting from my eighth year. The result was a sort of private exhibition. The pictures, however, were not hung on the walls but lay spread on the floor, on top of the piano, on the sofa and chairs. Every sketch, every study set up an almost bodily reminiscence. I found I could remember how long it took me to match the yellow shawl and the pink knee of the model. I remembered how reluctant the brown wall in the background had been to separate from the model's hair which was of exactly the same shade of brown, how I did not have enough green paint for the reflections of sun-rays playing on the grass, and how difficult I had found it to combine the horizontal ripples on the surface of the river with the vertical lines of the reflections.

I remember the stubborn resistance of the broad brush and the feeling of joy that came from applying a dab of paint to canvas. Not just any dab of paint but precisely that one lying in a dimple between those collar-bones.

I remembered the birth of that dab of paint on the palette: flesh-coloured ochre, light cobalt, whiting and a touch of violet, like clear fruit jelly.

Resurrected Years

With my memories of the process of work some conditioned reflex brought back space and time, people, and even scents of the past.

Here on a small canvas is a clumsy, thinly painted picture of a rowing boat, the sands, the sea and a pine-tree. On the back is the figure "1910," in my mother's hand.

That means I was nine when I painted that picture. Nearly forty years divide me from that day but I remember clearly the breeze and the scent of bilberries and the shower that drove me from the balcony of the little white seaside house near Riga.

Here is another date—1914. This canvas is no bigger, but the colours are deeper. A woodland path.

I remember that day too. It was very hot. I sat on a thick, humped root that jutted out of the ground, and painted the Tagan pine woods near Prince Volkonsky's estate outside Moscow—now the Architects' Rest Home. The paint-box kept slipping off my knees. The little brass pot of linseed-oil upset in the dry red pine-needles and poured over an ant. I spent a long time saving that ant with a twig. I remember a monk coming up to me from the near-by monastery of Yekaterininskaya Hermitage and standing for a whole hour in his dingy black cassock watching me paint. I liked that because the picture pleased me. I considered it not a scrap worse than "The Last Beam" in the book about Levitan my mother had given me shortly before.

The 1916-1917 album. On the first page my first sketch from the nude. That was done on a Saturday, I remember well. In Khotulev's studio at Krasniye Vorota. I started going there while I was still at school. On Saturdays there was a sketching class with a model.

I was very frightened that first Saturday. I thought something very special was going to happen. For the first time in my life I was going to see a completely naked woman close up—something very mysterious, indecent and shameful.

The model came out from behind a screen, wrapped in a big shawl. She passed us barefoot, sprang on to a low platform and dropped the shawl on to a stool.

And nothing special happened. There was nothing indecent about a nude woman, it appeared. Naturally not. "Nudity" is indecent only in art—in painting, on the stage, in books, and then only if the artist wants it to be so.

Next to the albums of sketches lie some large canvases which have been removed from their frames. Student work.

A large portrait of a girl in Russian national costume. Face ochre, arms and hands with blue shading, a red hair ribbon, a brown skirt. I remember Arkhipov praising me for that painting, much to my delight and astonishment.

A vertical canvas. A nude. A very white, pearly body and bright red hair. That was one of our regular models. There was a constant tussle going on over her between the studios. Everyone wanted her in his studio—Mashkov, Osmerkin, Konchalovsky, Malyutin.

And there on a stool sits another woman. Nothing beautiful about her, with the swollen body, the untidy hair with the straight parting, the small eyes and the childish lisping mouth. Yet she was a famous model: you will recognize those slanting eyes and that soft torso in many of the wood carvings of one of Russia's greatest sculptors—Konenkov.

These large canvases still seem to smell of the bitter odour of the smoke from the iron stoves we used to heat our studio with in those days.

They were wonderful, unique days. 1918, 1919, 1920. ... The difficult and hard years of the birth of a new land.

The armies of our enemies stood in Siberia, in the Caucasus, at

Arkhangelsk, in the Ukraine. The great main railway lines became short dead ends that always ended up at the front.

There were shortages of coal, of fire-wood, of bread. The street lighting was cut off. The trams stopped running. Frost crept into homes and offices. Wick-lamps burned in the dark rooms: thin wicks of thread stuck into vials of kerosene or oil.

And yet those were beautiful and happy days.

In the evenings, gathering for a supper of frozen potatoes or brown lentils moistened with green hempseed oil, we would tell each other how we had spent the day.

And that day always turned out to have been remarkable. For some reason or other we never felt tired, although each of us had covered tens of kilometres on foot during the day. Father was lecturing at many institutions in Moscow. He was one of the initiators and founders of the workers' faculties and of military-technical courses; he was planning new railway lines and big junctions and sitting on various state committees which were drawing up great plans for the new state. So naturally he had something to tell us every evening.

I talked about Lunacharsky's lectures, about the discussions in the Polytechnical Museum, about Lenin's visit to our students' hostel, about courses of philosophy at the university where I went after work in the studio, about my bearded students in the military courses where I taught the laws of perspective, and about the kids in the children's home where I taught drawing.

These evening meetings and talks round the table were always so interesting that we used to sit up late, although in the morning, before setting out for the distant centre of the city, we would have to saw and chop up fire-wood for the little stove, fetch water from the pump in the yard and patch our felt boots in order to start a long and highly interesting day—a day consisting of work we loved and of our dreams of the future.

The Curve of Quality

Probably just because it is so long since I painted, now that all the relics of my unachieved profession were strewn about the room I found it easy to look at my works with the dispassionate eye of a connoisseur and to say: "That is good, that is so-so, and that is rotten." And then I suddenly discovered a surprising curve that led me to an unexpected though unavoidable conclusion.

Comparatively successful works kept alternating with utter rubbish. Moreover, the bad work often turned out to be just those things which had pleased me most of all at the time of painting and which I had been most proud of.

My private exhibition started with a little canvas album of the year 1909 when I was eight years old.

What about those drawings? As yet there was no struggle to achieve anything. The drawings showed what "came out," not what I had been aiming at. With one exception, perhaps, when I had tried to show a galloping horse at a bend in a road. I could not manage the foreshortening. The horse would either run across the road and dash straight into the mountain-side or it would seem to be falling over. At this place the paper was almost worn through by the eraser but the horse and its rider lay on one side in a galloping position. The rest of the drawings were simply childish. Grey elephants wandering about a yellow desert. War in the mountains with hundreds of tiny mites with weapons in their hands scattered among rocks and caves.

"Illustrated tales" of this sort always seem splendid. Young children never have any trouble in drawing them, and the thoughtless ease with which they handle colour and form creates an illusion of quality which often deceives highfalutin or sentimental grown-ups.

When I was nine or ten years old I first came up against a definite task. I had to draw not the conventional "sign" of something, turned into an object only by the painter's inner fantasy, but the object itself.

It was my first contact with nature.

These works of mine were less effective in appearance and looked more helpless, but, nevertheless, they were honest. The infantile charm had gone but it had been replaced not by dilettantism but by sheer lack of ability.

My little canvas with the sea, the pine-tree and the rowing boat on the beach, which I referred to at the beginning of this chapter, would never have been accepted for an exhibition of children's work which teachers and connoisseurs of "children's creativeness" are so fond of arranging.

There was nothing striking in this little picture with its drab tones. I had mixed the colours very clumsily and assiduously because the sea I saw with my own eyes was not blue as the sea always looks to children and the sand I saw was not at all yellow like the sand I had painted with those elephants in the desert. All the same, through the lack of skill and the helplessness could be detected something achieved. The boat had form, not the form of any boat but of the one I had seen with my own eyes. One could see the greyness of the rainy sky, almost indistinguishable in colour from the faintly greenish sea.

And poor as this little painting was I can now see that it was a step forward.

Here is another study. The one I painted when I was thirteen, sitting in the pine woods and enjoying the fact that a monk was finding my work surprisingly good. Of course, the work was much more skilful than the grey painting of Riga beach but there was nothing in it to boast about to oneself, or to that monk. The "skill" of putting glossy paint and bright colours on to canvas is dilettantism, nothing more. Much later, when I was an actor, I learned that in creating a role this method was what Stanislavsky called "playing for effect." It is the easiest, and the most disastrous way of playing. The feeling of mastery of the brush has turned into a manner and the manner has become stereotyped. Even though still childish and naive, that stereotype had given birth to a coquettishness in brushwork, to over-brilliance and over-sharp contrasts. The "curve" had fallen.

Happily not for long.

In the winter of that year—1914—I painted a still life with the aid of my art teacher. I discovered that to paint something like a simple blue saucepan on a white table-cloth was not at all easy. Striving for external effect does not pay. The search for precise, not approximate colours and forms in early still lifes as in early drawings of plaster casts gave definite results. These works lie before me now and I can look at them without feeling ashamed. The "curve" takes an obvious upward turn.

But next to them lies a sketching album dating from the summer of the following year, and that contains some more very poor drawings. One of the worst is a sketch of a seated figure. It takes up only a quarter of a page in the album. Empty space surrounds it and across this is scrawled a presumptuous signature with the date.

What happened? Why did I have so much confidence in the value of this sketch that I even had to sign it?

I remember the reason well.

That spring I had been to a memorial exhibition of Serov's works. There, among much other work, were some sketches for illustrations to Krylov's fables. They were all under glass. Many of them were signed. Near some of them hung little tickets bearing the words "Sold" or "Acquired for the Tretyakov Gallery." I learned for the first time that sketches of a few lines were also works of art. Before that I thought that only finished pictures were considered works of art.

And so my enthusiasm for careless sketches was born. The means became the aim. The more careless the better. The important thing was not the house I was drawing or the man sitting on a tree stump: what was important was the speed and lightness of line. And in the brief spell of one summer my hand lost its ability to draw and my eye its ability to see.

Happily that ended catastrophically.

An artist took the next-door summer cottage. He heard that I painted, grew interested and said to me: "Come on, draw me." He sat on a tree stump and turned to me in profile. I opened my sketch book, drew him in five minutes, signed the drawing and showed it to him. He looked at it and scolded me. In the drawing his leg from thigh to knee was twice as long as from knee to ankle. He had no stomach at all and his legs sprang straight out of his ribs.

All this was explained to me with great force and utter contempt for me. I took offence and left him, but the shock was very severe. I suddenly understood how little I knew and how presumptuous I was.

In the autumn I drew from plaster casts with my teacher and gave up dashing off works of genius with my pencil; I had enough to worry about trying to place Niobe's eyes correctly. My teacher placed her head at a very difficult angle but nevertheless my drawing came off. If I could draw as well as that today I would be delighted. The "curve" began to rise again.

These ups and downs in the "curve of quality" were most interesting to observe when the fall took place slowly and I could clearly analyse the reason for it. In Khotulev's studio I drew a woman's portrait in charcoal on grey paper and put a high-light on the tip of her nose in chalk. Evidently the effect of the high-light pleased me very much because in following portraits the chalk high-lights appear with ever-growing frequency. The final result was a portrait consisting of nothing but high-lights. High-lights on the pupils of the eyes, on the nose, on the finger-nails. A pearl necklace on the neck was badly drawn. It did not cling to the neck, did not lie on the collar-bones, but every pearl was carefully high-lighted.

Arkhipov could not forgive things like that. He hated cheap effects and so in the work done in the Arkhipov studio some pictures are better than others but taking them in order you can see an accumulation of practical skill which was not an aim in itself and did not become showing-off. The "curve of quality" straightened and slowly mounted.

* * *

I do not know whether in the long run I would have become a real painter or whether on attaining a certain level of professional skill I would have stuck there. But, in any case, I am not at all sorry that I developed a passion for painting in my childhood nor that I studied art in my youth. On the contrary, a professional contact with the fine arts was probably a most valuable education for me.

It taught me to use my eyes, and in my present profession that is very important. I was taught to transform the world I could see and perceive into definite material—pencil, charcoal and paints. I studied anatomy and learned to understand the mechanism and plastic form of the human body; I modelled in clay and learned the movement of volume in space. In the graphic department I learned to etch and to make lithographs, woodcuts and linocuts.

I grew to love the smell of paint, wood and glue priming. I loved the portrayal of space and colour. I loved *materiality*. And the producer of a puppet theatre, where the image is essentially material, has to think in material, in texture, volume and size.

Had I never studied painting and drawing, had I never held pencil and brush in my hands as a professional, I would probably not have realized how many creative laws are common to the different arts, and if in this chapter I have involuntarily mentioned Stanislavsky in connection with painting, then later on, in writing of the theatre I shall, of course, mention Fedotov, Doré and the Kukryniksy.

CHAPTER THREE

The Path to the Stage

If anybody had told me as a child that I would become an actor I would simply have scoffed at the idea.

I had just as much chance of going on the stage as of becoming a doctor or an astronomer. Had I been offered the choice of being something other than an artist I would most likely have chosen to be a mathematician or a technologist, following in my father's footsteps, or a biologist, because of my enthusiasm for fish and pigeons.

Once, during my student days, I skipped an evening drawing class and went to the Moscow Art Theatre to see *Uncle Vanya*. Next day Arkhipov came into the studio and asked me why I had not turned up the previous evening; when he learned the reason he said: "Well, well! Here there was a nude waiting for you, and off you go to see some *Uncle Vanya*!" The reproach did not surprise me at all. Why, indeed, should I have wasted an evening on *Uncle Vanya* seeing I was going to be an artist?

And yet I became an actor and instead of daubing paint on paper or canvas I began to paint my own face, making up in the dressing-rooms of that very theatre which Arkhipov had scolded me for visiting.

Without an Audience

Every child longs to act; a love of acting reveals itself from the earliest age.

This urge to act underlies most children's games where children reveal powers of observation, of imagination and of truthfulness of expression that grown-up actors envy.

Little girls show remarkable acting ability as they put their dolls to bed, unswaddle them, take them to the doctor and scold them for being naughty.

Little boys, without for a moment doubting the veracity of what they are doing, gallop on imaginary horses, spread their arms to fly imaginary aircraft or, puffing and panting, accomplish complicated operations on imaginary goods trains.

If you ever manage to get into a children's game, which is not an easy thing for a grown-up to do, you will be astonished by the power of a child's imagination.

One day when I was already an actor I was playing Visitors with my nephew. He invited me to drink tea out of non-existent cups. Stanislavsky would have called this game a study of "affected actions" and the five-year-old boy would have been given excellent marks while I, the professional, would hardly have got a "fair."

My young partner always remembered exactly where he had put down the imaginary tea-pot, never forgot to remove its imaginary lid when he added hot water, and neatly turned the little tap of the imaginary samovar when, in his opinion, the tea-pot was getting full.

In the middle of our tea party the little boy was summoned to his real tea. His first reaction was to spring up and go but then, recalling that he was still holding a tea-cup (thumb and two fingers were tightly flexed as if gripping it), he came back, carefully put the "cup" on the table and went into the dining-room.

I, of course, went through this phase of pure, childish "acting." And to this day I remember many games of my earliest years; I remember not only what they were about but also the inner truth of what I was playing.

I remember being a "participant" in the fighting on the barricades in 1905. I was four and a half then. The "barricades" were my brother's upturned bed behind which I crawled with the girl from next door and a cat.

A year later, I remember, I was a "newspaper publisher and distributor." The newspaper I wrote myself with printed letters; the text consisted of scraps of grown-up conversation. I recall writing the phrase: "The Cadet Party is very angry" and I remember how hurt I felt when Father after a glance at my paper turned to another one.

I remember myself as a "cow" very well. My godmother Auntie Kapa stitched me a pair of cloth horns and stuffed them with cotton wool. I used to tie these horns to my forehead and run to graze on the green carpet in our lodger's room. There were flowers in the pattern and I used to "eat" them crawling on all fours.

I have never forgotten that feeling of being a grazing cow, a real cow, russet with white patches, although I was wearing nothing red at the time.

But I also remember that the moment I noticed a grown-up watching me at play I would break off the game. I would lose my temper or burst into tears and snatch my horns off. In this too I was no exception. As soon as children feel the eyes of grown-ups on them they stop drinking tea out of imaginary cups or putting dolls to bed or playing cows or aircraft or doctors.

And however well and truthfully children may perform in their acting games—and, generally speaking, they act very well indeed—there is not one of them you can be sure will make an actor, that is, a person who can preserve his inner seriousness and his belief in the truth of his acting in the presence of an audience. Only in the presence of the spectator does the art of acting achieve its full meaning.

If the first appearance before the public, often so decisive in the career of an actor, is difficult and dangerous for a grown-up, it is doubly so for a child.

Children who are modest by nature usually flatly refuse to "perform"; they grow shy and rude. They do not want to recite or sing for their parents' friends.

Children who lack this modesty eventually relish the taste of success and "perform" willingly, but their performances often turn into showing-off, into precocious coquetry and they start posing.

If some teachers and parents were more attentive they would not be in such a hurry to exhibit the gifts of their children to their guests and thus satisfy their own vanity and infect their children with it too; they would have a different attitude towards children in amateur talent circles.

I do not at all wish to blame everything that is done in children's amateur dramatics, but that work is attended by great dangers and sometimes does irreparable harm; so for myself, I am, on the whole, glad that I never took part in any dramatic circle as a child—either at home or at school.

By myself or with my friends I played at trains, at tiger-hunting and even at theatre and cinema games, but that was all without a public, as the participants in the games themselves played the "public" so that, in fact, there were no real spectators.

The Germ of Vanity

There is probably no other profession where the germ of vanity is so dangerous as in acting.

If through sheer vanity a schoolboy tries to get excellent marks in algebra there is some real benefit, whatever you may think of his motive. That schoolboy not only acquires knowledge, he eventually grows keen on the subject and later maybe even becomes a good mathematician.

But if someone—a child or a grown-up, it makes no difference—tries to sing or act on the stage only in order to achieve success, that is, solely out of vanity, then he will never make a good singer or actor.

The "curve" that I found in my early drawings left me in no doubt that there was a decline in quality whenever I tried to strain after an external effect or to show off my "skill." I did not call it vanity in those days but it really was vanity that lay at the root of the false effects in a drawing or painting.

It is to this wretched disease that Stanislavsky referred when he warned that "One should love the art in oneself, not oneself in art."

If this disease is dangerous for the artist who starts painting false, flashy pictures, it can be absolutely fatal for the actor. It devours his guts, it shows itself in every intonation, in every gesture. It destroys sincerity, and the art of being sincere is something essential to an actor, his main weapon.

An actor probably cannot learn to be sincere any more than he can learn to be talented but if he possesses sincerity he must learn to preserve it. That is difficult. It requires a ruthlessly severe teacher and a pupil who is equally merciless with himself. This sincerity did exist in our family singing circle. It was the songs themselves not our voices or our performance that we loved; the "germ of vanity" found no fertile soil in me at that early stage.

But gradually that soil appeared.

Because my voice was high and vibrant I usually led the singing. Friends or neighbours dropping in at our summer cottage would praise me and would often ask me to sing a solo. Like all children I must have been shy at first but then grew used to it. It began to please me to be invited to sing and so the song turned into an occasion for childish showing-off. Vanity had taken root and now I am grateful not to those kind, well-intentioned people who praised my singing but, on the contrary, to those who did not hesitate to tease me for my childish confidence that I was a good singer.

That happened twice, I remember. They must have been serious occasions for me to have remembered them so well.

Mother took me to my first opera, at the Bolshoi Theatre. What the opera was I can't remember because I was probably only about six then and naturally didn't understand what the opera was about. I think what interested me more was the applause. Grown-up people all clapping their hands like a lot of children, and making a terrific noise about it. Mother told me that always happened in the theatre when people were pleased with something. I was surprised that grown-ups should behave that way but I joined in their flippant pastime with pleasure.

My next surprise was the conductor.

The movements of his little stick coincided exactly with the sounds I could hear. I concluded that the sounds were made by that little stick itself and was quite offended when my nanny refused to believe me afterwards.

And my third surprise was the manner of singing.

To someone whose ear is not accustomed to that kind of singing the full volume of opera sound always gives an impression of a certain amount of *vibrato*. Especially in the upper register.

I did not find it beautiful, but every time the fat lady on the stage finished singing the audience stirred and applauded.

So that was the way one had to sing. That was good singing.

I do not know whether I grasped it at once or whether I worked it out later, but I recall how once that summer, sitting under an acacia-tree, I spent a long time "rehearsing," trying to make my voice vibrate. Then I climbed up the wooden steps to my godmother's room, sat on a step outside her door and gave her a demonstration of how well I could sing.

I tried to make my voice wobble on every vowel: "In the da-a-awn the little sta-a-ars shi-i-ine." But I never reached the end. The door opened and Auntie Kapa looked out in astonishment and asked: "What's the matter with you? Why are you making that horrid noise?"

That, I think, was my first conscious appearance as an actor, my first deliberate attempt to impress an audience; it was also my first acting flop. I burst into tears and hid under the verandah where I sat in a cobwebby corner until supper-time. Even the happy chicks which came up to me seemed to be against me and I drove them away with clods of earth.

If anybody else had criticized my singing I probably would simply have felt childishly offended and stubborn; I might not have admitted to myself that I had been showing off; I might not have felt ashamed of myself.

But after my parents there was no one I loved so much as Auntie Kapa and my affection for her was based on a profound respect and a recognition of her as an authority on everything.

Up to the last days of her life—and she lived until she was ninety—Auntie Kapa remained a person of great integrity, with a clear mind, demanding much of other people, decent and kind, without the least trace of sentimentality. She was a widow living in straitened circumstances and she had brought up all her children herself, including my mother whom she had adopted.

It was impossible to be idle in her company because she herself worked from morning till night and could not stand idleness even among little children.

She lived all the year round on her small estate at Potapovo near Moscow; it was called an estate merely for the sake of the past as everything had long ago been sold and there remained only a patch of ground with an orchard, an old wooden house and a few outhouses.

I shall never forget the weeks and months I spent with Auntie Kapa. They are among the most joyful and unclouded memories of my childhood, and I shall always be grateful to her for that respect for work which I acquired not from "educational precepts" but from personal contact with Auntie Kapa. She taught me to work in the garden and to look after the beehives, to handle a scythe and harness a horse, to darn stockings and even to mark the linen.

I owe much to Auntie Kapa but I think it is for the way she criticized my boastful singing that I ought to be most grateful to her.

There was no escaping her judgement, there was no loophole I could find from her verdict. Once she had said that I sang badly it meant it was true. And the most shameful thing was not that I sang badly but that she realized that I was showing off.

That is why I went on sitting under the verandah till evening.

An actor's sense of shame is one of the most powerful antidotes against the "germ of vanity" and I am grateful to Auntie Kapa for having administered this bitter medicine in good time.

The next occasion was two years later. At a Christmas party the children were dancing in a ring and singing: "Ah, I've caught you, little bird." They sang completely out of tune, not at all the way we sang with Mother and Father. Someone asked me to sing. Quite certain that I was going to show them how the song ought to be sung, I went into the middle of the ring and sang: "Ah why, dear children, do you want to have me caught?" Evidently I started on too high a note for my voice broke after the first few bars and everybody burst out laughing.

My Christmas party ended in tears and even the box of water-colours presented to me failed to console me for that public disgrace.

These two incidents were enough to stop any further attempts at solo performance. Since then I never again "performed" as a singer either at anybody else's house or at school concerts, although our family singing circle went on.

Unfortunately the "germs of vanity" possess a surprising capacity for reviving and in my later years these nasty germs caused me no little harm. The infection takes different forms and I shall have to return to the subject later, but now, in order to prevent any future misunderstanding, I warn the reader that I certainly do not consider as vanity the artist's pleasure in the success of his work or in the recognition of his success by others.

That pleasure is natural and it would be hypocritical to deny the artist's right to it.

But it must follow, not precede his work. If it precedes it the sum is radically changed—the plus sign becomes a minus.

If you have saved a man from drowning and he is grateful to you for it, then you have every right to feel pleased with his gratitude, the more so because you are as glad as everybody else that the man is safe and sound.

But if you jump into the water just to get a Life-Saving Medal—that's a bad thing.

In exactly the same way if an actor plays a part or an author writes a book, why shouldn't he be pleased if his work is praised? But if he has been counting on that praise beforehand and has worked on the role or on the book only for the sake of that praise instead of being moved by an inner urge, an inner enthusiasm—then that's bad too.

Moreover, parts acted that way, books written that way do not come off. That is a stern law of art. The "germ of vanity" kills every gesture of the actor, every phrase of the writer.

An Unexpected Incident

All the same, in the long run it was my voice that got me on to the stage.

They say that if a boy has a very high treble as a child, the operation of some biological law will see to it that he becomes a bass when his voice breaks. This law must be unreliable because when my high treble broke my voice turned out to be something between a baritone and a tenor.

However, it was still a singing voice and during our military training classes at school I became the platoon soloist.

People began to advise me to study singing properly. Of course, I had no intention of abandoning painting for singing but I did not see why I should not learn to sing better if that were possible, especially as one of those who advised me to was the son of Shalyapin who studied painting with me in Arkhipov's studio. And for me "the son of Shalyapin" was, after all, an authority.

On Myasnitskaya Street (now Kirov Street) stood the private school of A. G. Shor, which bore the name of a "Conservatoire."

I entered it. That must have been in 1919 or 1920.

There I discovered that I had a "short" voice and that among the other pupils there were many with far better voices. It is easy to be known as a good singer among non-singers but very much harder when one is in professional company.

Nevertheless I started singing scales and arpeggios and then the romance "A lovely castle stands with many rooms within" and spent so long learning to "cover" the top notes and to "hold my breath" that to this day I cannot bear to hear that song.

Two years passed, and one day we received a visit from our neighbour Natalia Baklanova, a violinist from the Musical Studio of the Moscow Art Theatre.

We scarcely knew her; all I had heard about her was that she was the sister of Olga Baklanova, an actress of the Art Treatre and a soloist of the Musical Studio.

The call was unexpected but even more unexpected was the fact that she had come to advise me to go in for a singing competition for entry into the Musical Studio.

She said: "I was passing your window and heard you singing and it seemed to me you might have a shot at it. It's a very interesting young theatre, you know. Have you seen *La Fille de Madame Angot*?"

"No, I'm afraid I haven't."

"A pity. It's a good show."

"I'll certainly go. When is the competition?"

"Today is the first round. If you want to enter you'll have to hurry. Otherwise you'll be late."

Had it not all been so unexpected and rushed, had the competition been not in half an hour but, say, on the following day, I would have had time to reflect, and, of course had I done so I would not have gone.

But there was no time for reflection. After all, why shouldn't I go? I had nothing to risk. If I failed I would be none the worse off.

I took the first song that lay handy, hurried to the Art Theatre and put my name down at a little table.

Nervous singers paced the corridors. They were all older than me; some were even grey-haired.

In dark corners they gargled and uttered short nasal sounds, typical of all singers testing whether their voices were "carrying" or not; some thumbed sheets of well-worn professional-looking songs.

The examination boards were at work on various floors and in various foyers of the theatre. I was summoned to one of these foyers. A bass sang, then a baritone. Both sang well. "Thank you," they were told as they left. I walked over to the piano and handed my music to the accompanist.

A dark-complexioned man with close-shaven cheeks said: "What's your voice?" I said: "I don't know. Tenor, it seems." The man found my answer surprising. "What do you mean: 'it seems'? Well, never mind, sing:" I felt no trace of nervousness. I found the situation more amusing than alarming. I sang Rubinstein's "Azra." "What else have you got there?" I sang a romance. "Thank you." Odd, they let me sing to the end. They had said "Thank you" to the baritone half-way through Figaro's arioso.

I went home fully convinced that I had not got through to the second round. After all, there were three hundred candidates.

Two days later I met Natalia Baklanova outside the house. "D'you know?" she said, "I read your name on the list. You've got into the next round."

At that moment all my diffidence and calm vanished in a flash. There were a few days left before the second round and during that time I practised regularly, examined my throat in the looking-glass, grew worried when I thought I had a cold coming on and polished up some lines of Balmont which as a child I had heard a distant relative, an actress of the Art Theatre called Durasova, recite. According to the terms of the competition I had to recite as well as sing.

There were fourteen of us in the second round. The examination board sat at a long table in one of the foyers of the Art Theatre. In the middle sat Nemirovich-Danchenko. I had never seen him before but someone pointed him out to me. Short in build, plump, grey-haired, he was smiling faintly. He was evidently in a good mood.

I sang Rubinstein's "Azra" again; my voice cracked on the top note. The blue-chinned man (by now I knew it was the chief conductor Bakaleinikov) said: "Last time you took that F sharp all right." I maintained an embarrassed silence.

"Recite something," said Nemirovich-Danchenko. I recited my lines of Balmont.

I was the youngest competitor and being blond looked younger than my years. Nemirovich-Danchenko must have thought I was quite a child for there was a hint of mockery in his voice when he narrowed his eyes and asked me my age.

The next day I went to the theatre myself to look for my name on the list. I found I had passed.

True, I was not offered a salary but, nevertheless, I had been taken on.

Before the second round my whole family had noticed how excited I was and how eager to pass. No one held that against me, the more so because, despite my youthful appearance, I had been married two years and had the right to be considered a grown-up, and grown-ups have to be responsible for their actions.

So, to some extent I was expected to come home with a feather in my cap. All the same, when I returned as a member of the Musical Studio of the Moscow Art Theatre the surprise was as great to my family circle as it was to me.

But, probably because of its utter unexpectedness nobody, including me, took the matter seriously. We saw it rather as an unexpected occurrence, more in the nature of a harmless adventure.

I felt convinced that painting would remain my main occupation, my life's work, with the theatre as a sort of a side-line.

During my early years in the theatre I went on attending the drawing department daily. I drew, I engraved, I took exams and even got into the fifth, that is the final year. Then the theatre went abroad for eight months—to Germany, Czechoslovakia, America. I went with it. It meant the loss of a year's studies, and on my return it was difficult to make the effort and catch up with the rest, especially as there was much to do in the theatre and it became impossible to combine the two. True, I took a few more exams and wrote a long work on "Colour in Dürer's Woodcuts" which I went as far as to present in the Academy of Arts. But those were the last flickers of my enthusiasm. My attendance at lectures at the art school became ever less frequent and, to tell the truth, I do not even know when my name was finally removed from the list of students.

CHAPTER FOUR

On the Eve of a Role

Like most people who have nothing directly to do with the theatre I had very little idea of what backstage life consisted of.

When I walked past a theatre—it did not matter which one: the Bolshoi with its vast Empire-style portico and the bronze quadriga on the pediment; or the Korsh Theatre which looked something between a church and a provincial railway station; or the Art Theatre which had been made out of an ordinary dwelling house with the addition of a flight of steps, heavy doors and a large projecting porch supported by chains in the Art Nouveau style—I always had the impression that in the day-time the place was asleep and that there was nobody inside—except, of course, the box-office attendant and the commissionaire.

I even pictured to myself the drowsy silence that reigned in the always somewhat eerie body of the theatre, in its dark auditorium with the curtain down, in the empty foyers and corridors.

Then comes evening, when other buildings gradually fall asleep, when offices, banks and schools empty and the doors of shops are bolted; and then the theatre awakens. The lamps are lit at the doors, the public streams hurriedly into the vestibule, to the cloak-rooms and down the corridors and finally into the auditorium. And after that, everybody falls into a dead silence together, laughs together, applauds or coughs. In the intervals they promenade in an orderly way round and round the foyers, stealing glances at each other or at their own reflections in the mirrors. They gobble up cream cakes in the refreshment room and hurriedly puff cigarettes in the smoke-rooms provided for that purpose and after the third bell gather again in the auditorium to stiffen with excitement, to laugh, to applaud. And then, when the last spectator has been handed his coat the theatre lights are lowered, the doors are locked and the place goes to sleep till the next evening.

Of course, I knew that rehearsals went on in the theatre as well as performances, but what they exactly were and what place they occupied in the life of the theatre I knew no better than thousands of spectators do.

In a Strange House

One day in the theatre was enough to shatter all my illusions of what went on in the theatre during day-time.

I discovered that actually during the day a far busier life went on behind the silent façade than during the brief hours of the performance.

At ten o'clock that first morning the corridors of the theatre were crowded with players. In the foyer a rehearsal of *La Périchole* began. In the middle stood a small table with a wobbly step-ladder close to it; on the table, for some reason, two chairs were placed. We novices sat apart, understanding very little of what all this meant. What was that curious construction? A throne or a balcony?

Men and women in ordinary dress, old and young, thin and fat, some more or less good-looking and some far from it—in short, quite ordinary people—were behaving in a strange and rather silly way. They kept waving their hands, shrieking and frowning in their efforts to be "Peruvians."

There was one man of medium height with a blue jacket and the drain-pipe trousers fashionable at that time who was behaving in a particularly odd way. He shouted louder than all the "Peruvians" put together and walked with a duck-like waddle, his legs so wide apart that they looked like a pair of dividers. I enquired in a low voice who he was but received no reply as the assistant producer shushed me. Apparently it was forbidden to speak at rehearsals, even in a whisper.

Nemirovich-Danchenko was taking the rehearsal. He smiled paternally as he watched the actor who was moving about so strangely, and lavished warm praise on another actor, a tall man no longer young who was calmly moving about among stools and chairs looking at the turbulent "Peruvians" and half-singing, half-humming something.

making, it seemed to me, no effort whatsoever to act. What then was the producer praising him for? What could that actor be doing if at first sight he appeared to be doing nothing? It was all very surprising and mystifying.

But it was not only the rehearsal that puzzled me. I was not merely a novice, I felt a complete stranger. As if I had dropped into a foreign land where people behaved differently, had different customs and even a different language. I felt out of my depth but inquisitive too, and very uncomfortable in this strange house.

Now I know that the people I had fallen in with were ordinary people, just like anybody else, but then they seemed to be far from it. The women's frocks were not particularly dressy but compared to what my college-mates, future artists, wore, these women I was seeing for the first time in the theatre, my new colleagues, looked the last word in elegance and *comme il faut*. I did not like the way they walked, their crimson finger-nails, the rings on their fingers and the way the men kissed their hands. Hand-kissing was something I especially disliked and I for a long time would not do it "on principle."

On that first day I heard a collection of words being used that I scarcely understood, and without going to much trouble to find out their meaning I tried to use them as often as possible when talking with actors—so that they should take me for one of them.

The point was that before I joined the Musical Studio I had not been at all attracted to the stage, even less to books about the stage; as a result my vocabulary was quite lacking in stage terms. And it was difficult to sort all those terms out at first. An actor will say of another that "he has not grasped a character," that he does something that the audience "doesn't get" and I could not understand just what it ought to "get" and what an actor ought to do to "grasp his character."

Man in Black

Gradually I began to feel more and more at home in this "strange house" with its peculiar kind of life and language.

My work began with studying according to the Stanislavsky method.

The exercises were similar to those I had done at the Shor Conservatoire where I had been made to sing "At the Noisy Ball" according to the Method. I understood little of the exercises at the Conservatoire, but here in the theatre I found things easier to understand, and much more interesting.

It was amusing to sew an imaginary button on to a jacket with imaginary thread or to improvise the behaviour of a man stuck in a lift. I did the exercises fairly successfully and my teacher was satisfied.

I was put on the pay-roll though my salary as an actor was very modest. The "strange house" had opened its doors to me not because I had caught Nemirovich-Danchenko's notice at the entrance exam but because some acting ability had been spotted in me.

But, to tell the truth, I have no right to say that I passed through any systematic acting schools before I made my debut on the stage.

My course of the Method was irregular and short and my actual study began on the stage itself.

When I joined the Musical Studio the main company of the Moscow Art Theatre was touring in the United States. Besides the productions of the Musical Studio, the Art Theatre stage was being used once a week by the Third Studio of the Art Theatre (now the Vakhtangov Theatre) for their production of *Turandot* and occasionally by members of the Second Studio (later the Branch of Art Theatre) who were performing *The Blue Bird*, where with other novices I was called on to play the "men in black."

Those who saw *The Blue Bird* at the Art Theatre will recall that a whole series of miracles take place in it. Plates come to life, a lamp falls and breaks, and out of it appears a character called Light; ghosts float through the air. All these miracles are the work of "men in black" dressed in black velvet costumes and hoods with slits for the eyes. They wear black gloves and black velvet overshoes.

All these "miracles" took place in semi-darkness, against a background of black velvet; all that the public could see were plates or the Roman figures of the animated clock which the "men in black" were carrying about the stage. They could see strips of gauze floating through the air; they were attached to long black invisible wands which the "men in black" waved.

In assigning these invisible roles to us our teachers were far from being activated by solely pedagogical motives. Anyway, they went on considering the exercises as the main thing in our studies of the art of acting. And I myself did not think at that time that being one of the "men in black" could be any sort of preparation for real acting. Now, however, when I cast my mind back to my early months of that new and strange profession of acting I feel that in a practical sense the exercises in which I had to improvise, playing a doctor or a tram conductor or a man committing suicide, were less useful to me than the job of being one of the "men in black." At first sight one might think there was nothing creative in that role, but I was being called on to do something definite and responsible.

First of all the fact that one was not seen diminished stage fright, which is natural to all beginners; one could, indeed, find no more convenient method for gradually mastering stage fright.

The most valuable feature of the job, however, was the fact that in playing this part one learned to be aware of the task to be done, which is something highly essential for every role. For even if the "man in black" was himself invisible his actions were visible to the public and, consequently, the responsibility for those actions was no less real than in any "visible" role. In a certain sense this feeling of responsibility was even enhanced, for the obligation to act was in a pure unmistakable form.

In the exercises I frequently experienced a certain sensation of falseness. It was not always easy to find the answers to questions like: "What am I doing now? what do I want?" To say "I am weeping," or "I am laughing" was untrue, since that defined a state of mind rather than action. Action arises only when you have an aim, in other words, volition. You can "truly" weep on the stage only if your tears spring from some desire, for instance, from the desire to be pitied. Then you can easily answer your teacher's questions: "What are you doing now? what do you want?" with the right reply: "I want someone to feel sorry for me." During the whole role, in every episode in it, the actor must go on wishing one well-defined thing, which means he must have a clear aim in view—and it is the same whether he has a silent or a speaking part, whether he sits still or moves about. Only then is he able to "act" and not merely "be" on the stage.

All those are the very rudiments of the Stanislavsky Method, but in my first exercises I found it very hard to grasp their sense fully. Not so much, perhaps, to understand as to feel their meaning. And so while my teacher was satisfied I did not feel fully confident that I had been acting truthfully.

In the role of "man in black," however, all the tasks seemed to be clear and straightforward. No sense of dissimulation, no sort of deception.

I liked the part. I was on the stage close to the actors playing Mytyl and Tyltyl, at the very side of the Cat and Night as they acted, spoke their lines and moved. The public could see them but not me. There was something very pleasant and amusingly uncanny about that.

My business consisted of waving a black wand which set in motion a long strip of floating gauze. But this purely mechanical task became, in fact, an actor's task. Didn't I have to make that piece of gauze represent the flight of a ghost? That meant I couldn't simply wave the wand in any direction; I had to watch the flight of the strip of gauze, feel the speed or smoothness of that flight, sense its power to frighten people, in other words, create the character of a ghost. It looked easy—something like a children's game—but, in fact, it was play-acting, for the spectator saw the ghost I was creating and I knew and felt that.

True, what was visible on the stage in those moments was not my physical self, but something I was creating; every turn of that floating ghost was an expression of my will and imagination.

And while in playing a doctor, beggar or suicide victim in the exercises I very rarely felt the truth of the characters, here I felt it completely and experienced pleasure from that sensation of truth.

In other words, in the sense of organic feeling the role of the "man in black" was again of great benefit to me. But that was not much either. For what determines the quality of a real actor most is probably his capacity of *communion.*

Far from every actor can always manage to look his partner straight in the eyes, listen to him and answer his questions—to respond to his emotions, not to his lines or cues.

This lack of communion was just what our teachers used to upbraid us for most in the exercises.

In the part of the "man in black" this communion did, in fact, exist, although I was in no direct contact with the actors. Tyltyl and Mytyl were "frightened" by the ghost, and that meant that I, the creator of that ghost's flight, had to frighten them. Their emotion of fear depended on the emotion in the flight of that length of gauze, on the sharpness of its turns, its sudden upward sweeps and downward plunges in its spiral flight. That was communion, that was dialogue—wordless, but all the same dialogue.

So I recall the "man in black" with gratitude as a first step on the way to the profession of actor.

Bad Excitement and Bad Calm

At last the occasion came for me to show myself to the public.

I was given the silent role of the scribe in *La Périchole*. I had to come on to the stage on the heels of two tipsy notaries, help them to their chairs and then hand La Périchole a pen for her to sign the marriage register.

Yakov Gremislavsky, the famous make-up artist of the Moscow Art Theatre, adjusted my wig and made me up himself. I looked in the mirror and saw two scared pale eyes looking at me from under black brows on an orange-cheeked, "Spanish" face.

When I made my entrance, supporting the swaying notaries, I had the feeling that the whole auditorium was looking at me and only at me and that there must be something wrong with my costume. La Périchole came over to sign and in my nervousness I jabbed the pen into her cheek. For a second La Périchole turned into the actress Baklanova. But she was not angry. She smiled. Naturally I should have been grateful to her for that, but I felt so awful just then that I would have needed far more than smiles of encouragement to get me out of my somnambulistic condition.

After a few performances I got over my stage fright, but, unfortunately, what replaced it was not the right emotional state for an actor.

When I came on as a notary's clerk and imagined that all eyes were upon me I was quite wrong. Neither on that first nor on any subsequent occasion did anybody look at me. The spectator's eye had no occasion to dwell on the clerk alone.

When I played the "man in black" the spectator could not see me. But his eye followed attentively that gauze ghost that I set in motion in the air. I sensed that; I felt myself to be an actor.

When I played the clerk on the brightly lit stage I was visible from all sides, but no one looked at me because there was simply no occasion for it. The spectator's eye wandered past me and turned towards the Viceroy or, in the other direction, towards La Périchole, Piquillo, the tipsy notaries or the fat Don Pedro.

Naturally, I settled down in the part but my calm was the wrong sort, something that in the actor's profession is even more dangerous than the wrong sort of excitement. The actor has no right to feel at home on the stage. This feeling corrupts him, it saps the life out of the character, it destroys the feeling of action. From the wrong sort of excitement—stage-fright—the actor ought to develop a creative, active excitement, a studied, organized calm, not that of indifference. If a trapeze performer suffers from an ordinary, human attack of nerves he is bound to fall; at the same time, if he is calmly indifferent, if he neglects to gather his strength, mobilize his inner forces and take an active attitude towards his work, if he lacks what circus performers call "pluck" he is just as certain to fall.

That is why neither in the first phase of human (non-creative) excitement arising out of stage-fright, nor in the second phase of human (non-creative) calm, turning into indifference, did the role of the notary's clerk benefit me. There was no question of creating a part or of feeling action. That meant there was really no role, despite the fact that I made my entrance, in costume and make-up, on a well-lit stage. If this first "visible" part may be considered to have enriched my experience as an actor with a sense of the stage then it must be seen only as a bad experience. It is very dangerous for a beginner to learn pure craftsmanship.

Second Half

I benefited much more from a role I played by pure chance, one which I was never given and which, moreover, I did not play on the stage.

I very much liked the Vakhtangov production of *Turandot* and I often asked for a pass which permitted me to sit on the stairs in the balcony gangway and watch the play.

What I especially liked was Shchukin's performance as Tartalia.

I learned to imitate his way of stuttering and in the intervals of *The Blue Bird* I would amuse the company with these imitations.

Somebody probably mentioned it to Nemirovich-Danchenko for I was invited to act as the compère in the part of Tartalia at a special New Year concert for theatre-workers.

Only my complete lack of experience made me accept the proposal. Now I would not risk doing it for anything in the world, and, what's more, I doubt if I could manage it.

But then, I sewed myself a jacket and a pair of short trousers out of some green material I found at home, stuffed a cushion under my belt, put on a cardboard nose with a pair of spectacles on it, and calmly appeared before the public which was sitting at tables.

It included poets, writers, actors from other theatres, and, finally, Nemirovich-Danchenko himself.

My turn went down well. I was led from table to table and introduced to various "celebrities."

How can this success be explained?

Was it simply that I was naively innocent of all the difficulties that lay ahead of me, of all responsibilities? Did my histrionic boldness and faith in the rightness of my performance spring from childish thoughtlessness?

Of course not.

That was not the whole story, although it was an important part of it.

Success came thanks to my having an organic feeling for the character. I could say anything, improvise, address the public, in short do anything I wanted to without going outside my role for one second. As if I had put the character on together with the trousers and the green jacket.

The happiness of mastering a role completely is great. The most gifted actors experience it in far from every role they play. Besides, even in successful roles they do not always maintain this organic feeling for the character from beginning to end. Their proximity to the character varies. Truth and falseness interchange. Sometimes the public does not notice it, but the actor always does. Because of these sensations there are parts of the role he likes and others that he dislikes. And what he dislikes is usually those very episodes when the truth of the role is eclipsed.

How was it that I, inexperienced as I was, could have discovered that happiness? How had I managed to get into the role organically, in such a way that for a whole evening I never lost it and lived inside that role easily, happily? The answers to those questions are not to my credit.

I succeeded because the way to that character was relatively easy. Every role, you see, consists of two parts—creating a character and then living it. The first part requires enormous creative imagination. It is impossible to live a character unless you can imagine the person you are playing, every detail of his psychology, of his behaviour and outer appearance.

The fuller and more concrete is the character in your imagination, the more easily, the more organically you will be able to live the role on the stage.

So, in fact, the entire first part of the work on the role I played that evening was done for me by Shchukin. It was his imagination that had created the wonderful character of Tartalia in all the details of its psychology, behaviour and outer appearance.

My imagination was not involved. All I had to do was to imitate, and as the character Shchukin had created was very clear and graphic, it was comparatively easy to imitate it.

Of course, there is acting in imitation too, but that acting is only one half of the business. I knew one actor who could imitate Stanislavsky brilliantly and who in the company of friends or at green-room "rags" could go on being Stanislavsky for as long as you liked, astonishing the public by his acting skill. But the same actor was hopeless in other roles. His powers of observation were adequate only to create an imitated character; to give birth to a new, independent but no less full and complete character one needs to have an actor's imagination too, the capacity to select, combine and unify the material gathered by observation. And evidently, it was just that capacity that the actor lacked.

That is why, despite its apparent success, I cannot consider my Tartalia to be my first role.

I had shown I had sufficient powers of observation to assume another man's character and some ability for imitating that character and of living it organically.

But to live a character is the second part of one's work on a role.

And how to manage the first part of the work, how to create a character itself, that was something I did not know.

CHAPTER FIVE

A Role

Nevertheless my performance at the New Year party rendered me a service.

Two or three days later I read my name on the call list: I was to rehearse the role of Terapot in *La Périchole*.

The role was very small. In the three acts it occupied no more than a few minutes, but those minutes belonged to it, and the role was, hence, a real one.

In addition to his responsibilities as master of ceremonies Terapot has his own definite line in the plot. He tries to make his niece the favourite of the Spanish viceroy, but the viceroy unexpectedly falls in love with the street singer, La Périchole; Terapot thereupon intrigues against La Périchole seeking to arouse the indignation of the ladies-in-waiting against her.

All that in fact takes place in one short monologue addressed to the ladies-in-waiting and the lines I took with me to the rehearsal were confined to a single sheet of paper.

Before a Locked Door

My rehearsals were taken by a small thin woman.

Now and again she put her hand to her abundant auburn hair and her attentive grey eyes changed expression: now they were stern, now alarmed, sometimes they expressed joy, and the next moment they were full of childish confusion.

I had always thought that producers had to be punctilious, strong-willed people who knew beforehand exactly what they wanted to get out of an actor.

Ksenia Kotlubai had nothing at all in common with that conception, and this surprised me the more because she had been a colleague of Vakhtangov's in the past and had produced *Turandot* with him.

As I shook her frail hand I did not know what that little woman was going to mean for me.

The first half-hour made it clear that I simply did not know how to rehearse.

For some reason I felt ashamed to read my lines. My audience of one made me shy. All the time I thought I was being affected and artificial and getting my intonations wrong.

When I waved the piece of cloth in *The Blue Bird* I was absolutely clear in my mind about what I was doing. I was creating a ghost. I felt quite at ease with Tartalia too: I was imitating Shchukin.

But what did I have to do now? How was I going to speak for a man whom I did not know, had never seen or heard?

True, I knew Stanislavsky's formula: "One must play oneself in the given situation."

But it was not as easy as all that. That "given situation" is in the character of Terapot himself. Without him the situation would be different. And, judging from the text, his character did not resemble mine, either in its inner content or in its outer expression.

I had read my lines several times at home and learned them off by heart; but that only made them seem the more strange.

How could I release those inner springs which enable an actor to transform himself and in the guise of another person live with that new person's feelings as organically as if they were his own?

With the help of Ksenia Kotlubai I went through the whole text, taking each "moment" in turn. We elucidated what Terapot meant by each phrase, how he revealed his intentions and where they reached their culmination. We began to imagine his looks, his gestures and manners. We decided that he was probably not a fat round man as my predecessor in the role had played him but a bent, withered-up old man.

All that was very interesting to talk and dream about, but the moment I had to turn those dreams into reality, the moment I began to speak or move, everything became artificial and petty again.

Every time I was brought up against something like a locked door, although that door already was glass-panelled and I could see what was going on at the other side of it.

To open that door I had to feel myself the material out of which the stage character was created and that feeling was something I felt incapable of summoning up.

A Roundabout Way

Then Ksenia Kotlubai suggested a method which no theatre actor had ever used before and which, of course, no producer had thought of.

At that time this roundabout way was probably the most direct and maybe the only possible way for me.

Ksenia Kotlubai knew that I was an artist by profession and besides she had once noticed that I brought a puppet of my own making with me to the theatre and that I had amused the actors with it as we sat drinking tea in the refreshment room. What she now suggested was that I make a puppet of Terapot, of that shrivelled-up, angry, bent old man who already existed in our imagination, and that I should try to rehearse my future role with it.

I was delighted with the idea and two or three days later had an old man with a beard and long hair ready.

I brought the puppet to rehearsal, slipped it on my hand and began trying to play Terapot with it. I did not worry about my lines any more. They remained my lines since I was the one speaking them, but they were also "his" lines because they belonged to the puppet. I lost my feeling of affectedness and at once came to life.

But it gradually became clear that my puppet did not much resemble the role.

We wanted a Terapot who was more cunning and mean by nature, more ugly. In short, the concrete, actor's imagination began to work: not a literary concocting which often merely hinders the actor from feeling the character, not a cerebral imagination, but the imagination of the feelings, organic for the actor and often very hard to put into words.

We decided that we needed a second puppet and I made a new Terapot. Bald, beardless, hook-nosed.

But that one too did not turn out to be what our awakened imaginations were now clamouring for.

We stopped, finally, with the third puppet. Its head was sunk in its shoulders; the face was asymmetrical. The large forehead dropped over one eye and the chin jutted out like that of Philip II in the Velásquez portrait. Judging by the folds beside the parched lips, Terapot's voice ought, probably, to be high, wheedling and sickly-sweet.

But, strange to say, we used the third puppet least of all during rehearsals. Just because it seemed to be exactly the right one and made us laugh a lot by the way it fitted the lines, we wanted to broaden the scope of its behaviour. My puppet had no legs, but we wanted to know how our Terapot would walk, how he would gesticulate. My puppet's arms were short and feeble, but we wanted them to be the long clawlike arms of an old hunchback.

The actor's imagination found its direction. Before my eyes a definite character grew. It was not an outer, physical portrait. Just the contrary. Terapot was to me a real living man and I wanted to play him, that is to personify in myself everything he consisted of: his psychology, his intentions, his physical behaviour.

Living the Character

The first half of the process of creating the role was complete; I began to work on the second half, that is, on merging myself completely in the character and learning to live it.

I found it interesting to set Terapot tasks quite different from those which were his on the stage.

I imagined that the foyer where we rehearsed was a picture gallery and that Terapot was one of the visitors looking at the exhibits. He is in company and for that reason moves about in a rather free-and-easy manner, emphasizing his desire not to be embarrassed by his physical handicap and to be independent and calm. I made Terapot do the most commonplace everyday things such as tending a samovar, chopping fire-wood or reading a newspaper, so that I could understand how Terapot himself felt when no one was looking at him, when, that is to say, he was not thinking of his appearance.

I grew accustomed to living inside the character in all and every circumstance: after all, people do not change in different circumstances but only reveal themselves differently, remaining the same at heart. That means that the stage character has to be felt organically, in such a way that it will stand up to any task set it. When that is achieved the role fits the actor like a new skin and that feeling of compactness gives rise to the sense of joy and inner freedom peculiar to the actor. When he feels that freedom the tasks set by the play are only a few of the possible ones, only a part of the life of the character and not its entire life, and then the fulfilment of those tasks becomes easy and natural.

When the time came for me to begin rehearsing with the rest of the company I could rehearse quite easily. My colleagues praised me. A new Terapot, a nasty, mean old man, was a surprise to them. They were interested.

At last I had to get into the skin of the character in the full sense of the words, that is, to go into costume and make-up.

As I had my puppet before me all the time I tried to make myself up to look like what was in fact the original of my role.

For that make-up paints were insufficient. I had to resort to cotton wool and gauze for a big glued-on chin and nose, and to soft paste-like plasticine for the protrusions over my brows, which I made meet the forehead to give the impression that the forehead was hanging over the eyes.

I had a lot of trouble with the costume too. At first the tailors made a special "truss," a sort of waistcoat with a hump on the back. After fitting it they made me a tunic with an enormous starched collar.

But as it turned out the artificial hump did not make me into a hunchback at all. I had to lengthen my legs and arms and shorten my trunk. To lengthen the arms the shoulders had to be padded and, strange to say, the sleeves shortened so that as much wrist as possible was shown.

To lengthen my legs very high heels were fixed to my shoes and, in addition, the shoes padded with cork soles.

Finally, to shorten my trunk, I had to wear a broad Spanish cummerbund wrapped so high round my waist that it came almost up to my collar-bones.

During the fitting all that was very interesting and I thought I would find rehearsing even easier and more interesting, because in the mirror I saw just the person I imagined Terapot to be.

But just the opposite happened.

The costume and make-up made the role go awry. I sprang out of the character and I felt lonely and uncomfortable.

Previously I had turned myself into a hunchback: I drew my head into my shoulders and lifted my shoulders. I "made" a face, screwing up one eye and thrusting out my lower lip. Now the hump and the face were not my own work but that of the tailors and the make-up artist. My shoulders were raised by cotton wool, my chin was glued on and the habit I had got into of making certain physical movements was now only a handicap to me. I had to rehearse everything all over again to make the costume, the heels, the chin and nose fit completely and become as comfortable to wear as my own jacket and my own chin. And only when I had come to like the sound of my high heels tapping, when my cloak became a help, when my hands forgot that they wore gloves, only then did everything gradually fall into place and Ksenia Kotlubai dare to show me to Nemirovich-Danchenko.

I faced an audience and felt so scared that I remember only the footlights, the sympathetic eyes of my colleagues and the tenseness of my whole body.

Of course I said and did everything I had to, but quite mechanically, though, no doubt, it was an accurate repetition of what had been instilled into me at rehearsals.

Nevertheless Nemirovich-Danchenko accepted my work and said I could perform in one of the next performances.

My comrades congratulated me. I was happy.

First-Night Flop

In the interval before the act in which I appeared Ksenia Kotlubai came to my dressing-room, scrutinized me thoroughly, said a few words of encouragement and went into the auditorium; I went upstairs to the small vestibule outside the ladies' dressing-rooms in order to turn over my lines once again with the "ladies-in-waiting."

Word had run round the company that I was a good actor and, as is usual on such occasions, the wings were quite crowded with people interested in seeing how the novice shaped.

All of which, of course, flattered me. I acted with a special sense of satisfaction.

I expected to see Ksenia Kotlubai in the next interval. It was for her to bring confirmation of my success from the auditorium. But something detained her and she did not come. Perhaps she was talking to someone.... Five minutes passed. Ten. The interval was over, the curtain went up on the next act, but there were no signs of her. I hurried to the stage door and learned that Ksenia Kotlubai had left the theatre during the previous interval, before my entrance. Feeling utterly at a loss I rang her up at home. "We'll have a talk tomorrow," she told me dryly, unkindly.

All the joy I felt from my first role vanished. I hated my false chin, my hump, my high heels. I lost no time in tearing the paste from my nose and brows, in freeing myself from my silk cummerbund.

Next day, in the same room we used to rehearse in, I met Ksenia, and she said to me in the same unkind voice: "Last night, before you went on, I went upstairs to hear you running over your lines. I felt nervous about you. I was afraid you would mix up everything. I didn't want you to catch my nervousness from me, so I listened from the corridor. And from your voice I could tell that you were enjoying your run through, you were acting your part before the ladies. In fact, you were showing off.

"At that moment your partners had become the audience for you; that's to say they'd ceased to be partners. Terapot's lines were just thrown to the wind. I detested your boastful 'play-acting' a few minutes before you had to take the stage and act properly. There's an enormous difference between a rehearsal and the performance. You can act only during a performance. At rehearsals you should test yourself, polish up, assemble the details.

"What's more, I'm sure that during the performance you went on acting for your colleagues standing in the wings. If I'm right, that wasn't acting but cheap vanity.

"I didn't want to see you doing that so I left."

I do not think I properly understood everything that Ksenia Kotlubai said then but I felt quite certain that I was guilty and that she had described accurately the state of mind I had been in during the performance as well as in the vestibule. What I had been thinking about was, of course, not the role, not my responsibility to the performance as a whole but things quite outside the role—vanity and other shameful things.

On my next appearance I had no such self-assurance in my performance and probably acted worse than ever, but from that time on I really began to enter into the role in relation to the stage and the audience and gradually recovered what I had learned during the rehearsals. The joy of living the part, without superfluous boastfulness, began to arise all over again.

My Teacher

It was only after several performances, and then without giving me warning, that Ksenia Kotlubai came to watch me from the auditorium. Next day she made a number of comments; praising me for some things, suggesting a few improvements. I was happy to find that she was not going to give me up as I had feared she might. Had that happened I would have felt like a blind man abandoned by his guide in the middle of a busy city square. It was not only that Ksenia Kotlubai would help me to correct and perfect the role. It was much more than that.

Everybody, not only the beginner, and irrespective of his profession, needs to be able to go for advice and assistance to someone he holds to be the final authority.

If you have that confidence in someone then, no matter how severe is the judgement of your behaviour or intentions, you will not search for any roundabout way of justifying anything false or dishonest in your work.

I had unlimited confidence in Ksenia Kotlubai from the moment I met her. For that reason meeting her meant much more to me than simply meeting a good, experienced teacher and producer.

Luckily for me, Ksenia Kotlubai did not give me up. She was pitilessly honest in her verdicts on my work and to the end of her short life remained my teacher in the fullest and broadest sense of the word, remained my actor's conscience.

As it turned out I worked on most of my subsequent roles with other producers, and later on, at quite another theatre, but I always applied to myself the strict criteria of Ksenia Kotlubai.

During the last weeks of her life I visited her in hospital. That autumn I had just transferred from the Nemirovich-Danchenko Musical Theatre to the Second Moscow Art Theatre. I was to understudy that fine actor Azarin. That was a responsible and risky job. In the Musical Theatre I was considered a capable actor though lacking enough singing voice for the stage; at the Art Theatre, on the other hand, I was considered a passable singer but there were serious doubts about my acting ability. The part I had to understudy became a test of the right to take my place at least among the novices, and, naturally, I was nervous.

When I went to see Ksenia in hospital I told her how anxious I felt about my new role.

First she smiled that special distant smile that you see on the lips of people who are seriously ill when some strong, healthy person comes to see them. Then she drew from under the blanket her frail little hands, laid them on the dead-white sheet and carefully turning her face towards me, said: "When you start rehearsing with partners, don't you dare think of it as a 'test'. Don't mind them seeing that you're deficient in skill or temperament. Rehearse the way you need to. Carefully, treating the character delicately, with feeling. Get the idea out of your head that someone might form an opinion of you during rehearsal. That would be shabby and unworthy. The main thing is the role, the future performance. The rest is much less important and can only harm you. Besides, if you think of your role only as a test, you'll flop on the stage too."

These words, the last piece of advice that Ksenia Kotlubai gave me, helped me through the early rehearsals with my new comrades. She never saw me in the role.

When I came to play it she was no longer alive, and had left me but the memory of my first and dearest teacher, one who gave me for the rest of my days that measure of responsibility for life in art that is so difficult to define in words.

CHAPTER SIX
Lessons of the Human Theatre

First of all I ought to explain what I mean by the "human" theatre.

Hard as I have thought, I haven't been able to find a more suitable definition to apply to every kind of theatre other than the puppet theatre. And I need one now because later in this book I turn to what is now my main profession, puppets.

How am I to distinguish those forms of theatre in which the spectator sees live people on the stage, played by no less living actors, from the theatre where he sees puppets?

You cannot lump all those theatres together under the description "dramatic," because that would mean genre and not a kind of theatre, and, besides dramatic theatres there is opera and ballet and variety. Moreover, there can be productions in the puppet theatre which we shall have to call dramatic, opera, ballet or variety. So it occurred to me to use the term "human" as the inverse of "puppet," despite the fact that the puppet theatre, like any other theatre, speaks only of man, treats man and that the physical inspirer of the puppets is, after all, an actor, a living man.

So the term "human" I have chosen distinguishes that form of theatre from the puppet theatre only in the sense that in the human theatre the outer visible character is portrayed by a human being whereas in the puppet theatre this is done by a puppet. In everything else the puppet theatre is as "human" as any other theatre.

I had to make this definition clear at this point so as not to have to dwell on it later and so that the reader should not reproach me for ambiguity or imprecision in use of terms.

In this chapter, I intend to say something about the "lessons of the human theatre," the lessons I learned from fourteen years of work first in the Nemirovich-Danchenko Musical Theatre and then in the Second Moscow Art Theatre.

Of course, I learned much more than I can tell now, and some of the other things I learned I will come back to later; now I will dwell only on the main thing: that which had direct influence on my conception of the theatre and on my present work in it.

I shall not list and describe all my roles. I shall refer only to those which, independent of their size or success, bring out the main points of the lessons most clearly, in other words, those in which I learned something important.

However, because I learned my lessons also as the result of observing the work of others and then drawing conclusions for myself I shall often have to digress from my own work.

It must also be borne in mind that in considering roles that now lie deep in the past I shall perforce judge them from my present position regarding art and draw comparisons with what is going on around me today. Some parts of this chapter may therefore seem over-theoretical but I would like to remind the reader once more that I have no intention of laying down the law to anybody. So please consider any theoretical statement I make simply as a rule which I am now trying to apply to my own work.

A Serious Warning

I find it hard to remember now whether Nemirovich-Danchenko saw my Terapot the first time I played the role or later on when I had more or less mastered it, but, in any case, I was very eager to have a talk with him to find out whether I was going to keep the role or not.

Nemirovich-Danchenko praised me. I kept the part and played it during the whole eight years of my work at that theatre. But my talk with Nemirovich-Danchenko turned out to be far more important for me than that.

He told me that on the whole he liked my Terapot, but added that there was a certain latent danger in my acting which I ought to know about because it could spoil the whole role in future.

I walked for a long while with Nemirovich-Danchenko up and down the semicircular corridor near the entrance to the auditorium; I felt that he was choosing his words carefully, as if he feared that because of my youth and inexperience I might not understand what he was explaining to me.

And indeed, that complicated relationship which exists between the actor and the character he is portraying—a relationship so difficult to define—took a quite unexpected turn during my talk with Nemirovich-Danchenko. He said: "You act Terapot as an angry, ugly, slimy, repulsive figure, and you are right for that is how he is and how he ought to be shown. But the repulsiveness and ugliness must belong to the character alone, to Terapot, and not be transferred to you personally. A character can be unpleasant but the spectator must not feel that the actor himself is an unpleasant or ugly man.

"This law applies not only to the actor but to everything the audience sees on the stage, everything within the range of sight, everything that is 'playing' on the stage.

"For instance, in *The Lower Depths,* there are some dirty rags lying on a bank. The audience realizes that they are dirty but it does not think for one moment that there are bedbugs in those rags. If it thought that, it would have a sense of physical discomfort. The Baron is filthy, repulsive, he never washes his shirt—if, indeed, he has one at all—but, all the same, the spectator does not think that the actor playing the Baron stinks of sweat and never washes.

"In just the same way the spectator must not think that the actor playing a bad man is bad himself. If the audience thinks that the negative qualities of a character are transferred to the actor himself, it will not like watching him. That's something an actor must understand."

I cannot remember the exact words but I recall what Nemirovich-Danchenko meant by them and I think I am conveying the sense accurately. I found the example of the rags in *The Lower Depths* particularly telling. I remembered those rags at once, I remembered how they had made on me an impression of absolute reality though it had never entered my mind that real dirty rags might have been used on the stage.

That meant that I, the spectator, realized somewhere in my subconsciousness that the rags were "acting" at being dirty; but until that talk with Nemirovich-Danchenko I had never suspected the existence of that subconscious feeling. That example of his made me test what was really going on inside me as a spectator, and I found out that Nemirovich-Danchenko was quite right.

And since the rags are accepted by the spectators simultaneously as fact and fiction, without the two being considered identical, it follows that the same unconscious duality applies to the relations between spectator and actor. The spectator simultaneously believes in the truth of the character but subconsciously separates character from player.

This same subconscious disassociation of fact from fiction on the part of the spectator applies to the action too. If, for instance, the audience thought for one moment that the actor playing Othello was really suffocating the actress playing Desdemona half the audience would rush out of the theatre in horror and the other half would storm the stage to rescue the actress. As that does not happen it means that here, too, the spectator makes a difference in his mind between a stage murder and a real murder.

This simple, logical conclusion was a novelty to me. I suddenly realized that there could be no question of an absolute identification of character and performer in the spectator's mind and that I had made too crude an interpretation of the creative practice of the Art Theatre and its demand that the actor be absolutely true to life on the stage.

Of course, Nemirovich-Danchenko was right, but how was one to put into practice what he preached? How could one play a scoundrel without looking as though one were a scoundrel oneself, yet at the same time preserving the organic feeling of the character?

Where did the watershed lie? It would be pointless simply to soften the character, to make Terapot less of a scoundrel, to reduce his ugliness, get rid of the hump. Besides, that was not what Nemirovich-Danchenko was asking for. He asked for something else and that, evidently, was not to be found in the character of Terapot but in my inner attitude to the character. I had learned that on the path to a character you can stray on to tracks that lead to the abyss. And if you fall into that abyss you risk being smashed to bits.

Nemirovich-Danchenko's warning was all the more grave because it concerned the very first role of my acting career. Obviously I stood in real danger and ought to be worrying about it.

In that sense I understood Nemirovich-Danchenko very well, but I had only a very hazy theoretical idea of how to avoid that danger, what I ought to do, on what paths it was dangerous to turn aside and what sign-posts those paths had. No actor was ever saved from anything by conceptions so purely vague and theoretical.

A Character Comedian

My next role after Terapot was that of Strymodorus, the leader of chorus of old men in *Lysistrata*.

One critic called this production "The Fire in the *Cherry Orchard*." And, indeed, it seemed to be the antithesis of everything the audience expected to see on the stage of the Moscow Art Theatre. After so many plays devoted to psychological subjects, to the searching analysis of individual characters and their personal fates, Aristophanes' frank farce was as unexpected as would be the sudden appearance of a Bacchante in Uncle Vanya's room.

The main characters of the play are the people, the crowd. The main plot turns on the decision of the entire female population of Greece to boycott their husbands so long as they went on fighting internecine wars; the main idea of the play is the struggle for peace, for health, joy and life.

The production was bold and brilliant. Some people were shocked by its "indecency," others praised it for its youthful freshness, its optimism, and, in the last analysis, for its purity.

Nemirovich-Danchenko produced, with Leonid Baratov as his chief assistant. The sets were by the well-known Isaac Rabinovich who was then only at the beginning of his career as a stage designer.

The stage was stripped of all wings, floats and backcloths and for the first time the audience saw it as a whole in all its depth and breadth. On the revolving stage against an unbroken background of strident blue, rose white columns and architraves, flights of steps, platforms and passage-ways, all in the same tone of white.

As there were no wings the stage could not be entered from the sides and on most occasions the actors came up from below stage through an enormous well with a broad flight of stairs in it.

There was no scene-shifting but each time the revolving stage turned, the group of snow-white columns looked different and presented new possibilities for the mise en scene.

The stage revolved and, consequently, the scenes changed with the curtain up and all the lights on. There is nothing new in that now, for many producers have used those methods since that time but that was the first occasion that the revolving stage had been turned in full view of the audience and it created a tremendous impression on people who came to the theatre unprepared for it, and still more so on regular Art Theatre supporters. The impression was all the greater because sometimes the acting went on while the stage was turning. The rapid dance of the young warriors or the slow walk of the old men sometimes went on in the same direction as the stage was turning, sometimes in the opposite. This created an extra sense of speed or slowness.

But the most notable quality of that production was the fact that with all the originality of treatment the main thing was the theme of the play, that moving theme of life, so precise in its political and social tendency. And it was surprising that the oldest in years of Russian producers should have turned out to be the youngest in spirit in those early days of Soviet theatre. That was something I did not realize or appreciate when I was rehearsing and acting in *Lysistrata,* but only many years later.

I shall have to return to *Lysistrata* in my second book when I come to write about my work as a producer; here I shall speak only of my feelings as an actor.

My role was far from being a principal one but nevertheless it was very actable. Neither Aristophanes nor his translator and adapter D. Smolin can be considered the author of that role; it was the "invention" of the assistant producer Baratov. He, as it were, split it up between two actors, one of them getting the lines, the other the emotion.

The main outer feature of Strymodorus was his extreme old age and helplessness. He could hardly move without assistance. He was carried on a shield, and supported by two warriors (also old men); he "floated" pompously about the stage issuing orders. But as he was obviously quite toothless it was impossible for anyone to make out what he was saying and therefore he kept an "interpreter" at his side, another old man who repeated every phrase clearly and precisely. So the entire literary text of the role belonged, in fact, to the interpreter, while all the emotions, all the text's inner content belonged to Strymodorus. The audience first grasped the sense of the unintelligible words from the intonation of the old man's voice and then received confirmation through the "interpreter's" loud, indifferent voice.

I was very fond of the role of Strymodorus. I liked the combination in him of absolute senility and the temperamental peremptoriness of a military "leader."

However, in the very first rehearsals I ran into a quite unexpected difficulty. As soon as I began to speak or move, my shoulders rose and my neck shrunk involuntarily. It was a conditioned reflex remaining from my previous role. When I went on to the stage in the role of Terapot my first and absolutely unconscious movement was to lift my shoulders and give myself the physical feeling of being a hunchback. This gesture was quite out of character with my new role and I had to fight against it for a long time before new elements of physical feeling appeared, or rather, before they became reflexes.

Later I understood that this "shoulder raising" was a fault I shared with others. Many actors starting in new roles are afflicted by conditioned reflexes carried over from the past. In my present work as a producer I run into such things all the time. The actor is not to blame for it for I know that the more successful his previous role has been the more difficult it is to adapt himself to a new one. The manner which looked an organic part of a role becomes a hopelessly unpleasant mannerism in the succeeding one.

I am not referring here only to external methods. After all, it is not very difficult to rid oneself of an external manner or characteristic. It is far more difficult to throw off inner manners, but they, too, disappear as soon as the new character enters into its own. The struggle against habits formed by a previous role has to be conducted mercilessly, otherwise those habits creep on from role to role and devour an actor like a moth devours a piece of cloth.

To judge from the reaction of the audience and the press notices my Strymodorus was, after all, a success, but as I acted that lisping ancient with the body of a mummy and the temperament of a bantam cock I always kept in mind my talk with Nemirovich-Danchenko and his example of the rags, and tried to realize where I might be running on to that dangerous path which led to the abyss. In my new role that fatal path was still more difficult to recognize for, to use theatrical terminology, Terapot was a "character villain," while Strymodorus was a "character comic" and as a result the attitude of the public to him was quite different.

Terapot was a dangerous enemy, he could do harm and was therefore not merely funny; Strymodorus was too helpless to be at all dangerous and was thus primarily comic.

The audience is angry with Terapot, but not at all so with Strymodorus. Terapot is a little Iago; Strymodorus is more of a clown than anything else.

The spectator's dislike of Iago may be transferred to the actor; of that I had been warned, but the public likes a funny clown and feels no anger about him.

Did that mean, then, that there were no pitfalls for me in my new role? It seemed so.

Yet during some performances and at certain places in the role I felt I was doing something wrong, and if, on those occasions, there happened to be someone I knew in the audience I felt scared to ask his opinion of my performance. I felt ashamed.

I could not have put into words just what I was ashamed of, but that inner sense of shame did sometimes arise, and I realized it had something to do with what Nemirovich-Danchenko had warned me about.

Look How Nice I Am!

One day Ksenia Kotlubai attended a concert at which I appeared. Afterwards she barely mentioned my performance but to my surprise asked me why in making my bow I had pulled my shirt-cuffs down. She spoke with asperity, there was a shadow in her eyes and I felt ashamed of myself. This time I clearly saw the reason for feeling ashamed. Ksenia was right. My cuffs had not bothered me in the slightest and I had pulled them down just to give the impression of behaving naturally. Pure coquetry. "Look, what a nice natural manner I have! What an easy smile! How modestly and simply I behave while you applaud. Look, I'm even adjusting my cuffs!"

And though it had been a success my concert turn was as good as spoiled for me by my exhibitionism.

I had allowed myself to do the very things that shocked me in others. At once a host of memories flocked into my mind.

I remembered a circus acrobat performing on a trapeze. She had a strong, nimble body. She stood on one hand, right up against the very top of the tent, then swept down, turned a double somersault and with astonishing precision grasped another trapeze. She was the very epitome of strength, audacity and perfect physical fitness; she conveyed these qualities to the spectators and every one of them wanted to match her in strength and agility, to be no less audacious, no less perfectly fit than she was. The public was in raptures about her magnificent feats.

But when she had finished, she sprang down on to the yellow sand of the circus ring and with a coquettish little "Ap!" slapped herself on the thigh; then she made a stylish side-step and smiled invitingly. Why did she have to do that? Surely her splendid acrobatic feats did not require it. Wasn't the public's joy and applause enough for her? Did she have to stimulate it with methods that have nothing whatsoever to do with art?

Why after showing us her remarkable body in all its beauty did she have to show its personal, feminine beauty?

Well, it seemed that I too had felt dissatisfied with my concert performance and that like the acrobat I had decided to stimulate success by making a personal exhibition of myself with my false modesty and winning smile. There was an element of prostitution in it, and that at its worst, "prostitution of the soul." I stood guilty before my severest judge, Ksenia Kotlubai. I had sinned against the public, above all against my profession.

But such personal exhibitions ("Just look how nice I am!") can take place not only when one is making one's bow.

Exhibitionism often creeps into the creative process itself and becomes the hard core of the role. It is that old "germ of vanity" again, but in a special form, the most dangerous, probably, of all its forms. If there does not happen to be a keen-sighted and ruthless doctor in the neighbourhood of the victim of this disease, a doctor in whose diagnosis the patient has unquestioning faith, then the unhappy fellow will find it very difficult to diagnose his own malady. And, besides, he can raise at first sight very convincing objections by affirming that, in art, exhibitionism is generally unavoidable.

True enough, every character, whether it be created by a writer on the pages of a book, by an artist on canvas or by an actor on the stage, has its origin in the author and comes to life through him.

The author's thoughts and feelings are the material of which the character consists. Whatever a writer speaks about in his works, his characters nonetheless pass through the emotions of the writer and his experiences during the act of writing.

On the stage, moreover, the physical properties of the executant enter into the material: his hands, arms, legs, his eyes, his voice. However much the actor changes his face, his gait, his voice, he is creating the character with the help of the physical means he possesses. And in just the same way, however far the spiritual qualities of a character may be from those of the actor himself, his own spiritual qualities are involved in his portrayal of that character.

That is all indisputably true; there is, however, a great difference between an actor who uses himself as material for creating and revealing a character (which is not already himself) and the one who uses a character to make a display of himself.

The first way leads to art; the second leads to exhibitionism, to prostituting one's talents.

Perhaps that is the reason why we find so few good leading ladies and leading men, especially in what is known as the classical repertoire. The performers of these roles have to have fine figures, good looks and beautiful voices and as a result they prostitute themselves willy-nilly and substitute themselves for the characters they ought to be playing.

I do not at all mean to say that there should not be any good-looking men and women on the stage, but it is one thing to create the character of Laurencia in *Fuente Ovejuna* with the help of one's personal gifts, one's beauty—and quite another to play Laurencia as a means of displaying one's own good looks.

The "sweet malady" of exhibitionism is by no means limited to the display of an actor's physical qualities. On the contrary, the prostitution of spiritual qualities is found much more frequently. "Look what a profound soul I have, see how subtly I feel, how sincerely I suffer!"

This path is all the more perilous because it is often "justified" by "emotion," something which Stanislavsky insisted on for actors of the Art Theatre school.

There is no greater name in the history of the Russian theatre than that of Konstantin Stanislavsky. Nobody has done so much to reform the theatre of the whole world. But Stanislavsky's terminology sometimes serves as a stronghold for actors and producers who would have horrified Stanislavsky himself and whom he would certainly never have considered as his disciples.

The word "emotion" has, in particular, given rise to many quite contradictory opinions.

Stanislavsky forbade an actor to act his feelings on the stage. He used to say that it was impossible to act joy or grief, impossible to act a "result." And yet it is just those actors who do nothing else but "act feelings," who suffer, pine, groan, who produce the most extraordinary tremulous sounds, who try to run up and down a gamut of at least two octaves in one sentence—it is precisely these actors who explain everything by saying they are acting according to the Method and building their roles on "emotion."

Stanislavsky maintained that all roles are character roles and that the spiritual beauty of the hero has to be assumed by the actor in the same way as a clearly defined "character" has to be. Yet many actors, juggling with that term "emotion," shamelessly prostitute their feelings on the stage without even trying to get into the character of the role.

If they find the term "emotion" inadequate to justify their behaviour they quote what Stanislavsky said about the necessity of "going out of oneself." This formula is useful and true, but in applying it you must really "go out of yourself."

If you really go from yourself to the character your personal qualities are turned into the qualities of the character; but if you take the wrong path, thinking less of the "going" than of yourself, you will only be prostituting yourself. To say the least, it is immodest to consider that one's personal spiritual qualities are as beautiful as those of the "Knight in the Tiger Skin," Juliet, or Zoya Kosmodemyanskaya. Especially as modesty was one of the distinguishing features of those characters. No actress will ever succeed in playing the role of Juliet or of Zoya if she considers herself as fine as they were, or thinks that it is sufficient for her to show her own purity in order to portray the purity of Zoya.

That is seen specially clearly in the concert hall.

A singer renders "Were I a little bird to fly in the sky" and puts everything into trying to show that she herself is that "little bird," hopping from the window-sill to the porch. You blush for a singer like that. You cannot look at her. The point is not whether she does or does not resemble a fluttering bird. The point lies in the immodesty of her behaviour, in her desire to play up her feminine qualities by means of the romance.

But once one gets rid of that desire everything gets into place. The crippled singer Zoya Lody, when far from young, sang "I am young and slender, come for me, I will hurry to the Rialto before sunset," and thanks to the fact that the singer made no attempt to identify herself with the heroine, the audience did not feel even the slightest pang of regret that the character does not match the singer in looks.

Zoya Lody saw the character "above herself" and built it up as something beautiful and independent, and thus was able to convey it to the audience.

The renowned Gypsy singer Varya Panina used to sing seated, almost motionless. Sometimes she sang male songs, but this did not seem inappropriate to the audience because she did not falsify the character in any way and never substituted herself for it.

And yet the same romances are often sung from the concert stage with such absolute conviction that everything conveyed by the words and music is directly related to the singer's own person that one feels really ashamed to go on watching.

Some singers manage to appropriate to themselves even Russian songs. A song which has the ring of genuine art on the lips of a peasant girl at an evening gathering is changed into something astonishingly immodest by the manner in which some variety actresses sing it, and, in any case, has absolutely nothing in common with the noble poetry of folk song.

Oh yes, I hear you saying, but what about Shalyapin? Surely when he performed—not only on the stage but on the concert platform—*he* did not limit himself to rendering the literary and vocal content of a song? *His* eyes and brows did not remain calm and motionless. The character *he* was portraying shone through every physical movement. In every turn of the head, in the expressive movements of his hands, in every gesture of his extraordinary body. He acted every romance as he sang it.

All that is true, but those of you who were fortunate enough to hear and see Shalyapin on the concert stage probably remember a very interesting detail that escaped notice at first. Although Shalyapin's concert repertoire was not very extensive, although he certainly must have known every romance by heart, he always came on with the music in his hands, and while singing raised a lorgnette to his eyes and glanced at the music. And in this way Shalyapin kept a constant, if very thin line of demarcation between himself, the singer, and the character in whose name he was singing.

That is why when the grey-haired Shalyapin sang "Black hair curls over my shoulders" the audience did not feel anything false. Shalyapin's art lay just in that ability to make his grey hair look like black curls.

Of course, the concert hall is not the theatre. The character on the concert stage is more graphic and it is easier to draw a line of demarcation between oneself and the character. Yet that line does exist on the stage, though in even thinner form. I could give dozens of examples of actors on the stage who, if not always consciously, turn their acting into prostitution.

Sometimes this process reaches a point when it becomes positively repulsive, being based on some "creative method," on a cynical principle that "guarantees success." Many producers and impresarios in foreign theatres and more especially in the cinema look for actors and actresses on the basis of their "sex appeal," to use an American expression. And so, instead of a character, instead of a role on the stage or screen we get outright prostitution: trade in calves, thighs, passionate sighs, "innocent" downcast eyes, luscious lips. None of that has anything to do with the character; they are personal qualities of the actor or actress; the role is simply a lucky chance for displaying them.

Even when the actor's appearance coincides with that of the character, his playing will not look like exhibitionism if he masters the subconscious feeling of the barrier between himself and the character.

The actress Maretskaya, using practically no make-up to alter her face, could create on the stage two astonishingly different characters—the cunning, experienced conqueror of men's hearts, Goldoni's Mistress of the Inn, and the pure, childishly-clumsy, tender, fifteen-year-old Mashenka in the title part of Afinogenov's play. Maretskaya could do that not only because she was talented but because she was fonder of the characters than of herself in them.

There, it seems to me, lies the secret of that demarcation line between the actor and the character which it is so important to keep. If the actor sincerely feels that the character he is portraying is more positive, more heroic, braver or purer than he is himself, then he will always remain conscious of that line.

This feeling in no way prevents the actor from genuinely summoning up all his personality. On the contrary: in attempting to give the fullest possible expression to the character the actor involuntarily mobilizes the best forces that are in him; when that happens, his personal qualities are not less but more visible than in the case of an actor who prostitutes his personal gifts. However, by being fully revealed they become the qualities of the character, magnified by the strength of the actor's urge to perfect the character.

The danger of exhibitionism and the methods of overcoming it are to be found in literature too. One would think that memoirs were the most personal of literary genres; yet among memoirs one finds some which one cannot read without blushing for shame, so boastfully and immodestly are they written, while there are others in which the author feels the theme to be much more important than himself—and in that case personal reminiscence becomes just a vehicle for helping to develop the theme, not an end in itself.

The memoirs of Protopope Avvakum are highly characteristic in this sense. Avvakum's hatred of Patriarch Nikon, whom he considered to be a heretic, and his fanatical belief in the cause of the Old Believers made every episode in his personal life a literary argument, a means of expression in the development of his theme. And literary argument is always an image.

Over a period of eighteen months Julius Fučik wrote his *Notes from the Gallows*. Every minute spent in prison was horrible in the extreme, and every second spent in writing an act of extreme heroism. But not once did Fučik describe his own feelings in order to arouse pity in a possible future reader, to win approval of his firmness or raise a memorial to himself. The theme of assertive life, of struggle, was for Fučik greater than the theme of personal suffering, and just because he did not think about it for one moment, he became the personification of heroism.

Lyrical poetry too is basically memoirs. But when lyrical poetry, even of a very personal kind, goes beyond the limit of personal biography in its theme, in its general conclusions, you have absolutely no feeling of exhibitionism. The lyrical poetry of Pushkin or Mayakovsky is in that category. But if you look at some of the poetry of Yesenin you find that exhibitionism sometimes gets the upper hand, and then the reader is more interested in the poem as personal gossip than he is in the image and the theme.

This element of gossip is sometimes unpleasant in the works of a poet as great as Yesenin; in lesser poets it is simply intolerable.

Ten years ago a young poetess published a little volume of verse. At the head of many of her poems stood dedications to a well-known actor. And the poems that followed described just what had taken place between the authoress and the person to whom the poem was dedicated. This was exhibitionism in its most extreme form.

The result was something like the game of Consequences: "Who? With whom? What did they do? What were the consequences?" One could fill in all the answers. Who? The poetess. Her picture was even provided on the dust-jacket. With whom? With the well-known actor whose name appeared in the dedication. Where? On the beach. What did they do? They kissed. What were the consequences? She returned to her husband with "tired lips." There was no reply, however, to the principal question: Why? Why did the reader have to know all that? Why was the incident important? What does it sum up? What does it show in people's lives? The poetess simply lacked the talent for that general conclusion which can turn the most personal event into a poetic image, and as a result the kisses on the beach remained nothing more than gossip.

Of course all this did not come clear to me at once; nevertheless, from that day when Ksenia Kotlubai reproached me for being coquettishly "natural" I tried to keep an eye on myself, not only during concert performances but in every new role too, especially in lyrical and psychological parts.

The actor in a lyrical role finds it much more difficult to create a complete scenic character and, at the same time, avoid "coquettishness" than one in a well-defined character part. I know several actors whose looks are all in their favour for the roles of lyrical heroes but who, strange to say, turn out to be sentimental and tastelessly affected in those roles while they are quite successful in creating subtle characters in character roles.

Speaking of my own experience, I felt the danger of exhibitionism most acutely when playing the small role of Prince Fyodor in *The Death of Ivan the Terrible*. My most difficult scene was the last one when Fyodor, a helpless child, learns of the death of his father and Tsar.

This is only a small episode in the role. Shrieking: "Father! Tsar!" the boy who does not yet believe in what has happened, runs across the entire stage and then, noticing the prostrate body, stops and cries once more: "Father!" and flings his arms round the man whom, perhaps for the first time in his life, he recognizes not as the Tsar but as his father.

In rehearsing this scene I always bore in mind that in another moment Fyodor's shriek would become pathological but that I must keep his despair within limits. I consulted some of the senior members of the company; one actor told me that in such cases he found it very helpful to think of some harrowing experience he had lived through in his own life. Recalling his personal grief he tried to relive it on the stage and his memories agitated him and helped him to draw on the particular feelings required in the role.

I found this advice simply appalling. Even in real life I little believe people who like to share their grief with others. Some of them do it so readily that their display of emotion becomes suspicious. And to behave that way on the stage seemed to me not only to dishonour the person whose sufferings or death was the reason for my grief but also to be false in terms of the theatre.

In my doubts I turned to Sophia Giatsintova. At that time Giatsintova was acting the part of Nelly in Dostoyevsky's *The Insulted and Humiliated*, and the perils of taking the wrong path of self-pity in that role were still greater than with my Fyodor.

Giatsintova convinced me that I was right. It happened that at the very time she was playing Nelly she had a heavy load of family sorrow to endure, almost analogous to that which her heroine in the play had to endure.

She told me, though, that in playing Nelly she tried to do exactly the opposite to what the actor I mentioned advised me to do.

In the scene when Nelly tells of the death of her mother Giatsintova made every effort to prevent a single side of her role, the slightest intonation, coincide with her own private experiences.

It was very difficult for her not to touch her own feelings while playing, especially when the grief she had to act coincided with her personal grief—it meant offending her personal feelings and hampering her stage feelings.

There are actors who are very proud that they can cry on the stage with real tears and thus show how deeply their feelings are touched, how thoroughly they enter into a role. But for some reason I was always bothered if from the audience I saw real tears in an actor's eyes. And, strange as it may sound, real tears became artificial and, far from creating for me an image of grief, destroyed it. I noticed, too, that my neighbours would point out the tears to each other and whisper: "Look, he's crying. Look, there are tears in his eyes, real tears!" At that moment the character disappeared and in its place was an immodest actor or actress—and that broke the continuity of action.

Of course, great sympathy for the character on the part of an actor may bring tears to his eyes, but it is not worth letting the audience see those tears. They will always remain personal and only hinder the public from believing in the character.

I played the role of Fyodor quite often but, to tell the truth, each performance was something of a matter of chance. Sometimes I found it easy; the lines lay like the links of a chain, connected with a sense of truth. The character of Fyodor was clearly, sharply chiselled. And then, suddenly, at the next performance everything would ring false, the stage grief would get mixed up with notes of my own hysteria and sound artificial and immodest.

The role of Ivan the Terrible was played by Alexander Cheban. He was an actor with a wonderful sense of communion, truthful, "correct" eyes easy to look in. Generally speaking, far from all stage partners are easy to look in the eyes. Whenever I felt I was going astray from the truth I tried to find my Fyodor by establishing contact with Ivan the Terrible, and myself by establishing contact with Cheban.

Sometimes this worked and then I regained the power of feeling myself to be in the scenic truth of the situation, but it was comparatively rare that I felt myself completely inside my role, every second, from the beginning to the final curtain. Most performances were patchy—a particle of truth, a particle of falseness, then again truth, again falseness. I liked Fyodor, liked him a lot, but I could not grow really fond of the role. Simply because I suffered so much all the time I was acting it.

I was suffering again in the role of Volgin in Afinogenov's play *The Crank*. Volgin is the main character in the play. He is a young, sincere, honest man with plenty of initiative. People consider him a crank because of his candour, his unwillingness to compromise, his romantic belief that truth always triumphs. In the play Volgin has to suffer many personal ordeals. His sweetheart marries another, his friends let him down, his first steps in social life lead to failure. But he copes with everything, summons up his strength for the struggle and, in the long run, the truth he believes in does triumph.

The role of Volgin was splendidly played by Azarin. I was chosen to understudy him on a tour. I had to prepare this big part on my own and act it with only one rehearsal.

Of course, I could say it was this hurried work that made my acting so inadequate, though, in fact, I did appear in several performances. But there was another reason too. The fault lay in my wrong approach to the part.

I liked Volgin very much. It seemed to me that I was perfectly fitted for the role. In the first place, I shared all his opinions and dreams. Secondly, we were the same age. And, finally, I bore a possible resemblance to him so that I hardly had to use make-up at all.

And yet this apparent resemblance turned out to be not only a hindrance, preventing me getting into the character, but a pretext for substituting myself for the character, for exhibitionism. The actor's imagination failed to function, the character failed to take on independent outlines and would not develop, it just kicked its heels. And if it is true that the only way to act lyrical scenes without flights of sentimentality is to be concrete and individual, then that too is the only way of removing elements of personal hysteria from dramatic scenes and emotions.

Eighteen years have passed since that time. And for thirteen of those years I have been off the "human" stage. However, not long ago I ran into Volgin again quite unexpectedly. The House of the Actor organized a memorial evening for the playwright Afinogenov who had been killed in Moscow during a German air raid. Everybody who knew Afinogenov was very fond of him, and the actors wanted to pay a tribute to his memory by acting excerpts from his plays.

Ex-members of the Second Moscow Art Theatre decided to put on scenes from *The Crank*. On the tiny stage of the House of the Actor there came together Bersenev, Birman, Cheban, Durasova, Lagutin and I.

All of them had appeared in the original performance. At that time, I, as an understudy, never had occasion to act with them. I had only dreamed of doing that, but the dream had been unfulfilled then. Now had come the moment of fulfilment and the strange thing was that with it also came the fulfilment of my attempts to establish contact with the character. I suddenly found myself understanding Volgin in his individuality. True, the contact was a brief one, but it happened that I had to act that very fragment of the role which had been worst of all in my original performance. It was where Volgin found out that his sweetheart was going to marry someone else; when everybody goes off the stage Volgin has a very moving monologue in which I always felt uncomfortable and uneasy. And now that apparently difficult monologue suddenly became easy and clear and my feeling of discomfort disappeared.

This happened, I think, because I understood the monologue—and the character as a whole, for that matter—in its age relationship. I had grown older than Volgin. We used to be the same age but that was eighteen years before and then I had not felt Volgin's youth to be an element in his character. Now, without considering myself an old man, I could not, at any rate, call myself young. Volgin, however, remained as young as Afinogenov described him, and so it was easier for me to grasp the typically youthful aspects of his character, it was easier to understand the type.

It may seem paradoxical, but when I originally played the part of Volgin it was just this coincidence of ages that hindered me from seeing the limits of the character. Now I saw it and as I had played Volgin before and lived the part, if only a few times, my new appreciation of it only pumped fresh blood into its veins.

I am very happy that now I have the right to say that after all I *did* play Volgin. I was able to compensate my sad memories about incomplete contact with the role by acting this short excerpt, and I am glad that my unexpected "relapse" at the House of the Actor did not turn out to be a flop.

Look How Nasty I Am

Ksenia Kotlubai warned me about the danger of prostituting myself that lay in a positive stage character.

Nemirovich-Danchenko had warned me about the danger of the negative aspects of a character possessing the actor.

But if one can understand the desire of an actor to vaunt his good looks, his figure, voice or "soul" what sense would there be for him in boasting of his personal defects, of trying to "sell" them to the public? Why should the actor say: "Look, how nasty I am"?

Does this mean, then, that the reason an actor allows himself to be possessed by these negative features is something other than the desire to boast of his personal defects?

Yet, however strange it may seem, Nemirovich-Danchenko and Ksenia Kotlubai were referring to the same thing, to the substitution of oneself for the character, to the "selling" of one's own features. It is certainly possible to find this in negative roles, indeed, it happens fairly often; it is found quite as frequently in comic parts as in lyrical heroic ones.

I remember seeing an actor playing the role of an old man with long, thin, shaky legs in tights. His legs were so incredibly thin there seemed to be no flesh on them.

The role was a grotesque one. Why should a grotesquely comic old man not have legs like that? There was no reason why not, of course.

And yet, for all the comic aspect of those legs, they evoked in me, sitting in the audience, a certain feeling of protest, of inner resistance against a character which somehow looked unpleasant despite the fact that the actor played the role fairly well. I blushed for the actor for risking to show such horribly ugly legs, for being so brash as to display his personal defects, his ugliness. He was not acting ugliness, he was exploiting it, in exactly the same way that some people exploit beauty—and that is something equally shameless and inadmissible in art.

I understood the full truth of this at a New York dime-show. There I saw two freaks dancing on a small circular stage: an enormously fat woman and a tiny old man, a dwarf. The public laughed. In a corner sat a man in evening dress who was joined at the stomach to the undeveloped body of another man also in evening dress. They were Siamese twins. The public gaped in surprise at these repulsive sights, and went on to the next room where an armless woman was using her toes to type out the name of whoever cared to pay her ten cents. Compared to all these things even the display of trained fleas that was taking place in a small room nearby seemed to be a noble feat of art.

I realize that the things I have just described have nothing in common with art and, moreover, that they are not considered that way by the unhappy people who are obliged to make a display of their misfortunes in order to keep body and soul together; nevertheless it is unfortunately true that in real art one often encounters a quite unjustified intrusion of a similar exploitation of physical defects. An actor will flaunt his stomach instead of creating the character of a fat man and parade his own haggardness instead of acting the part of a beggar.

Of course, an actor has to have some outward resemblance to the character he is playing. It would be difficult, if not impossible, to make a Don Quixote out of a little fat man, and very hard for a tall thin one to play Sancho Panza; but in this sort of part as in lyrical heroic ones it's a question not of the presence of this or that quality but of the way it is made use of. And here again that concerns not only external physical qualities but qualities of emotion, temperament, psychology.

I once saw a man acting the part of Iago and taking such pleasure in the villainy of the character that he was quite unpleasant to watch. And it was the actor, not his Iago, who was repulsive.

This is what Nemirovich-Danchenko had warned me against; evidently, when I felt ashamed of myself for some parts of my Terapot or of my Strymodorus, it had something to do with those places in my performance in which I was relishing their psycho-pathological features.

At that time I had not known how to fight against that feeling of shame, or rather against the reasons for it. Sometimes it seemed to me that I ought perhaps simply to reduce the negative aspects of the character and, to put it crudely, make it more "pleasant," but that, of course, was not only no solution at all, but simply dishonest because there are characters whose negative aspect cannot be reduced; neither the play nor the characters themselves permit of that. How could one present Goering in a "pleasant" light? It would be senseless, why— harmful, to do so. The worse Goering looks on the stage the more credit to the actor playing him.

But what then has the actor to do to prevent making himself repulsive? Only one thing: he must try to reveal the main theme of his role without ever letting himself relish negative details, for that inevitably leads to him being possessed by the features of his role.

I saw Kachalov act Richard III in a concert version and despite the actor's enormous powers of creation there was not the slightest indication that he took any pleasure in the villainy of Richard's soul.

Yet you sometimes find that happening not only on the stage but in literature too; a writer will give himself away in the negative side of his characters. He is so pleased by the utter degradation, the boundless villainy or contrariness of the characters he has created that the reader comes to dislike not only the characters but the author too.

To some extent this feeling is evoked by certain pages in Dostoyevsky about Smerdyakov or old Karamazov.

The pathological memoirs of criminals that are such fashionable reading abroad just now are based on a patently cynical prostitution of the author's own negative features; in them, art is wholly replaced by an exploitation of the basest instincts of author and reader alike.

In those cases the pathological aberration is clear in its repulsiveness, but though smaller doses of it may be less dangerous for reader and spectator they are quite fatal for a writer and even more so for the actor.

Radiolocation

There is a special sort of dream to which theatre folk are prone—actor's nightmare. No one on the stage is immune to it.

It takes different forms, of course. Everyone has his own nightmare. But the theme is always the same. Fiasco. An accident on the stage. You dry up, your wig falls off, you miss your entrance, there is an outburst of coughing in the auditorium so that not a word you say can be heard.

Every actor awakens from a nightmare of this sort his heart bouncing against his ribs like a rubber ball.

The things these nightmares are about take place in reality, otherwise they would never figure in actors' dreams.

As I mentioned above, I had to rehearse the role of Volgin very fast; only on the day of the actual performance was I able to run through the whole role with partners. The result was that I had only an outline of the mise en scene and the development of the plot.

Before the curtain went up I sat at my dressing-room table trying to joke with my companions in an attempt to convince myself that I felt calm, but with the second bell my stage fright had reached such a pitch that it was hard to conceal it, and when at last the curtain rose to reveal the dark chasm of the auditorium I was already in a vacuum.

I spoke a few lines. I answered my partners. I moved from table to sofa, from sofa to table. But all the time I felt catastrophe drawing nearer and nearer. A few more minutes and the performance would come to a halt. There was no play without Volgin and though I, playing that role, was on the stage, Volgin in fact did not exist: instead of him a somnambulist was moving and speaking, and that somnambulist was soon going to stop moving and speaking, for the panic I was in was soon going to get out of control.

Unfortunately for me there were, for some reason, a number of children in the audience. Perhaps there were no more than two or three of them but their squawking made it hard for the public to hear. A man's voice rose shushing the children and then other voices rose shushing him.

In short, I got the impression that no one was listening to me any longer and that the catastrophe had started.

All this ran through my subconscious mind and increased my stage fright all the more.

And then after the next squawk from the auditorium my partner Sergei Popov, playing the role of Igor Gorsky, with whom I was acting a friendly, lyrical scene, turned his back on the audience, smiled at me and said in a low voice: "What's going on? Brought a kindergarten to the theatre, or what?"

For him this performance was nothing out of the ordinary and so he was able to make a quiet interjection on the stage without losing his sense of the part or disturbing the texture of the performance in any way.

I summoned up the power to smile in response and quietly agreed with his comments.

His next words were already back in character, as was my reply.

The dialogue between Igor Gorsky and Boris Volgin continued but meanwhile I was having an inner dialogue with myself: If I had the power to hear Popov's aside it meant I was still "alive." If I could smile and reply with an aside too it meant that all was not lost and that I could fight against this hypnotic terror.

To check myself I deliberately paused a little before my next lines. I found I was able to maintain the pause and was conscious of its length. At that place in my role the conversation between Volgin and Gorsky assumes a note of arguing. I turned sharply on Gorsky and heard the audience react to my move. I could feel the tension in the silent auditorium. My fear had gone completely. There was no need to think of it again.

I could now act and live not with my own emotions but with those of Volgin. I could cross from sofa to table not according to the stage directions but according to the inner necessity of the state of mind in which Volgin found himself in his arguing with Gorsky.

I felt deeply grateful to Popov for having restored my stage sense. I was able to play the part to the end.

Stage sense is something quite unique. Not without reason the exercises set for an actor by the Stanislavsky Method include one of being alone in public. This teaches the actor the ability of existing under the eyes of spectators just as if they were not there; but this does not mean at all that the spectators vanish from the actor's subconsciousness. If that were to happen he would no longer be alone in public but in reality, and that sort of solitariness is essentially impossible on the stage. Except when the actor is in a complete state of panic. Even when the actor thinks that he has completely identified himself with his character and is living in it without having to add any extraneous feeling, he goes on sensing the audience every fraction of a second he is on the stage.

Moreover, this link—so difficult to define—that stretches like a tight thread between actor and audience is the principal source of joy in the process of the actor's creative work.

In professional jargon we speak of an actor's "apparatus." This term includes the whole sum of a given actor's qualities. This "apparatus" is not only a transmitting-set but a receiving apparatus. And if we compare the actor with a sort of technical apparatus then he resembles radar equipment more than anything else, and the process of his work radiolocation.

A radar sends radio beams in certain directions. These beams encounter a mountain, a ship, an aircraft, are reflected and turned back to be received by the same set that has transmitted them and which now uses them to record the object that has reflected them.

The actor directs his looks, his emotions, his voice at the auditorium, and the auditorium picks them up and returns them to the actor in the form of a reflection, and the actor's subconscious mind records the reflected beams that have emanated from his acting.

In this, probably, lies the main difference between the actor and concert performer on the one hand, and the writer, artist, sculptor or composer on the other.

The latter also address their work to the future reader, spectator, or listener but during the process of creation they do not depend on their public, for at that time it does not yet exist. They can presuppose a certain reaction and, to some extent, take it into account, but their work of art begins to act on the public only when the process of creation is complete.

With the actor, though, the process of creation goes on simultaneously with the process of conveying what is created to the public. And the interdependence of actor and audience is so strong that what happens is a sort of mutual act of creation. The length of a pause depends not only on the actor but also on the audience, because the actor's radar equipment hears this pause returned to him from the auditorium, and if his contact with the audience is real and complete the actor can neither prolong nor shorten that pause. The actor's subconscious mind registers not only every rustle, every cough or laugh: he senses the silence of the auditorium with all his being, and the tenseness of that silence too. He senses it and masters it. That is why actors often like to peep through the curtain before a performance: they need to know who will be their partner that night. For it is impossible to act any role on the stage without the active assistance of the audience.

If a play had the same audience night after night an actor would not last a run of ten performances.

The only reason why he can play the same role hundreds of times is that each time that extraordinary contact with the public is re-established and hence every performance is to a certain extent unique.

Second Breath

Sportsmen say that during long-distance running every runner has one specially difficult lap when his forces begin to flag and his heart and lungs refuse to function.

But if you can get through this terrible lap, they say, the organism adapts itself to the running, the heart finds a new rhythm, the blood a new circulation, the lungs breathe anew.

Tiredness vanishes and a man can run many more laps. This is what is called getting one's second breath.

And it happens too that when you are working on a role—assuming, of course, that the role is successful—suddenly at some often quite unexpected moment you get your "second breath."

The life of the character becomes so organic that you can act it without the fear of breaking out of role at any place, of behaving in a way that belies its logic.

In his book *A Story of the Past* Vladimir Davydov writes: "I was always shocked when an actor felt worn out at the end of a performance. All it showed was that something was not quite right in that actor's work. From what I noticed, this sense of fatigue is found only among actors who play, as they say, on their nerves, on inspiration. They are constantly anxious, constantly frightened about the forthcoming scene, about their role as a whole, about the points of stress. But if everything is thought out in advance and the whole framework built firmly and sensibly, why should the process of creation present any difficulties? On the contrary it is a keen pleasure, I would say, the highest rapture. Every scene you act fills you with inspiration, the sympathy of the public raises your creative forces. I have always worked and created on the stage easily and freely."

In these few lines Davydov gives a very clear analysis of the sensations of the actor on the stage, but, alas, his last words can arouse only a sense of envy. It has been the lot of but few actors to have "worked and created on the stage easily and freely." Even gifted and really great actors find that certain roles never quite come off, or fail to win complete freedom for creation in those roles.

That means that unfortunately not every actor—far from it—manages to get through this "difficult lap" in every role. As for myself I doubt if

I could list a dozen occasions in all my stage career at two theatres when I experienced the complete happiness of creation.

Of course I did not fail in each role I was given—had I done so I would simply not have been given the roles—but in almost every one of them were moments when I was spiritually out of step. Even in the role of Feste the Clown in Shakespeare's *Twelfth Night*, which both my colleagues and the critics considered one of my successes, there were blank spots; spells of happiness and freedom on the stage alternated with spells of alarm and constraint, followed in turn by a "second breath," that splendid sense of rapture of which Davydov wrote. And I suppose that the inspiration would be the truest description of that state of rapture.

But you must have noticed that in the sentences I quoted Davydov used the word "inspiration" twice. Moreover, in the first instance he is speaking about inspiration in a pejorative sense, as something harmful, a hindrance: "... this sense of fatigue is found only among actors who play, as they say, on their nerves, on inspiration," while in the second case the same word describes a correct sensation on the part of the actor: "Every scene you act fills you with inspiration."

Strange to say, there is no contradiction here. Inspiration does not precede work on a role, it crowns that work. If an actor considers "nerves and inspiration" as material on which to build his role he is making a grave mistake, for then nothing will come out of his work but senseless "auto-intoxication."

When you make a start on a role it is better not to think about inspiration. And when you have finished there is no need to think about it because inspiration comes of itself without your needing to summon it, at that very moment when you feel yourself to have full power over the role. No pianist, no violinist can feel a trace of inspiration until he has every note, every touch at his finger-tips, until he feels an organic power over every musical phrase.

The joy of possessing this power is precisely what is called creative inspiration. It is then that there arises a remarkable feeling of improvisation. The point is not that the actor is improvising words—that is something that the worst of compères can do—the point is that in every phrase of the role you feel its absolutely actual intonation, and in every pause an actual length. That is the actor's "second breath," something that can come only when an actor sees a character with all his being and feels it in every pore of his body.

When I was writing about my first sensations of play-acting in my childhood I said that to this very day I can remember myself as a russet cow cropping green grass. I remember that because I believed in the existence of that cow, utterly and completely.

I can say in just the same way that I remember myself as Professor Dossa the surgeon.

In that role my feeling of really living the part was as complete as it had been in the children's games.

Compared with the roles of Volgin or of Feste the Clown that of Professor Dossa was quite small, a mere episode in a scene from Deval's *Prayer of Life*, but I loved that role because I knew my professor through and through, like a personal acquaintance. His snow-white starched linen collar, the professional cleanliness of his surgeon's hands, his old-fashioned frock coat, the shine of his gold watch, the neatness of his trimmed little beard and his cynical familiarity with the sufferings and death of others.

In this role I had a feeling of "second breath" at every moment, but it is my opinion that the character of Professor Dossa would not have arisen inside me and that I would not have been able to establish my power over it had my actor's imagination limited itself only to the role itself, in isolation from the whole play.

I could not have envisaged the outward appearance of the surgeon so clearly and precisely without the main thing, the theme of the role. And that was something that did not exist in isolation from or in contradiction to the other roles and themes of the whole play.

Professor Dossa was indifferent to the death of the woman whom he attended as head of a panel of consulting specialists, but the dying woman was the only fine person among the rest of the characters of the play, conceited, lying hypocrites. She is the only character the audience loves.

The stiff white collar, the pince-nez, the well-scrubbed hands and the dignified way he nibbled biscuits as he told his colleagues the details of a similar case of "lethal ending," pocketed his fee and glanced at the thermometer, the professional calm of Dossa's movements were insulting, as insulting as flies on a corpse's face. That, in fact, was the theme of the role.

And I have come to think that the actor's imagination which gives birth to a character, can call up the concrete elements he needs for the character—the true, not the accidental elements—only when his imagination is stimulated by the theme of the role in comparison with the themes of the other roles, or rather in mutual relationship with them.

The interdependence of the themes of roles cannot be understood unless the theme of the play itself is grasped. And that is something that every actor in every role must do—and not only the producer of the play.

If the actor's imagination starts "inventing" the character, instead of bringing it to birth out of the theme then the starched collar, the pince-nez and the white hands, and, besides, every intonation, every gesture, will be nothing more than useless naturalistic rubbish that destroys rather than creates the character.

The role of Professor Dossa which brought me the joy of "second breath" was my last role; I acted it on the last day of my work in the "human" theatre. Since then—that was thirteen years ago—I have not once made up my face or worn a stage costume.

But in spite of the fact that I remember my last role as having given me happiness as an actor, in spite of the fact, even, that only quite recently I met my once incomplete Volgin—if only on the concert stage—and that this meeting was also a joyful occasion for me, I have no regrets whatsoever for having left the "human" stage.

My present profession has ousted the dramatic actor from within me and I am not sorry for that because I am fully absorbed in my present work.

All my imagination, all the creative forces I possess are involved in work. I have not the feeling that some part of my potential is lying idle.

At the same time, though, I am not at all sorry that I was an actor of the "human" theatre, no more than I am sorry that I spent so many years studying art.

What I learned in the "human" theatre I value highly. I learned important things there, things I needed to learn. And I am boundlessly grateful to the people from whom I learned my lessons—sometimes without them knowing it.

CHAPTER SEVEN

Counterpoint

There is a form of musical composition in which several melodies or themes are played simultaneously. This is known as counterpoint. In combination these melodies harmonize in a chord, but each note of the chord belongs to an independent melody. You can sing or play any one of the melodies separately and it will be quite complete, yet all the melodies exist together without clashing, although not one of them can be called the main one.

The life of a man is like counterpoint. It is composed of very many different melodies, many themes of distinctive nature. And although all the themes of human life are interwoven and make up life only in their totality, nevertheless every theme can to some extent be separated from the others.

You can single out and describe the physical life of an individual man (the date of his birth, his height, state of health, his illnesses, his death); you can investigate his family life; you can examine separately the theme of his social work and, finally, of his profession.

There are moments when all the themes of a man's life concur successfully, and then you get a harmonious chord in which each note belongs both to its own theme—that is, it exists in movement, is felt in time—and to the chord, that is to the moment of concurrence.

Perhaps it is just in those moments of contrapuntal harmony that a man experiences complete happiness.

The inner dialectic of human life consists simultaneously in the conflict and the mutuality of its contrapuntal themes; human will tries to combine these themes in a harmonious chord.

But you cannot write the life of a man in the way a composer writes counterpoint. That would mean making it run horizontally and at the same time viewing all its complex nature vertically.

For a composer it is easy: he gives a theme to each stave and sets down note upon note. When the instrument sounds the listeners hear a vertical chord while the line of beats moves the life of those sounds along a time-horizontal.

But what is one to do if one wants to write the counterpoint of a human life? It's not possible to draw staves for each theme and write in one of them that a man is suffering from a headache, and at the same time in another stave lower down that he is worrying about his little boy's school marks, and still lower down that he is inventing a new aircraft engine.

The reader cannot read all these parallel lines at once in the way a conductor reads the score by whole pages and hears within him violin, bassoon, drum and cymbals simultaneously.

And yet every day a man lives in all his themes at once. And this means that anyone who is describing the life of a man will lead the reader along one theme, stop, turn back and tell how his subject was living in another life theme. In other words, you have to separate the lines of the different melodies and write them in sections one after another.

However, even that single solitary melody I chose to write about—the isolated theme of my profession—has turned out to be contrapuntal, for in my profession too many themes have run on simultaneously. I have already had to take the reader back to the beginning three times and start all over again; otherwise I could not possibly have disentangled the themes of the counterpoint. It was not my intention simply to write memoirs in chronological order.

When I wrote about my first contacts with art—about songs and fairy-tales, about my enthusiasm for pets and about the books of my childhood days—I brought the record up almost to the period of my youth, for I was getting on for fifteen at least before I gave up pigeon-fancying and playing with tropical fish.

But then I had to make a break and go back to the time I was barely eight so that I could tell you about my drawings and paintings, that is to say, about a theme that is specially important for me—the theme of the professional artist.

I carried this narrative up to the time I was twenty when, dropping my profession as an artist, I went on the stage; but here too I could not simply proceed with the story but had to stop and turn back once more to the years of my earliest childhood, for my play-acting began, in fact, earlier than my painting stopped and went on in the time of pigeons and fairy-tales, of drawings and paintings.

The preceding chapters have run in leap-frog fashion, but that is not because I was trying to be original. I could not write about everything at once, I had no other choice but to turn back, for otherwise I would have given the impression that every new theme of my profession simply sprang out of the air; in fact every one of them had its organic origin, its roots, and without explaining what those roots were I could not hope to make clear what my profession as a whole is composed of.

So now I shall have to stop once more and begin all over again in order to introduce a fresh theme, a different melody in my counterpoint.

In the previous chapter, while describing the lessons of the "human" theatre, I brought the story up to the year 1936 when I played my last "human" role on the stage. It was in that year that my present profession became my one and only profession; but I cannot take up the tale again at 1936 as by then I was already well launched in that profession whose origins lay back in the years when I had listened to fairy-tales and drawn grey elephants in the yellow desert and which had existed in the years I studied to be a professional artist and later when I worked on the roles of Fyodor or Feste.

In a relay race the baton is always passed on at the run. It saves time.

I was not thinking in terms of a relay race at all, but it happened of itself that my present profession grasped the baton from the profession of stage actor at a moment when it was already going at full speed. And so the transfer took place without my noticing it. There was never a day of which I could say I suddenly changed my life in art. By 1936 I had not only some thirteen years of concert performances behind me but had been made a Merited Artist of the Republic for my concert work and had been in charge of the State Central Puppet Theatre for over three years.

For that reason I cannot turn to the theme of puppetry and start my story from the day I quitted the "human" theatre. I shall have to start with the time I met my first puppet, which happened when I was seven.

The Toy

That was the year Mother gave me a funny little doll. It was called Be-Ba-Bo and consisted of a celluloid head and a blue dress which you could slip your hand into like into a glove. The forefinger went into the head and the thumb and middle finger became the doll's arms. If you wagged your forefinger the head would nod and if you wagged your thumb and middle finger the arms moved in a funny, quite life-like manner. Be-Ba-Bo could pick up a pencil or a match-box, he could scratch the back of his neck, wipe away tears, in fact do anything you liked.

He had a very funny little face with protruding eyes, practically no nose at all, just the nostrils; the mouth was wide and long and on his head he wore something between a fez and a dunce's cap.

Be-Ba-Bo's facial expression was somewhat indefinite. When his arms were flung apart his eyes registered surprise: when they were brought together as if he were applauding he seemed to be laughing; if they were brought up to grasp his head Be-Ba-Bo's face assumed a frightened expression, while if the head was lowered and you tightened your clenched fist Be-Ba-Bo cried.

Everything Be-Ba-Bo did was funny and rather touching. I loved him, and I pitied him too, the way little children love and pity a kitten. I even took him for walks with me, tucked into the sleeve of my winter coat, peeping out at passers-by, at the policeman, at children on the Chistoprudny Boulevard or at the windows of Einem's, the confectioner's near Myasnitskiye Vorota, which was not far from where we lived at that time.

Among the cream cakes and confectionery in Einem's windows there was always some sort of mechanically operated advertisement before which both grown-ups and children would stop.

One of them, I recall, was a house on fire with funny little firemen pumping water through a fire-hose. Little men from Mars were very fashionable among dolls in those days. I really don't know why. Maybe it was because just then astronomers had discovered lines on Mars looking like canals and the newspapers were writing that there was human life on Mars; anyway, whatever the reason, Martian dolls of all kinds were on sale: people, dogs, cats, and all with great protruding eyes. These firemen I am writing about were Martians too. I remember as plain as day how each in turn stooped over the pump of the fire engine. Their feet were attached to the floor and the little figures stiffened up, then squatted, up down, up down. One Martian's foot had come loose and it shook comically as he went down.

I was so keen to see the firemen close to, that I slipped under the iron rail that protected the plate-glass window from the elbows of interested spectators.

Of course the live dolls were interesting, but if you stared at them for a long time you saw quite clearly that they were not alive at all but dead. Only the loose leg moved slightly differently every time but everything else—heads, arms and fat Martian bodies—moved at measured beat without the least variation, like the pendulum of a clock or one of those carved wooden toys in which a bear and a peasant bring their hammers down in turn on an anvil. Even that toy was more interesting, for you could vary the speed of their blows; you could make the bear and the peasant lazy or, if you wanted, you could have them working madly. But here there was nothing new to see, however long you went on standing at the window. Up down, up down, up down—that was all. And that made the Martians' faces look so stupid and inert.

Compared to them my Be-Ba-Bo was a real little man. He could clean the window with his sleeve in order to see better; he could applaud like somebody at the theatre; he could bob up and down making fun of the Martians; he could look over his shoulder at a lady with a little dog on a lead; he could turn and look in various directions and everybody around started looking and laughing at him instead of at the Martians. Even the little dog grew interested and began to sniff at him which brought him a biff on the muzzle from Be-Ba-Bo. The dog sprang back in surprise and took refuge behind the lady with a bird on her hat.

By now everybody had lost interest in that silly fire in the confectionery display in Einem's window—Be-Ba-Bo had triumphed.

But my hand felt frozen and I slipped it out of Be-Ba-Bo, shoved him into my overcoat pocket, breathed on my fingers, put on my mitten and walked home with Nanny.

I expect it all looked very much like what I do now when I perform with puppets at concerts. There too I slip a puppet over my hand, make the audience laugh as the puppet moves like a living being, draw pleasure and joy from the performance myself, take off the puppet and walk home.

Actually, Be-Ba-Bo's performance outside Einem's window may be considered my concert debut. In that case I have practised my profession for over 40 years. But who could have thought at that time that there could be any sort of profession in it, let alone a serious profession around which a whole big theatre has been organized, a theatre with actors and artists and ushers and even a commissionaire with gold braid on his coat?

Of course neither I nor my parents ever let such a foolish thought enter our minds.

"I'm going in for art"—that was something indisputable. No one took any notice of sly little Be-Ba-Bo and when with my childhood the toys disappeared somewhere—my Be-Ba-Bo went the same way as Bishka the plush dachshund, the mechanical piglet, the fur cat—and his place in my pocket was taken by dried sunflower seeds, a penknife, a catapult, a transparent envelope full of stamps from the Congo and Nicaragua, a live white mouse or a squat little tube of oil paint.

Relapse

Childhood passed, school days were over, I had succumbed utterly to paint and brush and in 1919-20 the theme of painting rang like the trumpets of Jericho in the counterpoint of my life. Nothing, it seemed, could muffle it; the memories of Be-Ba-Bo that arose occasionally in my mind sounded like a gnat-squeak beside it, without making any claims to an independent place in the score.

But that was just where Be-Ba-Bo was so clever.

If he had expressed the slightest ambition in life I would have erased him from my memory as absolute nonsense.

What time had I for hobbies? I was busy enough without that.

I spent the whole day painting and drawing, and parts of the evening at the university studying all kinds of philosophical "substances" and "things in themselves" and "syllogisms," and in between that I had to earn a living by giving drawing lessons, teaching perspective, making models, charts for museums, designing posters.

But in the long run it is boring to draw columns of varying height representing the membership of the woodworkers' union or natality graphs for the Museum of Mother and Child Care.

So it was quite natural that I should have remembered the merry little Be-Ba-Bo of my childhood and proposed to my friends Maria Artyukhova and Tatiana Martynova that we should try and make comic puppets for sale.

There were few toys in those days. Children needed them and we would certainly have no difficulty in selling them. Even among our friends and acquaintances. The little heads would be easy enough to make and the dresses could be made out of rags. Not much was required and every family would be able to find some bright bits and pieces.

Maria made two little old women, Tatiana a "Violet Lady" with a red wig and I a piccaninny.

The fun started when we brought the puppets to the studio. Maria's old women made the sign of the cross very comically. Violet Lady walked proudly carrying a little handbag and my Piccaninny poked his nose into the paint-box, sniffed the paints, peeped from behind the easel and scurried away in fright.

We did not sell a single one of our puppets. Either we did not find any customers or we were poor salesmen. But the main reason, probably, was that we found it hard to part with such jolly puppets. It was not worth our while to make any more, for after all we found it took a tremendous amount of time. In terms of cash drawing charts was more profitable.

My Piccaninny's head was made out of a black sock with bits of an old astrakhan collar for the curly hair. The whites of its vertical eyes bulged like Be-Ba-Bo's. The pupils were formed by glossy buttons off children's boots. The gown-like costume was check pattern—a bit of old shirting.

And, as if I were a child again, the Piccaninny lay in my overcoat pocket, though now that overcoat was not of blue serge but of uncovered sheepskin, one I had been given as a teacher at military courses.

And as in my childhood days my puppet would creep out of my pocket to mock passers-by asking them how to get to Krivokolenny Street.

"The Tumult of the Ball"

Perhaps my friendship with the Piccaninny would not have gone beyond japes like that and ended the way my friendship with Be-Ba-Bo had done had the little fellow not started poking fun at singers or rather not at singers but at my own singing lessons.

As I mentioned earlier, for some time I took singing lessons at the Shor private Conservatoire.

At that place, as, by the way, at most schools connected with the actor's art, they had lessons given according to the Stanislavsky Method.

Stanislavsky's books are in fact only an introduction to a full explanation of the whole Method; at the time I was studying singing, however, there were no books at all on the subject, which meant that there was no possibility for checking the correctness of the way other people were expounding Stanislavsky's methods. That, probably, was why there were so many people eager to take up the idea. Anybody who was in one way or another connected with the Art Theatre could set up as an expert on the Method although it had reached him, maybe, at fourth hand. Moreover there was no guarantee that he had understood it properly even if he had it from the horse's mouth.

Even today, if you were to bring together all Stanislavsky's former pupils, his biographers and the theoretical exponents of his ideas, and organize a discussion, they would interpret the Stanislavsky Method with a surprising amount of variation.

I have been present at discussions of that sort between people who all had full right to consider themselves experts on the subject.

That is why I am unable to say whether the woman who taught us the Method at the conservatoire got it right or wrong. And besides, I do not know whether I understood her properly and for that reason I do earnestly beg her, should this book fall into her hands, not to take offence at what I write now, all the more so because I have the pleasantest memories of her, as of my singing teacher Raisa Barkova and of the late Alexander Shor.

I ought to be specially grateful to them because it was really in their company that my present profession was born.

Now I shall try to give an honest account of the way I took lessons in the Method; if it sounds funny I alone am to be blamed for it, not my teacher and still less Stanislavsky whose name I revere and who, I am proud to say, saw my puppets and thought very highly of them.

The second—or it may have been the third—romance which was assigned to me in the singing class was Chaikovsky's "Tumult of the Ball" transposed for baritone, the top note being E, which presented no great difficulty; it took relatively little time to learn, and I had not managed to grow tired of it. I sang it at the end of the lesson and enjoyed doing so.

But when I sang the same song to the teacher of the Stanislavsky Method she told me I was singing it the wrong way and that she would teach me the Method on that very song.

If I wanted to sing the romance the right way, she said, I ought first of all to fix my mind on some event in my own life like the one the romance was about. To remember, if not a "tumult of the ball," then at least an evening party with dancing. To remember a situation when I was forsaken and alone.

To evoke all those memories I had to concentrate and make myself feel I was again in love with a girl who had dropped me on some occasion. Only then could I beckon to my accompanist to start the introduction—for otherwise how could she tell whether I was in love yet or not?

This sign to the pianist had to be done very discreetly, with a nod of the head, a movement of the hand or a glance, so as not to distract myself from my state of tender passion or frighten it away.

All of which struck me as being not so difficult as silly, like a spiritualist's seance or a feat of amateur hypnotism.

Once one of those amateur hypnotists tried to convince me that I could hear the tender strains of a violin and could taste chocolate. I could hear nothing, taste nothing, but I felt so embarrassed for the hypnotizer's sake that I told him I could taste chocolate and, for his greater satisfaction, added that it was nut-chocolate. He was delighted.

It was the same now. I stood near the piano concentrating; the accompanist waited, the teacher waited, the other pupils waited, all waited until I, at last, fell in love. Profound silence. I tried to remember a "tumultuous ball," but in 1919 the very idea of such a thing was absurd, there were no such occasions—and as for those that had taken place in earlier years, well, I had been too young to be taken to them. I had no better luck in trying to remember girls who had forsaken me—there were not any—and anyway I felt shocked at the idea of thinking about one's personal emotions of love under the eyes of so many other people.

But the minutes passed. I went on standing at the piano and finally I realized I could stand there silent no longer: I had to beckon to the pianist to begin.

I sang my song. The teacher praised me. I returned to my seat. Up to the piano stepped a baritone and started concentrating to make himself feel he was a noble robber and fit to sing "Before the Voyevoda he stood, his head inclined, his eyes downcast." Again the spellbound pianist waited, the teacher waited, we all waited till we heard that fine romance turned into a poor monologue, sentimental, tasteless.

Back at home I took my Piccaninny and made him sing "The Tumult of the Ball" the way my teacher wanted me to sing it. The Piccaninny obliged with great pleasure and made everybody in the room laugh uproariously.

I produced my Piccaninny at the next lesson in the Method. He concentrated, beckoned carefully to the accompanist and then, sometimes with his chin in his hands, sometimes dashing away a tear, he sang and suffered about the girl he loved.

Everybody laughed—the accompanist, the teacher, my classmates—baritones, basses, tenors and coloratura sopranos.

The enjoyment was general, and my share of it was as great as anyone else's. It was very much like one of my present-day concert performances except that then there was no screen and I showed the puppet over the back of a chair.

And now whenever the compère at a concert announces me he often adds to my name: "Romances with puppets." This title gradually clung to my concert performances and it was my Piccaninny who actually began a series of romances with a rendering of "The Tumult of the Ball" sung according to the Method.

I was not making fun of the romance itself. It was a parody of the manner of executing it, or more precisely of false sentimentality. Later, making fun of sentimentality became one of the fundamental features of my work in the concert hall, and partly of my work on the stage.

If then I could have foreseen that the Piccaninny born of my memories of Be-Ba-Bo would himself give birth to a profession, I ought to have celebrated his debut with suitable ceremony but, without a thought of that, I slipped him into my pocket and went off to paint a still life.

The Birth of a Troupe

Having so unexpectedly acquired a "concert repertoire" my Piccaninny of course began to sing Chaikovsky at the University as well as in the studio, and as the audience laughed and applauded he had to look round for an encore.

At first he encored with a rather silly tale about the way he went hunting and, one after the other, shot a bird, a hare, a wolf, a bear and an elephant, putting each one into his bag.

If this tale had been told by a man it would have been simply ridiculous, but on the lips of a tiny puppet with serious, rather sad eyes it became naively comic and even rather touching and poetic.

At that time I did not pause to reflect on the origin of this quality of poetic humour that a puppet possesses; in general I played with my puppets without a thought in my head and it was only later on that I realized that the convincingness of this humour had its origin in the amazing capacity of a puppet to remain serious in any circumstance and situation; I realized too that the reason for this seriousness was simply the immobility of the puppet's face, its "concentratedness."

It is just this habit of concentration, surely, that makes a kitten look so funny when it rolls a pencil on a table top with an expressionless "face," or a monkey when it is examining its finger-nails.

Charlie Chaplin used this mask of fixed concentration on the screen.

It was only because his eyes and brows retained an expression of utter seriousness that Chaplin was able to get away with the most eccentric and improbable behaviour.

He turned comic clowning into something tender and lyrical.

The behaviour of puppets goes through the same process.

The serious expression they keep often neutralizes the over-acting of whoever is manipulating the puppet.

It was just because of the seriousness of my Piccaninny's sad-looking eyes that the tiny gesture with which he signalled to the accompanist to begin brought a roar of laughter to my first audience and won its heart. And it was his serious dead-pan expression that enabled him to tell, with complete belief in the possibility of the impossible, the story of how he had put the elephant he had shot into his game-bag.

However, though I did not then know that a puppet had this power of expression, and was unable to define it, at least I sensed the presence of some special quality in the puppet and took great pleasure in using it.

It very soon became clear that my Piccaninny's repertoire was hopelessly inadequate. I had to invent something for my friends' and my own amusement.

The first thing I thought of was to make an old woman like Maria Artyukhova had designed. I used cotton wool and a strip of jersey for her. She wore a blue sarafan and a traditional head-dress. She and the Piccaninny sang Chaikovsky's romance "We were sitting alone." Why they in particular had to sing this romance and what it all meant I had no idea at the time. They just sang, that's all. And the effect was funny.

Later on one of my friends made me a present of an old, moth-eaten plush monkey—a toy brought back from Leipzig many years before. It may have been a contemporary of my childhood companion Be-Ba-Bo, and was quite probably a relative of his. It could be slipped on to the hand like the Piccaninny, so that you could manipulate it with your thumb and two fingers. Its eyes too were formed of shiny buttons.

Despite its crudeness (because of it, in fact, I understood later) the monkey acted very well and soon elbowed the old woman out of her part in the duet with the Piccaninny. It was made to be worn on the right hand. The Piccaninny was worn on the left and as it is easier to play with the right hand the monkey took the initiative in the duet.

So my old woman became "unemployed." However, an unexpected partner turned up. This was one of the discarded Terapots: the one with the beard and the long hair. At home he had for some reason come to be known as Professor. He matched the old woman perfectly, especially when I gave her a silk dress and a hat with a feather in it.

I made a tiny guitar for the Professor and the two of them sang Borisov's romance "It was a happy day."

This time it could be understood if only from the plot of the romance why it is sung by the Old Lady and Gentleman. The romance describes how the two met on a rainy autumn day but were so much in love that an autumn became spring for them. After many years' separation they met again, this time in spring ... and "My passions have cooled and yours become ice and in our grey hairs no trace of love is more to be found"....

At that time the song was rather popular and was being sung seriously; my puppets, however, being puppets, made fun of its sentimentality.

So besides the Piccaninny's solo repertoire I had two duet numbers: the Piccaninny with the Monkey, and the Old Lady and Gentleman.

But apparently the Monkey did not feel quite at ease in the love duet, and as I had come to love him no less than the Piccaninny I decided to give him another monkey as a partner.

I wanted my new monkey to be an improvement on the one I had been given. And, in fact, it turned out much more like a real monkey. It had arched eyebrows, the eyes themselves were deep-set and close together, the lips were thick and the paws long and bony. And yet it "acted" nothing like so well as the original one. At the time I did not realize that this was due precisely to its naturalism. Only later did I learn that the more conventional the treatment of the outward appearance of a puppet the better it "plays."

All the same the new monkey replaced the Piccaninny.

Before very long the two monkeys besides Chaikovsky were singing Vertinsky's romance "Just a Minute." This romance was also highly popular in those years but its subject was just the opposite to "It was a happy day." Borisov's lovers meet in autumn and part in spring; Vertinsky's meet in spring and part in autumn. Borisov's romance is written in the Russian urban tradition, the so-called "Gypsy romance" style, while Vertinsky's was of a form that was novel in those days, the intimate little song with a touch of decadence, about a girl with the "foreign" name of Lulu and with the first rendezvous taking place on the beach, a setting hitherto not used in romances. Borisov's romance was meant to be sung seriously, Vertinsky's, as usual, with an element of irony. That, incidentally, was why the puppets demolished Borisov's romance more thoroughly, making more fun of it than of Vertinsky's song where they only underlined the irony and removed the touches of sentimentality. Even the pretentious name of Lulu sounded sarcastic when addressed to a monkey.

Both these romances remain in my repertoire to this day, and both the old couple and the pair of monkeys appear from time to time before the public, especially if I am performing on my own and not as part of a programme of other turns.

Borisov, by the way, was not in the least offended with me for letting my puppets make fun of his romance. This composer, who died shortly before the war, was an outstanding comedian who appeared frequently on the stage and concert platform. We often met at concerts and he always asked me to include "It was a happy day" in the programme and would stand in the wings looking and laughing at my Old Folk.

CHAPTER EIGHT

Plagiary

Failures and fiascos in art take place for many reasons but they are especially hard to bear when one has had great hopes and confidence in success.

In such cases, probably, a failure is almost inevitable and the only consolation that one can draw from it is that it is a lesson and a warning for the future.

So the earlier one learns that lesson the better.

My first fiasco with puppets took place long before puppetry became my profession and I must be grateful to fate that it gave me a graphic lesson of the truth that one can joke and play the fool with puppets but one cannot exploit them.

Extraordinary Night

It all began with the Musical Studio of the Art Theatre and the First Studio deciding to arrange an Extraordinary Night in the main theatre building. It was to be a sort of Green Room Rag, a semi-serious entertainment for a highly exclusive audience. All the box-office receipts were to be used for the support of poor actors.

The year was 1923—the year of the New Economic Policy. NEP had set astir the former business community—the world of tradesmen, employers and profiteers. Private shops, cabarets of doubtful reputation, privately-owned race horses and even gambling-houses had reappeared. A special character known as the "Nepman" turned up in our lives. Such people celebrated the temporary concession to private trade as a victory for themselves. They opened wholesale warehouses, started furnishing their flats and ordering Paquin models from Paris for their wives.

It was essentially such people's loose cash that the Extraordinary Night was supposed to rake in.

I have no clear recollection of the programme of that "rag" but it was extensive and pretty varied. I recall that a "potted" opera by Ilya Sats called *The Battle of the Russians with the Kabardinians* was staged. There was also a parody consisting of an orchestra of backstage noises: a long wooden box with dried peas bouncing in it to imitate the sound of waves on a beach, a revolving drum for the wind, a sheet of metal for thunder, strips of wood which when struck made the sound of galloping horses, and an apparatus for imitating a train.

All these instruments were played in all seriousness by musicians under the baton of Vladimir Popov who had invented most of them himself. Popov too staged a wonderful parody of a conjuror's act.

I remember a scene in which "savages" spoke some outlandish gibberish. Mikhail Chekhov compèred the whole programme and at the end invited the public to ride on the revolving stage—for a fee.

There was something almost sacrilegious in riding on the stage which was used to shift the scenery of *The Cherry Orchard*. That was something worth paying for. A merchant is always a merchant.

But the Extraordinary Night was not limited to a mere stage show. In one of the foyers an American bar with a jazz band and "Negroes" was set up, in another "Gypsies" sang, guitars twanged and a fortune-teller sat in a corner; in the upper foyer we organized a restaurant and called it "Krynkin's Restaurant on the Sparrow Hills."

In those days there were still people in Moscow who remembered that famous restaurant. True, our stuffy foyer had no Moskva River, no plantations of bird-cherry in bloom, no nightingales, no view of the sunrise over the towers of the Novodevichy Monastery: but there was everything else—food and vodka and a samovar and a "Russian Choir" conducted as in the old days by Krynkin's son, Alexander, who was employed at the Art Theatre. He conducted well, for he loved and knew much about Russian songs.

Well, since this stylization of the "good old times" was being put on, somebody remembered that among the young actors was one who was fond of puppets and who, therefore, could contribute reminiscences of the Russian Petrushka to the programme.

That was how I became a solo turn on that tremendous evening which created a sensation in the theatrical life of Moscow.

I had not forgotten my success in the role of Tartalia at the New Year's Eve party. I expected my Petrushka to be no less successful.

Looking for the Real Thing

There was little time to prepare but I wanted my turn to have an authentic touch. I wanted my lines to be the real thing, the words that had been handed down from generation to generation and heard on the lips of popular puppeteers in courtyards long ago. I wanted the puppets to look right too. And I had to have a hurdy-gurdy to play for no Petrushka ever performed without a hurdy-gurdy.

But how was I going to manage all that?

Petrushka men had not been seen on the streets of Moscow since long.

There were traces of Petrushka in Stravinsky's ballet, in Sudeikin's stylized drawings, and on peeling notices beside the gates of Moscow yards—"No entrance for ragmen and Petrushka men," they ran, those cold-hearted witnesses of the ruin of Petrushka.

True, I did once manage in my childhood to see a Petrushka in the yard of our house, but I had forgotten the details I needed. All I remembered was something endlessly lively and funny.

I recalled that Petrushka had a very high, quite inhuman voice and that I could hear him squeaking comically from inside the folded screen that his master carried into the yard. And then Petrushka popped over the top of the screen and everybody laughed at his long nose. He talked in turn to the Gypsy, the Doctor and the Constable and smacked them all with his staff. Then a black dog appeared on the scene but the performance never reached its end because at that moment a real constable strode into the yard and to the bitter disappointment of the public turned the performers out. Both the Petrushka man and the hurdy-gurdy player.

These reminiscences were not enough to help me do everything the right way, but in a second-hand bookshop I found a little book published by Sytin which gave the full text of the lines of a popular Petrushka man, written down, apparently, by some extremely conscientious fellow straight from the lips of a professional. The book had illustrations and though they were poor they sufficed to enable me to make the puppets.

I made all the puppets I needed, learned the text and rehearsed the whole turn.

All that remained was to get myself a hurdy-gurdy. That was all the more important since I had already persuaded an actress to play it for me. She was going to sing Russian folk songs to the instrument, and sell "fortunes."

In those days there were still a few hurdy-gurdy men to be found wandering about Moscow. Most of them lived somewhere in the old Moscow suburb of Maryina Roshcha. As they were all very old and a hurdy-gurdy was a fair weight they rarely brought their instruments any nearer the centre of Moscow than Trubnaya Square.

I had luck, for on the first day of my search for one I ran into a hurdy-gurdy man near Samotyoka Street. Moreover, he had a parrot.

To find out what tunes the instrument played and whether it was possible to sing to it, I joined the street urchins that trotted along after the hurdy-gurdy man and went into a yard. The hurdy-gurdy man stopped in the middle of the yard, took his big box off his shoulders, placed a rod underneath it to keep it steady, looked up at the upper-storey windows where potential listeners might be lurking and began to turn the handle.

A loud, unexpected, many-strained sound burst out of the shabby old box and filled the yard. At first I could follow neither tune nor rhythm: the music sounded like a lot of trills and ringing sounds. Then I made out the strains of "The fires of Moscow raged and roared." I joined in the singing. The hurdy-gurdy man gave me a hard look, the drab white parrot put its head on one side and clicked its thick tongue but I could not tell from that whether either of them approved of my singing.

I doubt if they did.

I may even have offended them. Why, if anybody now were to take me up and start singing with me at one of my concerts I would be furious and deeply offended at the lack of respect shown to my profession. But that idea did not enter my head then. I followed the hurdy-gurdy man into two or three yards and sang almost all his repertoire: "The Parting," "Ah, why this night?" and "The sun rises and sets."

I found that though it was not easy to sing to hurdy-gurdy it could be done. I reached an understanding with the hurdy-gurdy man about hiring the instrument together with the parrot. So I had a genuine text, I had puppets that resembled the originals, I had a real hurdy-gurdy and even a real parrot which knew how to pick out "fortunes." All I lacked was a real screen. My own screen was heavy and clumsy, and, as I recalled, the one the Petrushka man carried from yard to yard was a very light folding screen.

I Visit a Pro

Nikolai Bartram, the director of the Toy Museum, supplied me with the address of the only man who could tell me how to have a folding screen for a Petrushka show made.

This man was Ivan Afinogenovich Zaitsev.

He lived somewhere in the neighbourhood of the Novinsky Boulevard. Pocketing my Piccaninny—I thought it might help to introduce myself —I set out in search of the man.

Zaitsev turned out to be a broad-shouldered, wide-faced man of about sixty. Blue eyes looked gravely at me from a clean-shaven face. With a polite, calm dignity he invited me to enter. The room was tidy and clean. Zaitsev asked his wife to make tea. He addressed her by her full name Anna Dmitriyevna.

"Very well, Ivan Afinogenovich," she replied.

Her face too was broad and composed and her eyes were the same shade of blue as her husband's.

I sat down and told them my business. Drawing my Piccaninny out of my pocket I showed them how he went shooting and bagged "a bird, a hare, a bear and an elephant."

Evidently my Piccaninny made no impression on Zaitsev. He did not smile once, though I must admit he said nothing disapproving.

He showed me how the folding screen was made, but though he sounded willing I thought I could detect a note of regret in his voice. There was so great a difference in our ages and in the times and worlds we belonged to that I could not win his confidence.

In fact, I felt quite uncomfortable and looked round the room with embarrassment.

The walls were adorned with multi-coloured ribbons and caps made of glass beads—all that remained of Zaitsev's show-booth theatre and merry-go-round; wooden marionettes clad in bright costumes decorated with ribbons, beads and bugles hung on long threads.

Zaitsev took down one of these marionettes—a juggler with a ball—and adjusted the threads that led from the figure to a double cross made of wood, the cross beams of which rotated on their axes.

With a calm and grave expression on his face Zaitsev began to manipulate the frame and the marionette walked across the floor, its legs jerking comically. Then it dropped on to one knee and started tossing into the air a number of balls suspended on a thread. One of the balls bounced on to the tip of its boot and from there on to its head. The little man sat down, lay on its back, stood up and went on juggling with the balls all the time.

All this was very life-like and extremely funny. But I could not laugh aloud; there was not the trace of a smile on Zaitsev's face. And Anna Dmitriyevna, her arms folded across her chest, stood watching the marionette with an equally impassive look.

I asked Zaitsev to show me how Petrushka was made to speak in that high shrill voice. Taking a small paper bag out of a drawer he removed from it something wrapped in a piece of cloth which he carefully unfolded. It contained a small silver squeaker, made of two pieces of metal with a thin strip between them.

Zaitsev placed the squeaker in his mouth, pursed his lips, evidently to get the squeaker somewhere deeper, and suddenly said in a shrill Petrushka voice: "I'm dy-y-y-y-ying!"

Anna Dmitriyevna took up the dialogue immediately.

"Are you dying?"

And the little voice replied: "I'm dying."

"And where is your death, Petrushka?"

"Digging potatoes beyond Tverskaya Gate..." and the voice laughed with that gay silvery note in which only Petrushka can laugh.

The lines they were speaking were the ones I had learned from the book I picked up, but now they sounded real, full of life. Now I recalled that during the performance in the yards the hurdy-gurdy player had slipped in questions now and again, and I realized that this was necessary because it was not always easy to make out what Petrushka was saying in that shrill voice of his: the questions helped to make the meaning clear.

The kettle on the little stove came to the boil and Anna Dmitriyevna hastened to take it off, while her husband, neatly tucking the squeaker into his cheek with his tongue, went on talking without her help, alternating his own voice for Petrushka's.

We drank tea, but I could not rid myself of the timidity I felt in the presence of these real pros, these genuine connoisseurs of an extraordinary art form now dying out. I kept thinking that both my Piccaninny and my wish to use Petrushka for a quite incidental occasion must have disappointed—not to say offended—these worthy folk. Had I known at that time what wonderful lives Ivan Zaitsev and his constant and faithful companion Anna Triganova had lived I would have felt even more embarrassed.

Anyway, I left them, taking with me drawings of a folding screen which I at once ordered from a joiner and had covered with red silk.

A Flop and Its Causes

I had everything ready several days before the dress rehearsal; my comrades foretold success.

But I flopped. I understood that the moment I opened my mouth. The lines which sounded so gay and comic when spoken by Zaitsev and Triganova sounded simply silly on my lips. My Petrushka did not raise a smile, let alone a laugh.

The failure was so complete that there could be no question of rescuing anything, of revising or changing the details. It was quite useless from beginning to end. Dull, uninteresting, cheap. Everything, except the real hurdy-gurdy and the parrot. It was suggested to me that I take these round the corridors selling "fortunes" but I was so depressed by my failure that I could not do even that.

What was the reason for this flop?

What had I done wrong?

The easiest way out, of course, would be simply to shrug and say that art's not arithmetic and that you can't always find where the mistake in the sum is and, hence, the reason why it doesn't "come out."

But it's no good doing that, because in most cases you *can* find the mistake, and if you can it means you must.

Of course it's not always pleasant to reveal your own mistake in all its ugliness, but that is another matter. At any rate it's better not to play hide-and-seek with oneself, to stop being a hypocrite, and, when you fail, to examine your work thoroughly, from beginning to end.

Sometimes an examination like that shows that the mistake was nothing atrocious; in such cases it can be easily mended. And if the mistake turns out to have been a big one, something beyond correction, then to acknowledge it can of itself be something of a warning against repeating the mistake in future.

Well, what was my mistake? What had I done wrong?

Perhaps it was because I'd rushed everything, been in too much of a hurry?

But that far from always leads to bad results. Sometimes a thing done in double quick time acquires a special quality of hitting the mark.

No, the trouble was not there.

It was something much more serious, and I could not explain my failure by merely attributing it to hasty work.

That being so, the reason, perhaps, lay in the fact that my approach to everything was a serious one, that I had tried to get as close as possible to the real Petrushka, whereas the rest of the programme for that Extraordinary Night was stylized, parody. Perhaps, alongside the parody of jazz, of a Russian tavern, of an opera, my turn, which was certainly no parody of Petrushka, had appeared flat.

But this explanation, too, failed to explain my flop, for I was convinced that had Zaitsev himself appeared in the programme he would have been a success. Admittedly, it might not have been quite the same sort of success that he used to enjoy on the fair ground or at Easter-tide celebrations but it would have been a success nevertheless.

In that case I had to assume that I did not possess Zaitsev's acting ability, and lacked his skill in handling puppets; perhaps those were the reasons why the puppets were dead in my hands.

This theory would have been plausible had I met with no success hitherto with puppets. But that was far from being the case. At that time I had my Piccaninny and my monkeys and although I had not yet thought of showing them at concert performances they always won laughter and approval from my audiences.

I am sure that if I had performed at the Extraordinary Night with my monkeys or my Old Folk I would not have failed. After all, I am still showing them at concerts and must have shown them at least a thousand times in the last twenty-five years.

So it was not lack of acting ability or of mastery in handling the puppets that had prevented me from matching Zaitsev's performance.

My mistake, or rather my guilt, lay in the fact that I had no real aim. A sort of aim I did, of course, have: I wanted to be a "success." But success cannot be a real aim. It can only be the result of achieving a definite aim.

The aim of a work of art can only be its idea, or rather the complete communication of that idea to those towards whom the work of art is directed. And that requires that the executant perceive that idea as his primary task and put everything he has into the theme which is used to fulfil that task.

The theme of a dramatic work is found in the plot, and the plot unfolds itself in the behaviour of the characters and, in the long run, in the text. In other words, the performer has to be enthralled by the material as a whole as the means of working out a given idea.

To take an analogy, the process of creation is like that well-known episode in the Russian fairy-tale in which Tsarevich Ivan finds a chest from which he takes a hare; from the hare he takes a duck and from the duck an egg and from the egg a needle. The hare tries to run away, the duck to fly away, the egg to sink below the water. All this complicated chain of events would be senseless and silly if the needle to which they all led had been an ordinary one. But the significance lies not in the needle itself but in the idea that when it is broken Kashchei the Deathless will die and then Vasilisa the Fair will be saved and good triumph over evil.

It is the same thing when you are working on a show or a role: you only start really creative work when, in going through the lines, the action, the plot, the theme, your aim is not simply to reach the end of the job but to reach its main thought, its idea.

After all, I was after one thing only: to prepare a turn "like Zaitsev's." I spoke my lines, made my Petrushka buy a horse from the Gypsy or beat the Constable or the Doctor with his truncheon. But I never asked myself why all that should be interesting to the audience and what, in fact, it all meant. Without admitting it to myself I had been insincere in my acting, and, as Zaitsev was undoubtedly sincere in his, it was impossible for my turn to come out "like Zaitsev's."

Ah, that was my sin. Lack of sincerity, lack of being thoroughly involved in the plot, in the text and, the main thing, in the theme of the Petrushka scenes I was acting.

For Zaitsev, every component, beginning from the type of puppets he used, their costumes, the manner and form of their behaviour, and ending with each single phrase in the text, had the quality of being absolute. They corresponded exactly with his taste, his outlook on life, his sense of art.

Zaitsev did not consider it as abstract "folklore"—he never used such words—for it was his "personal" art too. For him the words "fairground entertainment" were not pejorative; nor did they define a "style" for he used the term "fair-ground art" only to refer to a particular form of theatre, combining in it the technical construction, the place of performance and the composition of the public.

The Constable whom Zaitsev's Petrushka beat was a real constable, like the one who might appear in the yard at any moment. But my Constable was a dead, non-existent one and my relations with him were, so to say, retrospective.

For Zaitsev, as for his audience, the line: "I'm Doctor Quack from under Kamenny Bridge" was not just a stylized popular saying, it was a quip against some charlatan who really existed at the time or against exclusive upper-class doctors.

But for me the line was essentially only formal and my attitude in speaking it was, after all, purely aesthetic.

I too of course could have poked fun, if not at doctors, then at least at certain types of patients, but for that I should have found a new subject and a new text that would have been congenial to me; then I would have been sincere.

The "Gypsy" whose back Zaitsev's Petrushka belaboured was not an ordinary Gypsy, but was above all a tradesman and if I had thought about it I should have understood the character in terms of those very "Nepmen" before whom we were performing.

But I did not think of that either. In fact I had no idea at all in mind, I did not think of giving any particular sense to Petrushka's behaviour. I just made him talk about nothing.

For that attitude art takes a cruel revenge and deals some very painful blows.

Unfortunately, although I felt the pain, I did not at once understand that the question, "What am I going to tell the audience when I play this or that turn or put on this or that play?" is a question of prime importance. You cannot even start work unless you find the answer to that question.

Later I was to receive further blows for my lack of attention to that question, but the desire to imitate the work of others left me once and for all. In that sense I ought to be grateful for having been given such a graphic lesson—for all its sharpness.

If I had imitated Zaitsev's sincerity, if, in examining his work, I had understood how important it was that the contact between an artist and his material should be organic, my imitation would have been creative: but I imitated only the external form and thus lost the possibility of being sincere, as all mere copiers do.

Sincerity sometimes makes up even for lack of technical skill, permitting an actor with little experience to play a role well, the beginner to write a good book.

The absence of sincerity always cancels out the value of the work of even the most experienced professional.

Sincerity often makes a real work of art out of the inexpert drawings of children. The absence of sincerity kills the work of pseudo-primitives.

You can see the hand of live and sincere artists in old clay toys, in the primitives of the *trecento,* in Maori carvings, in prehistoric rock carvings. But how dead and false are the works of those of our contemporaries who imitate the "primitive" in their painting and sculpture!

Leonardo da Vinci said: "Never imitate anyone, because if you do you will cease to be Nature's son, you will be her nephew." What a pity I had not read those words before I started to show my Petrushka!

Postscript

The theme of this chapter is exhausted, but as I have described my meeting with Ivan Zaitsev I ought to add something about the life of this remarkable man. It belongs chronologically to the subject of later chapters as I grew to know Zaitsev well and learned the details of his unusual life when he came to work at the State Central Puppet Theatre.

As soon as that theatre was opened I invited Ivan Zaitsev and Anna Triganova to join the company. As artistic director of the theatre I was Zaitsev's superior but the shyness I felt in his presence did not leave me, especially as my respect for this splendid man went on increasing in proportion to what I learned of his life in my talks with him.

We are told that the first impressions of people are the most reliable.

It seems to me that this is not so. In any case, I have often found first impressions to be quite deceptive and have frequently had to change my opinions of people as I have grown to know them better. But in forming an opinion of people of great integrity first impression rule is to be relied on. In that case your later impressions do not make you change your opinion, they only strengthen it as the person discloses himself to you as an organic whole.

All the facts I learned about Ivan Zaitsev's life were remarkable, but none of them conflicted with his appearance, his manner of behaving, because he was a man of integrity, a man complete in his aspect, like a good piece of sculpture.

He was already about seventy when he joined the theatre but despite his years he was incredibly strong and powerfully built. There was good reason for this. Zaitsev was an Old Believer and never touched alcohol or tobacco. I do not know what sins this highly respectable man considered he needed to repent of, but in his search for redemption he took a pledge to make a sign of the cross every day with a sixteen-kilogram iron weight. In fact this gesture became a daily exercise in gymnastics; this septuagenarian could put any one of us on our backs in less than a minute.

I also learned why Zaitsev always addressed his wife with the formal patronymic. Many years before, it turned out, he had been married to another woman, and she was still alive and lived somewhere else with grown-up children. During his travels the actor had taken up with Anna Triganova, a fair-ground performer like himself. She became his partner, friend and, except in a formal sense, his wife. His religious feelings, however, did not permit Zaitsev to divorce his first wife or to consider his relations with Anna Triganova quite proper, although they had lived together for dozens of years. Perhaps that was what he considered the sin that had to be redeemed; yet I have rarely seen two people so true and devoted to each other, rarely seen so fine, austere and pure a love as that of Ivan Zaitsev and Anna Triganova.

Step by step, Zaitsev's whole professional life was revealed to me, and this despite the fact that it was no easy matter to question him about that life: he was highly modest and rather taciturn though you could never have called him unsociable.

His professional life had been devoted entirely to the art of the fair-ground and the circus, of which he was a past-master.

He was barely seven when he made his debut in the circus ring. He went through every genre. He had been an "india-rubber boy," an acrobat, a sword-swallower, a "savage from the island of Ceylon," a conjuror, a clown, a ventriloquist. He had worked in the Guinet Circus, in Weinstock's Fair, in Tarvit's Mechanical Theatre. He knew the scenarios of the fair-ground pantomimes "The Capture of Plevna" and "The Surrender of Osman Pasha" and the texts of the short programmes, half-play, half-pantomime, of the mechanical theatres: "The Arrival of the Shah of Persia and the Funeral of the Pope" and "The Russo-Turkish War on Land and Sea with the Blowing Up of a Turkish Monitor."

He handled the figures of a Petrushka show to perfection, playing with genuine artistry; he used to refer to the puppets as "top 'uns," the fair-ground way of indicating that they were figures worked from below.

But he was just as adept with marionettes and, besides the performance he called "Circus," knew the folk play "The Journey of the Merchant Sidorych to Heaven and Hell," with a plot highly reminiscent of Faust (wasn't Faust played by marionette theatres before Goethe?).

Zaitsev's long life had taken him to many Russian towns, wherever a fair-ground theatre existed. But most of all he had worked in Moscow. At Christmas time, on Shrove-tide and in Easter week he had wandered through the fairs in Sokolniki Park on Devichye Polye, at Cherkizovo, on the Blagusha and beyond Pokrovskiye Vorota. And on saints' days he went with the fairs to the walls of the monasteries: to the Simonov, the Novodevichy, the Androniev, the Novospassky, the Danilovsky, the Rozhdestvensky.

Because Zaitsev's art was traditional and absolutely complete in form, he could not merge into the troupe of our young theatre. Moreover, we did not insist on that. On the contrary, we helped him to restore his puppets and screen to the form he was accustomed to. He recognized no other form. He could not understand the sketches of our artists and the puppets of our sculptors. He performed with puppets that he made himself, and Triganova dressed them up and adorned them.

He put on his Petrushka show, his marionettes and tricks, visiting schools and clubs right up to the day when he was taken to the hospital he was never to leave.

Shortly before he fell ill, our theatre recommended him for a state award. Our request was granted. Zaitsev was a Merited Artist of the Republic when he died.

That was in 1936 when there were already many puppet theatres in the Soviet Union and when the names of many people working in those theatres—the Yefimovs in Moscow and Demmeni in Leningrad—had become well known, but the first puppeteer to be made a Merited Artist was Ivan Zaitsev, the "Last of the Mohicans" in the art of the fair-ground.

His services to the public were to be measured by the thousands of kilometres of streets and alleys, highways and country roads that he trod, taking his screen and his hurdy-gurdy through the fairs of Russia from Moscow to Yaroslavl, from Yaroslavl to Nizhny Novgorod. They are to be measured in the laughter and the happiness of the spectators—working-folk, artisans, peasants. They are to be measured in the honesty and absolute sincerity of his work.

Not long ago I saw an excerpt from a book which registered the graves in a cemetery in Czechoslovakia.

I read the name "Mattei Kopecký. Vagrant."

Kopecký, like Zaitsev, travelled for thousands of miles over the roads of his country, showing his Kašparek (the Czech Petrushka) and his marionettes. Like Zaitsev he belonged to the representatives of the art of the fair-ground in the 19th century.

Recently Czechoslovakia commemorated the anniversary of Kopecký's death and raised a monument on his grave.

The people of Czechoslovakia know and love the puppet theatre and hold the name of Kopecký in honour, but Mattei Kopecký died a beggar.

Zaitsev too might have died a beggar.

Pre-revolutionary Russia could go to see the ballet *Petrushka* and stylize decorative pictures in the folk art manner or performances in arty cafés, but the real representatives of the folk art of the fair-ground died as beggars.

The fact that the last of them, who lived to see the new Soviet Russia, died bearing that honoured title which opera singers and theatre actors bear so proudly is something very remarkable, fine and new in its conception.

Zaitsev occupies an honourable place in our theatre museum. The glittering bugles of his theatre hang there, with his Petrushka puppets, his marionettes, the humble paraphernalia of the conjuror, the worthy old hurdy-gurdy and a large bronze medallion with a bas-relief profile of Zaitsev executed by one of the country's best sculptors, Ivan Yefimov.

CHAPTER NINE

A Home Theatricals

And yet, though I smarted from a sense of shame after that flop I did not lose my enthusiasm for puppets. Evidently, they had lodged so firmly in my heart that they could not be so easily removed.

Without search of gain or fame, in fact with no practical aim in view at all, I went on pottering about with puppets for my own and my friends' amusement.

In the screen that was left from the Extraordinary Night I made inside pockets in which the puppets could be kept.

When folded, the screen was quite light and handy to carry. I could get about with it fairly easily and even take it into a tram.

This at once widened my audience for it meant I could take the screen with me when I went to parties.

There is not a hostess who when inviting her guests is not happy to know that one of them at least can be relied on to "entertain the company." No matter how—by playing the piano, singing to the guitar, telling funny stories or, at a pinch, doing card tricks.

That probably is the reason why professional pianists, singers, and actors are always reluctant to visit homes they do not know very well.

They are afraid that the other guests will press them: "Oh, do please play something. A Liszt rhapsody, perhaps?"

I was not a professional concert performer. I did not consider puppetry to be my profession and was not in the least offended when asked to show my puppets.

On the contrary, I loved showing them. I used to do it without a screen, holding the puppets up from behind a chair or over the edge of the table; now with the screen it was more interesting and convenient.

Gradually the number of "home concerts" I gave grew, and though my audience grew too I often found myself showing my puppets to the same people more than once, and this made me think about extending my repertoire: it would be more interesting for them, and for me too. So when I got back home after a day-time rehearsal or after an evening show at the theatre I used to carve puppets' heads, glue strips of papier mâché together, sew in buttons for eyes, make hair out of thread or fur, and cut out costumes.

But for those home theatricals and showing the puppets to visitors, and taking the screen about with me when I went to parties, I would never have made puppetry my profession.

Among my friends there were, of course, many artists and actors and so my audiences were qualified to judge my work, and my performances, over which I took an increasing amount of trouble, imperceptibly became semi-professional.

At almost every performance there would be someone in the audience who would come up to me afterwards and ask me whether I would show my puppets at some school or sanatorium or somewhere else, and I would readily agree.

Besides the schools and the sanatoria I appeared at the Gnesins' Musical College, the Triada Literature and Arts Circle, the literary circle of "the Nikitin Saturdays," and at Pronin's "Mansard."

Some of these performances were purely professional. For money.

At paid concerts I sometimes had to perform with well-known artists, and of course I was glad that my puppets went down well on these occasions, but I did not attach any special importance to my "successes" and considered these professional concerts as more or less incidental occurrences.

What did I show at that time? Was it any good? To tell the truth it was no good. Today I would not show one half of those numbers I put on then: they seem thoroughly bad to me.

But my failures were not due to a lack of seriousness or honesty. The reason was my complete helplessness. I did not know how to analyse the reasons why such and such a number was successful any more than why I failed.

That was why I often wandered off the straight path and ran into blind alleys.

In that space which is called the art of puppetry I moved like a blind man—without a guide or even a staff: sometimes I wandered in circles, sometimes I bumped my head against a wall. But there was some advantage in that blindness too, for it would happen that I sometimes fell on an untrodden and very interesting path. Perhaps, had I been in full possession of my sight I would have gone past it without noticing it at all.

True, when I did chance on one of these paths I would soon turn off it and lose it; but later I would remember these true, if very small, ways, and many things that disappeared as a result of my helplessness in those years came to life again in later numbers or at theatre performances.

The Puppets Do Not Want to Speak

The first sharp turn that I took in those days was to give up romances and start trying very hard to switch over to vernacular speech and to constructed dramatic scenes.

Psychologically this turn was a natural one as the illustration of romances by puppet acting had come to me not as a conscious creative method but as a chance joke, with the Piccaninny singing Chaikovsky.

By inertia I then applied the idea of the puppets acting as I sang to the monkeys and then to the Old Folk.

I worked out another vocal number by staging a rather vulgar comic song by Agnivtsev called "Santuzzi."

But despite the not inconsiderable success I enjoyed with performances at home and in other places with my "Just a Minute," "I Remember That Day" and even "Santuzzi" I went on considering the genre I had found as something accidental, irregular and purely ephemeral. And for that reason alone I did not dare perform my romances at the Extraordinary Night.

At that time I knew very little about the aspects and forms of puppet theatres and the various methods of acting with puppets. I only knew that the Russian Petrushka was not unique and that in England there was someone like it called Punch, that Germany had its Hans Wurst, France its Polichinelle and Czechoslovakia its Kašparek. In all these cases the puppets performed scenes or plays. The text of these plays consisted of monologues or dialogues, that is, the lines belonged to the characters themselves and not to the reciter explaining the behaviour of those characters; the words I was singing, however, were in fact a reciter's text.

That meant, as far as I could see, that to extend my repertoire and give the puppets greater acting scope I should have to give up my illustrative singing and find the right literary material so that I could play something like short dramatic scenes with the puppets.

In an old album called *Recitation and Declamation* I found two tales: "The Husband" and "Tooth-ache." These tales were written in dialogue form and it was quite easy to dramatize them. I have forgotten both the characters and the plot. I remember only that I had to make three or four puppets including one to play the part of the wife. As a certain amount of stage properties was required and I, naturally, had no curtain, Petrushka and the Piccaninny became the "servants of the proscenium" who shifted the scenery under the eyes of the public. Once they had a bed to carry in, another time a dentist's chair.

I put on this number for the first and last time at a party in the house of Andrei Globa, the writer. One does not "fail" when one is among friends. But in fact it was a failure. Ksenia Kotlubai reprimanded me for my bad taste in choice of tales and that, of course, was enough to make me drop the number for ever.

The trouble however was essentially not so much in the literary material as in the fact that the puppets acted very badly and that I, the performer, felt disgusting.

The only amusing moment was when the Piccaninny and Petrushka dragged in the big bed. At that scene the audience laughed and I found it very easy to act. I could have gone on playing about with the Piccaninny for hours, making him adjust the legs of the bed and test whether it stood firmly. But I had only to bring on the main characters of the play, or rather, to make them speak, for everything to become senseless and boring. And despite a comic plot and an amusing text, the puppets were not at all funny when they acted and, what was worse, they were not organic.

And yet, had that text, with all its faults, been acted by human beings instead of by puppets it would have been funnier and more interesting. So puppets did not enhance the humour of a text, they rather diminished it. Then why use puppets at all?

I found myself at a puzzling deadlock. I had stopped staging romances just because I thought that by doing so I was narrowing the field of possibilities of the puppets, and yet as soon as my puppets tried to act a dramatically constructed plot their possibilities were narrowed still more, and it was precisely in the dialogues that I felt most helpless. The puppets refused to speak.

Why was that?

Evidently because up till then my puppets had not spoken a word from themselves, the only exception being when the Piccaninny related how he had been out shooting. My voice had not belonged to the puppets. It had always remained my own voice.

The audience hears an invisible singer behind the screen sing: "I remember that day. Ah, that was happiness. You and I met for the first time on that day..." and meanwhile above the screen appears first an old gentleman with a guitar, then an old lady with a head-dress, then they walk up to each other and the old gentleman, laying aside his guitar, ceremoniously kisses the old lady's hand. The text refers to the past, relating something that happened long ago, but the puppets are acting that past in the present.

To which of the puppets do the words and voice belong at that moment? To neither of them. The voice belongs to me, the singer, the relater, and the puppets are silent.

For just that reason the question of making the voice coincide with the puppets did not arise when I sang "Just a Minute" or "I Remember That Day."

Of course in rhythm and even in timbre the voice bore some relation to the puppet but it did not in the least claim to be the puppet's voice.

But in the dramatized tales I had chosen to perform, the voice did claim to belong to the puppet and everything became incredibly difficult. Besides I had to make my voice jump from puppet to puppet, playing the "old lady" one moment and the "old gentleman" the next.

But what about Zaitsev? By himself he acted a whole series of separate scenes with many puppets. How is it that it turned out all right with him?

I had suffered one defeat in creative competition with Zaitsev. Then I had put it down to the fact that to me the style of the literary material was not organic, and to my being insincere in it. Now I had chosen quite different literary material, had myself adapted it for the stage and had done that with absolute sincerity and utter enthusiasm. Then why was it that once again I was at sixes and sevens with the dialogue and the roles? Was it because I lacked acting ability? Yet I seemed to have more or less enough ability to play roles in the theatre.

Evidently in this particular case the point was that in playing with his Petrushka Zaitsev used two quite different voices. For Petrushka himself he spoke with a squeaker, that is to say, not with his own voice (when you use a squeaker the vocal chords do not function), while for the other characters he used his own voice. Those characters, it needs to be remembered, never address each other. Each in turn meets Petrushka, and only Petrushka, and so there were two timbres, different in principle: the "human" voice—that of the Gypsy, the Doctor or the Constable, and the "non-human" voice belonging to Petrushka.

And if one reflects, one gets a surprisingly dialectical interchange of conceptions. The conventionalized human speech on a shrill squeaker combined with the conventionalized puppet becomes a "natural" puppet-voice, while the natural human voice in combination with a puppet becomes conventionalized.

The conventionalized and the natural are interchanged.

Besides, Zaitsev evidently did not pretend that his own voice was that of the puppet. In any event when he spoke for the Constable, the Doctor or the Gypsy he scarcely changed the timbre of his voice, just faintly disguising it with an accent. Quite unconsciously, probably, simply according to the tradition of the style, there was in Zaitsev's own intonation something of a third person, a touch of the intonation of an elocutionist.

When an elocutionist reciting Chekhov or Krylov at a concert changes his voice, according to whose words he is speaking at the moment, he will not—assuming he is a good elocutionist, a good story-teller—alter his voice completely. He will not speak in full falsetto when he is representing a woman or child. He will only "colour" his voice, he will remain an elocutionist, he will not become a ventriloquist.

The elocutionist turns into the characters he is speaking for, but not for one second does he cease to be an elocutionist.

If, in dramatizing those tales, I had not gone so far as to introduce dialogue and had kept them in the third person, then in principle those "tales with puppets" would have been no different from my "romances with puppets," and then, maybe, I would have managed all right.

But I did not do that. I tried to speak completely for each puppet and that turned out badly.

I did not realize that my songs with puppets were a discovery—albeit a chance one—that deserved attention.

Chance discoveries in art (and in science, too, for that matter) are not necessarily bad. It was only after many years of work that I discovered this simple truth.

But even if I had wanted to broaden my scope by including dialogue scenes in my programme I ought to have studied the experience of the "romances with puppets" and to have adopted a more attentive and careful attitude towards the "talking puppet" which is subject to the law of conventionality. It may be that I would have understood that it is not a question of voice alone but of the need for the actor's emotions to coincide with the puppet's; even with its size.

The Yefimovs

Although I had suffered a failure in dramatizing those tales I was still eager to base the acting of my puppets on the spoken word.

I thought out a dialogue between a theatre manager and a budding actor. I made a new puppet for the role of the Manager: a fat man in evening dress. My Piccaninny played the actor. The dialogue was a sort of theatre review and now I would not dare put that turn on before an audience, because, when all was said and done, the text was crude enough.

All the same, I managed to handle the dialogue. I succeeded, probably, because my Piccaninny spoke with a stammer, as he had done in his hunting tale, and had become such a past-master of a stammerer that he could manage any text in that manner of speaking and always sounded comic, always discovered some new gestures and tricks.

The Manager simply spoke in my voice; I made no attempt to characterize him in any way. Like the clown's partner of the circus ring the Manager was only a handy sheet of litmus paper with which the reactions to the real clown, the main comic, could be easily registered. My Piccaninny was the real clown in this act, which was essentially not a dialogue between two comics but a comic monologue consisting of replies to the questions of an impersonal Manager.

However, despite the superficial success of the Theatre Review with my audiences of those days I did not want to go on looking for a repertoire in the direction of dialogues and verbal quips and sallies; I still dreamed of creating dramatically constructed scenes.

At that time the Yefimovs' puppet theatre existed in Moscow. This was a most interesting place. It was founded by two people: Ivan Yefimov, the sculptor, and Nina Simanovich-Yefimova, his wife, a painter.

These two made their own puppets, staged their shows and acted in their own theatre.

Their theatre was the home of a real artistic culture and of an enormous, an almost ecstatic love of puppets.

At that time I saw their "Krylov's Fables," "The Princess on the Pea," a short scene with Petrushka and the "Dance of the Animals."

Some things I did not like very much; the acting seemed naive or pretentious; but I greatly admired much of their work.

Ivan Yefimov taught sculpture at the art school where I had studied, and although I had been in the painting and then the drawing departments I knew him slightly and this provided me with the excuse of calling on him and his wife at home.

They lived in a large block of flats near Krasniye Vorota. I climbed the dark staircase up to one of the top floors, groped for the bell and rang.

At this point I shall interrupt my story and quote a few lines from Chapter 3 of Nina Simanovich-Yefimova's book *Notes of a Petrushka Player*.

"Ever so often, about three times a year, when we open the creaking door of our flat in reply to a timid ring there enters a young stranger. Always a different one. Sometimes forgetting even to give his name which, on the whole, is of no consequence because the name would probably not mean anything to us, he begins with: 'I saw your performance and came to find out how to make puppets.'

"When a traveller steps on to the porch of a farm house and is met by the hospitable lady of the house the watch-dog in the corner nevertheless rattles his chain and leaps out jealously; the fowl, gathering to peck their daily ration of oats, scuttle off fussily to the shelter of the nettles, and a flock of sparrows twitter shrilly on the fence.

"The short question of the innocent youth arouses at once in us all those different feelings: the jealousy of the dog—I can hear him growling within me, how the chain rattles and how he growls through his old yellowing teeth—is my love and jealousy for Petrushkas: things I intended to do scuttle away because I would have to answer his question and answer it seriously; the sparrows of my thoughts had flown away—they had flown away for a long time, perhaps for ever; but the housewife of hospitality predominates—in other words the joy that someone has called, someone who is really thirsting to know about Petrushkas.... But where are to be found these young searchers for the truth about puppets after the door has closed behind them? You will never see him again.... Yes, the door shuts behind them, you look round the room, at the floor which has come to look like a battle-field—you sigh and say to yourself: 'In a few more years when I am no longer alive and my knowledge has been scattered among clumsy, incompetent, perhaps untalented or even dishonest hands, people will scold me for having wasted the idea of Petrushka. But after all there is a hope that some puppet enthusiast will turn up who will work in a new sphere, discover undiscovered islands, open new horizons, create quite new plays and draw from the treasure-house in which it is so hard to delve but once you have delved, you can go on drawing from it for a thousand years.... There ought to appear some young actor who has the bravery to face his teachers, energy and independence before his comrades, and who risks hiding his pretty face behind a screen. He cannot be prettier than Yefimov who, nevertheless, emerges from behind his screen only to make some announcement about the puppet theatre, when we are playing before grown-ups.' "

I have introduced these lines because immediately after her book was published in 1925 Nina Simanovich-Yefimova presented a copy of it to me with the dedication: "To the young man of Chapter 3" telling me that she started to write that chapter immediately the door closed behind me.

This dedication did not strike me as being particularly kind because I had learned from the look in Nina Simanovich-Yefimova's eyes that it was not me she saw as the successor to their theatre: "the jealous watch-dog" had growled pretty loudly on its chain when I called. Nor do I think that she considered me to be that later on—all the less so because I was not that at all. I, like them, loved puppets, but I loved them in a different way.

True, that "jealous dog" did not prevent us from meeting, especially as I did not at first hear his chain rattling. I called on the Yefimovs several times. I brought them my puppets and asked them for advice. I examined the puppets of their theatre; they had a wonderful ballet dancer which could spin on one foot, a "Grandad Krylov" in a blue gown, a wolf with enormous chattering teeth, two splendid fabulous mice with large heads and free hanging folds of cloth for their bodies.

Of course I benefited very much from my first visit as from all succeeding ones to the Yefimovs. Above all because I grew to know people who were utterly devoted to puppets, not dull, commonplace people but people possessing individuality and talent. Besides, I saw puppets made in all kinds of ways. I found it highly interesting to examine them, to slip them on my hand and try to play with them, especially as many of them had much in common with the dramatically expressive, dynamic pieces of Yefimov's sculpture in clay, forged bronze, wood or porcelain that stood about the room.

But, unfortunately, I could not get from the Yefimovs an answer to the chief question that was nagging at my mind—the question of repertoire. It was not only that my failure over the Petrushka show had once and for all driven from my mind all ideas of imitating anybody. Nor was it that we were of such different age and had different aesthetic tastes. It was something else. It was the difference in principle between the possibilities the Yefimovs had at their disposal and mine.

Although there were individual scenes or interludes in the Yefimov theatre which Nina Yefimova played alone, the performances as a whole resembled a real theatre with curtain, proscenium arch, backcloth, and various decorative elements.

The Yefimovs played most of the plays and scenes together, some with three players (their son helped them occasionally). That meant that they could have as many as four or even six puppets on the stage at a time—a puppet on each hand of an actor. Besides, the Yefimovs had at their disposal voices of two altogether different timbres—male and female. All that remained for either of them to do was to find different tones within their vocal ranges. How could I hope to compare my programme possibilities with those of the Yefimovs?

But I did not envy them in the least. I did not want to turn my performances into mere theatre and to look round for partners. On the contrary, I liked presenting my puppets on my own from behind a small screen. I liked having no curtain or scenic effects and being able to fold my screen up and pack it away under the eyes of the audience. The less time passed between the moment I dived behind the screen after announcing my turn and the appearance of the first puppet, the more gratified I felt. The speed gave an effect of ease and simplicity, and these were qualities I attached much importance to.

And as I had only two hands I could only manipulate two puppets at once. I did not mind that two different characters, two different puppets worn on human hands had to have the faculty of living and moving in different rhythms which did not always synchronize. On the contrary, I enjoyed training my hands to move to different rhythms, to play simultaneously two characters who might be described as possessing physico-rhythmical differences.

To put it shortly, I was a jealous guardian of my solo role behind the screen. Maybe I was in this way continuing the tradition of the popular Petrushka player; however, that tradition placed me under many an obligation and, above all, obliged me to look for a repertoire which an actor could manage single-handed.

Unused Success

Because of my failure in staging those stories and also because I wanted to get away from literary "dialogue" subjects, I took another sharp turn: I dropped dialogue altogether and took up a purely "physical" subject, in other words, pantomime.

The desire to do this evidently rose from those dumb "proscenium servants" who had dragged in the bed so comically and had stolen the show from the main characters notwithstanding the latter's capacity of speech.

I wanted to take some quite ordinary physical act of an essentially narrative character and make the puppets carry it out. Setting up a samovar, for instance.

I bought a very nice little samovar at a toy shop. It was quite like a real one. A bright, shiny, brass samovar.

As the Piccaninny was still one of my favourite and most "playable" puppets I used him to "set up the samovar."

He lifted it above the edge of the screen, went out, only to return immediately with a tiny bucket filled with real water.

He took the top off the samovar, lifted the lid, poured in the water, put back the lid and then went out again to fetch a glowing splinter. Plunging the splinter into the chimney of the samovar he puffed at it from above and below through the little holes until the tinder caught fire, and then went out again. Next he brought in a small boot which he struck upside down on the samovar's chimney and carefully kneaded it, concertina-wise, to puff air into the samovar.

At this point the pantomime was interrupted. While waiting for the samovar to come to the boil the Piccaninny perched himself on the edge of the screen and stammered some nonsense to the audience. Carried away by his chatter he did not notice that the samovar had come to the boil. I had made a little tube through the lower part of the samovar and puffed talcum powder through it by means of a rubber bulb. The samovar was enveloped in a cloud of "steam." The Piccaninny sprang down from his perch, tried to pick up the samovar, burnt his fingers, blew on them, grasped the samovar again, and burnt himself once more.

In the long run the samovar made off by itself; it simply waddled away round the screen and disappeared.

The distracted Piccaninny ran after it.

That was all. The performance ended with that.

For my future work this turn had great significance because it showed that it was really most interesting to give puppets purely physical tasks. The puppet is created to be mobile. Only when it moves does it become alive and only in the character of its movements does it acquire what we call behaviour. And in its physical behaviour the puppet's character is born. Of course the text, assuming there is one, has enormous importance but if the words a puppet speaks do not correspond with its gestures, they become divorced from the puppet and hang in the air. Gesture and movement can exist without words, but in any role, especially in roles played by puppets, there cannot be words without gesture. I am, of course, referring to words which come from a source the audience can see; words can be spoken off stage in any theatre, including the puppet theatre.

But as continuous gesticulation with every phrase seems senseless, and as the unavoidable limitations on the gestures of a puppet lead to an irritating repetitiveness it is very often necessary to replace gesticulation by giving the puppets physical tasks to do.

In the turn with the samovar these tasks were pure and simple.

Although the scenario of the "physical plot" of this number was short, it was a success in that it revealed possibilities of puppets.

But I quite threw away this success.

Even in training studies, in school exercises, one must not set tasks of purely physical action. First of all because physical tasks do not exist in life in a purely abstract form.

If someone does something, he does it with some aim in view, with a certain attitude towards that physical task. It is precisely that attitude which creates physical behaviour, that is to say, the movements of a thinking being, not a robot.

There is even a difference in the way every man chops wood, depending on whether he is in a hurry to warm up a chilly room, or wants to show off his strength and skill before the eyes of a girl watching him through the window.

The character of a physical act is radically changed according to its theme or task.

But in life we do not think about the theme and task of physical acts because they are always there; on the stage, however, you must know them clearly before you open your mouth or make a gesture as otherwise your actions will be pointless.

I succeeded in thinking out the physical actions and did not pay the least heed to *why* the Piccaninny had to light the samovar or what, after all, my turn meant. Naturally this senseless, pointless item could not remain in my repertoire although there was much that was amusing and entertaining in it.

This was all the more regrettable because in that number there was another of my unexploited successes.

Back in my childhood I often used to make my Be-Ba-Bo turn over the pages of a book or the sheets of a newspaper and draw his hand along the lines as he read. I made Be-Ba-Bo, and later my Piccaninny, play a little tune on the piano, or pluck at the strings of a guitar and take fright at the sounds produced; I made them take a pencil or paint brush in both hands (puppets can pick up nothing with one hand alone) and draw funny faces on a sheet of paper or on canvas.

The contact between a conventionalized puppet and something natural, belonging to the world of man—a pencil, a newspaper, a guitar—created a peculiarly amusing and piquant effect. It made me laugh, and it made others laugh too, but for some reason I never attempted to show this in my programme. On the contrary I tried to make all my stage properties belong, in form, scale and material, to the world of puppets rather than to that of human beings.

I thought that the toy samovar I had bought would also have a puppet character, but it was so large and the material it was made of was so real that beside the puppet representing a human being it looked like a real samovar. And the same effect was given by the water, the glowing splinter, and the fire.

The juxtaposing of the Piccaninny and these real objects was so amusing and charming that it was essentially this and this alone that brought a certain amount of success to a number which otherwise was quite senseless.

Plot and Theme

The second of my pantomimes was called "Rejuvenation."

A patient comes to consult a doctor. The doctor examines him carefully, listens to him through his stethoscope, taps his chest and back. The patient draws a deep breath. Then the doctor takes a large knife—a real one—saws right round the patient's neck, grasps his head firmly with both hands and starts twisting it, first to and fro and then round and round, as if unscrewing it. Finally the head parts from the neck, the doctor takes it away and brings in another one, a young and beautiful head. This second head is not at all easy to attach to the body because the headless patient wanders about like a blind man. At length the doctor catches the right moment and manages to get the head on to the neck and then to screw it on tight.

The patient feels his new head with his hands, is obviously satisfied and, shaking the doctor by the hand, goes out.

On that the number ends.

Compared with the "Samovar" number "Rejuvenation" had more plot; there was a definite dramatic design; but just for this reason the complete absence of theme and idea made the number even more futile.

At least I ought to have known who that doctor was and who was his patient. But I neither knew nor cared.

And yet my physical scenario about rejuvenation might have led me to a satire on manners or to a political pamphlet.

Imagine that the patient is some not very honest parliamentary candidate and that he comes to the doctor with the request to change his head and give him an appearance which will impress his constituents and conceal his true likeness. That would put the number on the right lines at once. The theme would have shaped the characteristics of the participants and the nature of their behaviour, it would have enabled the idea, the point of the number, to be expressed and at the same time would not have upset the effectiveness of the little scene.

And this effectiveness was quite considerable because the number was in no way an imitation of the human theatre. It was puppetry through and through. Yet I did not know how to exploit my success. I mistook the effectiveness of the plot for a theme.

The only thing I can say in my defence was that even professional playwrights often make such mistakes. They fail simply because they mistake the plot for the theme, whereas the best plot in the world, for all its elaborate dramatic situation, is a still-born child if it lacks a theme.

The Theme and the Time Factor

My third pantomime was "The Piccaninny in Love."

In contrast with the "Samovar" and "Rejuvenation" this was not a single scene but a whole series of scenes.

In the front of the screen I made a square opening with moving curtains and made the action take place, sometimes in the centre of the screen—in a space like a little stage—and sometimes on top, in the place where my puppets usually appeared.

I do not remember clearly how the action went but the main idea was that the Piccaninny meets a blonde and falls in love with her. As he can speak only English and she only Russian he cannot declare his feelings to her.

That is where the pantomime begins. All the rest of the play takes place without words.

The ardent Piccaninny flings a noose round his neck and jumps down from the top of the screen. At that moment I slip my hand out of the puppet and the Piccaninny hangs on the rope quite inert.

The girl returns. She combs her hair. Suddenly she notices the Piccaninny and falls into a swoon.

One of the monkeys runs in (the monkeys were acting as proscenium servants), stumbles over the prostrate girl, takes fright, starts back, notices the hanging form of the Piccaninny and dashes headlong away to summon the second monkey.

Both monkeys carefully pull up the rope, free the Piccaninny from the loop, listen to his heart, give him some artificial respiration by flinging his arms up and down, listen to his heart once more, waggle his arms again for a little while and listen to his heart. The Piccaninny is obviously breathing because the monkeys leap about joyfully and waggle the Piccaninny's arms faster.

Finally one monkey runs away. I needed that because I could not bring the Piccaninny back to life until I had freed one hand from a monkey.

The Piccaninny revives. The monkey points to the prostrate girl and tactfully leaves. That gives me a hand free for the girl. The Piccaninny gesticulates over the girl and breathes carefully and tenderly on her face. The girl recovers consciousness and they fall into each other's arms. Curtain.

The two previous pantomimes had soon been discarded from my repertoire as despite the effectiveness of the physical plots they lacked themes, and hence ideas. This new pantomime not only possessed a physical plot that was quite suitable for puppets but it had a theme too. A modest theme, no doubt, but, all the same, a theme. With a conclusion, an idea. An idea which might be formulated as: "Love needs no words. Lovers can understand each other without words."

Why then did this pantomime, too, have so short a life, even shorter than "Samovar" and "Rejuvenation"?

Because its plot was bigger than its theme. The small, naive theme would have been suitable for a short satirical jest.

That would have been amusing, it would have conformed to the requirements of the genre. It would not even have seemed naive or small. But a theme of that sort could not possibly serve as material for a comparatively long, protracted melodrama, admittedly ironic but nonetheless a melodrama.

The plot must not be bigger than the theme. And that is just what happened in "The Piccaninny in Love."

There are people who spoil the funniest stories by spending too much time telling them. They make the point of the joke sound simply silly.

That is what I did. I spent too long on telling the love story of the Piccaninny and the Blonde and spoiled a theme that was very small to begin with.

There is a strict law of proportion between theme and time. And as besides the general theme, in every theatrical production each act, each scene, each episode and even each phrase has its theme, the time law is one of the most serious of all laws. It is far more complex than such phrases as "long," "drawn-out" or "boring" suggest.

Things are not always improved by simply shortening time. Sometimes you have to increase the theme of a phrase, episode or act and thus restore the proportion; at other times, on the contrary, you have to throw out whole scenes or acts.

The time law in the puppet theatre is probably stricter and harsher than in any other kind of theatre; in my work as a producer I now try to pay much attention to the time composition. But in those days I did not guess the reason for my failure and therefore was not able to reconstruct the composition of my pantomime.

The Reasons for Success

And so I have described most, if not all, my work during the period of my "home theatricals" and have rated it not particularly high.

How then is one to explain the success that nevertheless my performances with puppets enjoyed? Not only at home or at parties but before qualified audiences of actors, writers and artists.

How am I to explain why the magazine *Krasnaya Niva* published as early as 1925 a longish and favourable review of my work by Pavel Sukhotin the writer?

I attribute that to three reasons.

The first is that in these very imperfect things I was sincere.

After all, I am criticizing that work now from the position of my present views on art. And of course, were I to try and play the "Samovar," "Rejuvenation" or "The Piccaninny in Love" today, I would, despite my twenty-five years' experience, not be able to act them half as well as I did in those days. And that only because I have lost my faith in them and have realized what is wrong with them. That means I could not be sincere today. But in those days they did not strike me as being bad and I took a sincere delight in the way the Piccaninny lit the samovar.

If my Petrushka perished through lack of sincerity, the presence of sincerity saved my very imperfect pantomimes.

The second reason for the comparative success of my performances was the novelty of the genre.

My audiences of those days knew little, if anything, of puppets.

The very fact that the puppets moved in a lifelike manner interested and entertained them.

If I showed all my early work to present-day audiences, especially those in Moscow and Leningrad, before whom I have performed hundreds of times, failure would, of course, be inevitable. It would cause nothing but bewilderment. But in those days the appearance on the concert stage of a man carrying a small screen and showing puppets was quite new and, therefore, most interesting.

My puppets did not repeat the old forms, they copied nothing, expressed no stylization and did something original, however imperfectly.

And, finally, the main reason for my success was that of the kernel of all my performances. I always retained two of the oldest of my numbers: "Just a Minute" with the monkeys, and "It was a happy day" with the Old Couple.

And those numbers had certain positive properties.

Firstly, they were up-to-date at that time, for both romances were well known to the audiences.

Secondly, those two numbers were very precise in form.

And thirdly, they were quite new in their genre—the founders, in fact, of that genre—of "romances with puppets" which had not been seen on the stage before.

That is why the success of my performances rested on those two turns.

It was they who saved me from complete failure.

The Audience as Friend and Assistant

I suppose autumn 1925 ought to be considered the end of the "home theatricals" phase of my work.

It was interrupted purely mechanically by my departure on a long foreign tour with the Musical Studio of the Moscow Art Theatre. This was to take me to Germany, Czechoslovakia and the United States.

On my return to Moscow I was soon appearing at concerts as a professional and my puppet performances assumed the character of regular concerts. That is why on looking back now for the last time at the whole course of my pre-professional career I recall not only my helpless steps but also many of those people in whose company I worked and without whom I would probably not have taken a single step.

I meet my present audiences only during my performance in concerts. Their relation to my puppets is defined by laughter, silence, applause. Of course, it sometimes happens that some friend in the audience shares his impressions with me afterwards, but considering the number of concerts and still more the total size of the audiences, the amount of verbal criticism I get from the audience is very small.

During my "home theatricals" phase, on the other hand, I learned the audience's reaction immediately after each performance and could tell just what had turned out well or badly.

The audience became my teacher and assistant.

Naturally I find it difficult now to remember and quite impossible to list all those who assisted me with their advice and practical help.

But some of them I must mention, for their names fix both the time and the character of my performances with puppets.

Among those to whom I owe a debt of gratitude I ought to make special mention of the man who was not only the audience at my concerts but who also arranged them.

This was Boris Pronin. We met first at a students' evening at the Shor Conservatoire when I showed my puppets.

Of course, Pronin might have been called an "adventurer" but no one could accuse him of working for his personal advantage or of trying to make a career for himself.

On the contrary, in all his ventures Pronin was prouder of the people he involved in them than of his own role as organizer.

He loved the art world and was always trying to bring together actors from different theatres, artists and writers around some jolly and always creative idea or other. He had a real unselfish affection for his friends: for Moskvin, Alexei Tolstoi, Kachalov, for poets, sculptors, guitar-players.

He was constantly spotting some new talent and always in a hurry to show his latest discovery to his friends.

One fantastic idea pursued another in Boris Pronin's mind. He was always organizing something. Some club or other, a tiny theatre, a concert in some surprising form or simply an evening party during which there would be some sort of turn: an elocutionist reading verses or a play, or a new Gypsy singer he had discovered.

Pronin was a successful failure. He was successful because many of his fantasies were at first realized. People liked him and responded to his appeal, and his ardent temperament overcame all technical obstacles.

But this very temperament destroyed the project and it would explode like an iridescent soap-bubble.

As soon as he caught sight of my puppets Pronin evidently reacted to them as he did to one of his usual "discoveries." He at once decided to organize a puppet theatre. And it had to be in a cellar. There had to be beams in the ceiling and wooden benches and a hanging iron lamp. All rather medieval.

He did not find a cellar. There was not one available. But he found an attic and at once got the idea of opening an arty club called the Mansard.

This idea was realized.

At the opening of the Mansard Club there were performances by Vasily Kachalov, by the Negro singer Coretti Arley-Titz and by the poet Vasily Kamensky. I and my puppets also performed.

From that time on, right up to the time the place closed, I was often at the Mansard Club. We had no Art Workers' Club in those days. The Mansard was the only place where actors, writers, artists and musicians could meet each other.

True, the place was run on the money obtained from a high entrance fee which "outsiders" had to pay to get in.

The "outsiders" were the Nepmen with their eccentrically dressed women.

But people of the art world were admitted free of charge and among them were many great and talented names. You could hear wonderful music at the Mansard, romances were sung, poems were read and heated arguments about literature and the theatre took place.

I found it so interesting and important to meet the big names in art that I often sat on at the Mansard into the early hours of the morning drinking everything in with my eyes and ears.

I was probably the youngest of the company gathered there but everyone treated me as an equal. My puppets were popular and sometimes they would monopolize an entire evening.

That is what I should thank Boris Pronin for. I needed friendly, well-intentioned criticism from leading, talented people in the art world, and after every performance talk and advice flowed freely. Some liked one thing, some another.

But, of course, there are others besides Pronin and the habitués of his Mansard who deserve my gratitude for the help they gave me, especially as many of the friends I made at that time remain my friends to this day, and some of them have, like me, taken up puppetry professionally.

Maria Artyukhova, who made her first puppets at the same time as I, now makes puppets for many theatres. The writer Andrei Globa in whose home I once presented my unsuccessful stage version of the stories has since written a play for the puppet theatre, called *Jim and the Dollar*. It was with this play that the State Central Puppet Theatre opened under my direction in 1932.

My first pianist, Natalia Alexandrova, later became the accompanist and composer at our theatre and wrote beautiful music for a number of productions.

But I have lost many of my best friends, people who helped me and who saw the birth of my profession. My friend and teacher Ksenia Kotlubai, and Ivan Zaitsev. When I started to write this chapter Nina Simanovich-Yefimova was alive and well; she telephoned to tell me that she intended presenting our theatre museum with her puppets as she and Ivan Yefimov had long ago given up performing with them.

On a sunny frosty morning a few months later I attended Nina Yefimova's funeral at Lefortovo Cemetery.

Now the Yefimovs' puppets, the ones about which I have been writing, stand in a big glass case in our museum.

Over twenty years have passed since the death of my first wife Sophia Obraztsova-Smyslova.

It was she who made the costumes for my first puppets: the Piccaninny, the Old Couple, the White Lady. She stitched the flowers on to my first screen and made a cover for it to keep it from getting dirty when being moved about.

She was the first spectator and critic of every new number.

On November 28, 1949, my father, Academician Vladimir Obraztsov, died. Our professions were quite different. What could there be in common between a railway engineer and a theatre worker? A puppet-theatre worker at that! Yet my father had a very great and profound influence on my work. My father was immeasurably sincere and frank about everything: in everything he did, every judgement he passed.

He possessed an enormous capacity for work because the main motive force in his work was the creative vision, a concrete vision of the future of his country. Of the growth of cities, the exploitation of its forests and minerals, of new railway lines, of factory construction and the building of new schools and holiday centres.

His grasp of art was also characterized by creative approach, and at the same time very concrete. He took an interest in my work, saw every one of my new parts on the stage, every new number with puppets, every one of my new productions. And his unprofessional but straightforward and candid judgement was often of more value to me than the opinion of professionals.

My father did not live to see this book published, but he read it all in manuscript and so I feel justified in dedicating it to him.

CHAPTER TEN

In Foreign Lands

Taking everything into account, I am glad my profession began as a joke, as pure fun. I am glad I started from scratch and that I knew nothing of any use about the art of the puppet theatre.

If it had been otherwise, if from the start I had decided to take up puppetry seriously and had set about studying all forms of puppet theatres past and present, I would never have thought of performing romances and arias with puppets. Very likely, too, I would have acted and made my puppets quite differently.

True, I often marked time, often "rediscovered America," but the result was that by the time I came to learn more about the puppet theatre—either from books or from personal contact with my more professional colleagues—I had already acquired a certain "immunity." I was glad when I found things that coincided with my ideas on puppets, and firmly rejected what was alien to them.

Naturally, I learned something from others, including people in foreign puppet theatres, but I think I benefited more from what I did not like in their work than from what I did like. After all, one learns from other people's mistakes as well as from their innovations.

Other people's mistakes are more obvious than one's own. Besides, in the mistakes others make you can sometimes find those you make yourself. They often turn into a line of buoys marking the edges of your own fairway.

And the other boats which have run aground in the shallows or struck hidden reefs show you more clearly how to avoid dangerous directions.

In a Toy Shop

I did not see a single puppet show in Berlin. Not because there were none there in 1925, but because I had no idea where to look for them, and had little time anyway. I was fully occupied at the theatre.

In the toy department of the big Wertheim stores I found some little plush monkeys very much like that first foreign monkey I had once been given. I slipped my hands into a pair of them and tried them out, much to the surprise of the shop-assistant who could not have suspected that they possessed such gifts. But the monkeys were obviously made for children's hands; they were less easily manipulated than mine, and I left without buying any.

There were also some human puppets on sale there, but they had heavy wooden heads and arms. It was quite difficult to play with them, and, besides, they were ugly.

The look of these puppets showed that though they were the work of talented people with a genuine folk tradition, the passage of time and mechanical repetition had exhausted this talent and the tradition had become moribund.

Spejbl

I was much luckier in Prague.

I met there Professor Vesely, the editor of the puppet magazine *Loutkář*. He was very kind to me and gave me several copies of his magazine. From him I learned that Czechoslovakia had many puppet theatres—over two thousand. In most of these theatres they used puppets worked with strings and usually known as marionettes. I say "usually" because in many countries the word marionette is sometimes applied to theatrical puppets of all sorts. In English terminology the distinction is made by referring to marionettes and glove puppets.

In Soviet books on the subject glove puppets are usually called Petrushka figures. This, in my opinion, is not a very happy expression. Our modern puppet theatres have nothing in common, either in their repertoire or in their characters, with Petrushka show. It is silly to use the word Petrushka for a puppet representing Tsarevich Ivan, a reindeer or a dog. The real popular puppeteers never did so. They referred to their puppets either as "top 'uns," that is, ones which the puppeteer holds up, above him, or as glove puppets, that is, ones worn on the hands.

In most parts of Europe, including Czechoslovakia, glove-puppet theatres are comparatively few. I had the impression they were rather looked down on as something a bit primitive.

Most puppet theatres in Czechoslovakia used marionettes and I became quite familiar with the work of one of these theatres. It was called "V Říši Loutek" which means "In the Realm of Puppets."

We were received with the greatest kindness by the actors of this theatre. They put on a special show of several plays for us: Gozzi's *Princess Turandot*, Shakespeare's *Twelfth Night*, and the fairy-tale *The Sleeping Beauty*.

After the show they took us to a small restaurant and treated us with most touching kindness.

Naturally, I was deeply impressed by the fact that whole plays—plays by Shakespeare and Gozzi, moreover—could be done by puppets. Much in the performances pleased me. Sir Toby Belch was played most amusingly, especially in the scene when Malvolio reads the letter. Sir Toby falls on the stairs and rocks with laughter. I liked Tartalia in *Princess Turandot*. And I liked the decoration for *Twelfth Night* with its solid white columns and statues.

Some things however I did not like at all. In *The Sleeping Beauty* the giant was played by a little boy of about eight. He certainly looked enormous beside the puppets, but in comparison with the real living person the puppets looked dead and the boy looked unpleasantly naturalistic and clumsy. In a word, they didn't go together at all, they clashed, and this scene spoiled the truth of the performance.

Of everything I saw in Prague what I liked best was the puppet whose photograph I saw printed in the magazine *Loutkář*. It was called Spejbl and was the work of the sculptor Nosek and of the actor and producer Skupa from Plzen.

In addition to the photograph this copy of the magazine printed a series of drawings. The first drawing was a portrait of Skupa in profile, done without any distortion. The next drawing showed the profile somewhat simplified, with the introduction of an element of caricature. In the third the generalization was carried further. Gradually the profile became more and more that of a puppet. Finally it turned into the head of Spejbl.

I do not know whether that was the way Spejbl actually was conceived or whether it was just a joke on the artist's part; after all, by introducing changes by easy stages you can turn an elephant into a siskin (if you did not see the intermediate drawings Spejbl did not look in the least like Skupa). Yet this series of drawings brought out Spejbl's main features: though the generalization was highly conditional he kept a peculiar individuality and never became schematic.

Spejbl had big bulging eyes that squinted slightly, and protruding nose, and bat-like ears, but at the same time his head was surprisingly harmonious in shape. It had not one sharp angle, not one edge, it was solid and sculptural in the full sense of the word. The eyes, ears and nose were logical parts of its form and looked not at all exaggerated. It was interesting to note that whereas the first few drawings immediately after the profile of Skupa looked like caricatures, Spejbl himself was no caricature at all but a real independent well-proportioned being.

For all his conventionalized character there is nothing forced about Spejbl; and, what is most important, he is truly and pleasantly comic. With a touch of lyricism, even.

I suppose it is true that every good comic character has a touch of lyricism about him.

Later on I heard that Spejbl had become a popular favourite and was appearing constantly in many plays. He had begotten a son Hurvinek and a daughter Manečka.

And so a whole Spejbl family was created. Spejbl became a children's toy, he found his way into books. He became as proverbial as old Kašparek. A folk character. It is greatly to the credit of an artist when a puppet of his creation becomes one of the nation's favourite characters.

The Puppet and the Violin

I visited two puppet theatres in New York.

One of them was known as the Jewish Marionette Theatre, although they used glove puppets there.

The stage was arranged like a "human theatre" with wings, floats and painted backcloths.

The decoration and puppets were very formalized in appearance, somewhat reminiscent of Chagall's painting. As I did not understand the language I found it difficult to follow the plays, but, judging from the characters, the manner of acting and the reaction of the public, the play was a satirical comedy of manners.

I liked the people running that theatre. It was obvious that their work brought them no gain and that the theatre existed only because its founders believed in the art of puppetry and in its social function. There were Communists among them and they greeted me, the actor from the Soviet Union, from Moscow, like a brother.

But although I watched the performance at this Jewish Marionette Theatre in New York with keen pleasure and very much liked the whole atmosphere of the place the puppets themselves did not make much of an impression on me.

Outwardly they were effective, with strongly marked features, but they were not so much stylized as abstract, and somehow lacked charm. It may be, however, that I got this impression after trying out their acting possibilities and finding them somewhat limited.

My puppets did not have those little tubes used to lengthen the arms and neck of a puppet. That made them a little short-limbed and frog-like, but it meant that the arms kept the life-like movements of the human hand.

I put one of my monkeys on one hand and a puppet belonging to one of my American colleagues on the other. Beside the monkey the American puppet seemed clumsy with its big heavy head and stick-like arms.

The puppets greeted each other and patted each other on the head. They expressed their sadness about something, they rejoiced together, they even danced. As I acted for both of them, the competition in acting was purely between the puppets. Personally I thought my own puppet clearly had the better of it. Its movements had greater expressive possibilities.

But there was one feature of the production that I envied then. My puppets had never performed to the accompaniment of an orchestra. It was, however, not the orchestra itself that impressed me, for it was very small, consisting maybe of no more than three instruments. But in that trio there was a violin. The violin is an instrument that has a special sort of temperament. It has no physiological *forte*. Its strings and its bow do not permit that. I refer not to the rhythmical temperament but to that of the sound itself. The violin can create an impression of *forte* but it cannot make *forte* actually. The sound of the violin is "drawn sound," but the drawing is that of the brush rather than of the pencil. On the violin there is no sudden jump of a half-tone between C and C sharp as there is on the piano, the harp or the mandoline; the violin takes an uninterrupted path up or down the scale.

All that is strangely like the play of a puppet actor, especially when he is using a glove puppet.

The puppet actor too has no right to the full physiological temperament of a sound. Neither the size nor the physical properties of the puppet permit him that. Like the movement of sound on a violin the physical movements of a puppet worn on the human hand are not tempered. If the puppet is on threads and is thus held at some distance from the actor, its movements possess a measure of "approximation" and consequently take place in jerks, sometimes only barely perceptible; the glove puppet, however, moves as plastically and precisely as the human fingers do. And the human finger is a highly precise instrument of co-ordinated movement. I like the glove puppet just because its movements are not tempered: there is something infinitely small about them, that "understatement" which plays so important a role in art of any kind.

And when at that New York puppet theatre I saw and heard how the puppets were being accompanied by a lovely Hebrew melody on a violin I too wanted to link my puppets with the violin one day.

In the theatre I run now, we have a large, real orchestra. It contains many instruments of all sorts and I have come to understand that it is not always, and far from only, the violin which ought to be used to accompany puppet play; however, the selection of instrumental timbres is a serious problem which I still face when the question arises of the musical accompaniment to puppet shows.

Three Fingers

The other puppet theatre I saw in New York was the one directed by Remo Buffano.

When I arrived for the show I found Buffano sitting on a small chair playing an accordion. In front of him on the same sort of small chair sat two puppets a little less than life-size. By pressing pedals with his feet Buffano set the puppets in motion. One puppet beat a big drum and the other played the cymbals. The result was a comic, gay little orchestra.

Then the performance started. It consisted of several short plays acted by marionettes as well as glove puppets.

In all theatres where marionettes are used the operators stand behind the backcloth, stretching their arms over the top and manipulating the strings which run down to the marionettes. The actor's head and arms are out of sight behind the top curtain. Remo Buffano removed this top curtain. The puppeteers were visible. Consequently the whole mechanics of controlling the marionettes was seen too and it was amusing to be able to see how the figures were brought to life by the skilful hands of the actors.

Of course, I have no right to pass final judgement on the work of Remo Buffano on the basis of a superficial knowledge of his theatre, but surprising as it was to see the operator moving the strings in sight of the audience, this sense of surprise lasted only for the first few minutes. After that the puppeteers even began to distract the spectators, for, after all, the method that was revealed was no more than the means and broke the theme of the show without adding anything to it.

I also saw enormous puppets, twice life-size, at Buffano's.

They were marionettes (though in this case the operators required ropes rather than strings) but, in order to set those puppets in motion, such muscular strength was needed that there could obviously be no question of that subtle understatement to which I have referred above. Figures of this size can, of course, be used as an exception in episodic roles but I did not feel tempted to put on a whole show with these figures alone.

So of all the many impressions I brought away with me from Buffano's theatre only two features of it struck me as being really original. The first was that jolly little orchestra consisting of one human being and two mechanical puppets. I liked that immensely. The second was something I really envied at first.

Looking closely at one of Buffano's puppets I noticed that it had only three fingers on each hand. I asked Buffano the reason. He replied: "They don't need any more. Anyway, the audience doesn't count." This reply was not only simple, it was logical. A puppet often has no fingers at all, only a fist. Usually you give it a thumb and leave the fingers solid. Sometimes you need to detach the index finger too. But when you make all the fingers separately, three is quite sufficient, for four creates a rake-like effect.

I liked those three-fingered hands, but later on I realized that they were far from always being convincing or satisfactory. There are times when the character requires rake-like hands (as for instance with Kashchei the Deathless); then there can be no question of chopping off the fourth finger. So Buffano's discovery turned out to be an important lesson to me of the way a puppet's anatomy may be determined, not by any requirement to copy human anatomy faithfully but by the demands of the puppet's character and behaviour.

Sifting Time

But why was it that from all the many puppet shows I saw abroad the only things I really liked were Spejbl, the violin, the half-mechanical orchestra and the three-fingered hands of Buffano's puppets? Didn't I like anything else? Was the quality so low?

No! On the contrary, I liked much of what I saw, very much indeed. Moreover, the very fact that I met many people who had dedicated their lives to the puppet theatre was highly important and significant for me. But these contacts did not have a concrete, tangible influence on me. And that was mainly for the reason I mentioned at the beginning of this chapter.

I had formed a personal conception of puppets—an unconscious one, no doubt, but quite firm. It was this that rejected anything foreign to it, especially as then I was not dreaming of founding a theatre and therefore saw nothing directly in common between large-scale performances and my little screen. I derived pleasure from watching them, but they did not correspond to my own work.

Besides that, most of these shows were done with marionettes, and these had never attracted me at all.

Some things I liked, some things surprised me. But all in an abstract way. I felt it was not my form of art. I did not want to play with those puppets.

So on my return from abroad I picked up working with my own

puppets to all intents and purposes at the point where I had stopped eight months before.

Besides, in art one sometimes learns far more from people working in different fields of art than from one's own colleagues.

I do not know whether that rule can be applied generally, but it is undoubtedly true as concerns my work in the puppet theatre.

When I watch performances in other puppet theatres I frequently find myself protesting, carrying on an inner argument with myself.

As I see it, this is not the result of lack of good will or of any feeling of jealousy; it is caused by the sometimes unavoidable clash between my aims and taste and those I find in the work of others. Anyway, after seeing a puppet show at somebody else's theatre I do not always feel I have acquired any new knowledge or ideas. I benefit much more from seeing things in other theatrical genres.

I could list hundreds of instances when things I have seen inspired me and made me ponder and reconsider my positions, sometimes reinforcing them, sometimes rejecting something that till then had seemed right to me.

True, I never feel I want to transfer to the puppet theatre as a whole any work by a producer or actor which has given me pleasure in performances in other theatrical genres. On the contrary, I always wanted to define the exact limit of the possible in each genre. But I learned much from separate moments in productions on the stage, from ballets, plays, operas, and cinema: precision in choosing a theme, a sense of contemporaneousness, perfectness, a sense of music and clarity in characterization.

But it may be that my work has been influenced less by adjacent genres than by more distant forms of art: painting, music and especially literature.

Naturally, however, the greatest and most concrete influence has been exerted by the direct perception of life around me, especially those sensations which take the form of images.

For everybody working in art this transformation of sensation into a visual image takes place subconsciously as part of a habitual process.

And so if the impressions from the puppet shows I saw in Prague and New York had no direct influence on my work, the impressions of the tour as a whole could not but be useful, as they were impressions of life itself.

Over twenty years have passed since then. The sieve of time has discarded first impressions but what remains has become all the clearer and sharper.

I remember the romantic Hradčany at Prague and the puppet-like figures of the Apostles who come out at noon on to a tiny balcony at the front of the Old Town Hall clock. (The building was damaged in a German air raid during the war.)

I remember the little, toy-like houses in the Street of the Alchemists, on one of which sat an ordinary cat which looked like a tiger compared with the size of the roof.

I remember the stone vaults and the wooden beams of the five-hundred-year-old beer cellar U Fleku with its tasty dark beer, its slices of bitter radish and Prague students' songs.

It was my first trip abroad. It took me through three different lands: Germany, Czechoslovakia, the United States. The cities, the people, the class distinctions, the unusual customs, speech, habits and rhythms of life—all seemed to me strange, contradictory, and full of unexpected contrasts.

At first it was difficult to link the tidy, patriarchal, family hotel in Charlottenburg with Friedrichstrasse in the evening, with its two streams of prostitutes flowing up and down each pavement.

I remember coming out of the underground railway station Am Zoo and buying a copy of *Pravda* with Soviet money, and at that very moment seeing my first live fascist. He was riding a motor bike and shouting something. On the handle-bars flew a flag with a swastika on it. That was the autumn of 1925.

I recalled that fascist very clearly when early one morning in July 1941, standing with a fire-hose in my hand on the roof of my house in Moscow, I saw a swastika on the wing of an aircraft.

The foreign tour dislodged in a surprising way several concepts of space and time that had seemed immovable. Between Leningrad and Stettin we ran into a storm. Rocky islands swayed like ships at a landing-stage and the ships we met in the dark green sea looked like helpless toy boats. The Baltic looked enormous, powerful.

On the other hand the Atlantic looked as tiny as a saucer. It remained unchanged throughout our voyage across it. Only the colour changed. There was not an island to be seen, we never met a ship. There was nothing with which we could judge our speed or reckon distances. We floated on that multi-coloured saucer for six days and turned up in America. That taught me a lesson in the law of relative values that I have never forgotten, and that was something much more important and applicable to my work than the lack of a finger I discovered in Remo Buffano's puppets.

Our tour took us to several American cities. We were in Chicago, Cleveland, Boston, Detroit, Cincinnati, Washington. But it was New York that made the deepest impression on my mind. A stuffy, noisy, light-hearted, reckless, ruthless city. Difficult to forget its skyscrapers; the washing hanging up in the centre of the city; the fantastic sky-signs that every evening illuminate the corner of Broadway and Sixth Avenue; the tasteless food in the cafeterias; the carefree New Year celebrators with crackers, paper trumpets and masks, filling the city streets; the three-ring circus with its thousands of spectators, the small dime-shows and the Negroes with the happy smiles and sad eyes.

I shall never forget that sensation of being deaf and dumb that I had during the first few months of life in America, before I learned enough English to be able to speak and understand a little.

I shall not forget that constant longing for home, for one's own people and country. From over there, across the ocean, it rose in one's mind more huge and near than ever.

That surprisingly new sense of being near to one's own land across thousands of kilometres of sea and land gives a greater meaning to the very understanding and conception of the word motherland.

I doubt whether in art you can do anything worth while without fully feeling and putting yourself in harmony with your own land.

An Essential Postscript

In September 1948 I wrote the last chapter of this book and handed the manuscript in to the publishers. It went to press, and early in November the State Central Puppet Theatre set out for Poland and Czechoslovakia on a long tour.

Actors, orchestra, electricians and scene shifters travelled in three passenger carriages; two luggage vans were provided for the scenery.

During two and a half months we visited many towns and cities, gave 95 performances and did not return until the end of January 1949.

On my desk I found the long galley proofs of my book waiting for me. I began to read them through and when I reached the chapter "In Foreign Lands" I realized that after having revisited Czechoslovakia I should have to add something to it.

About the trip as a whole and the puppet theatres of Czechoslovakia and Poland I shall write in the second book when I deal with the work of the Central Puppet Theatre. Now I shall merely add that the Spejbl who 23 years ago delighted me so much on the pages of *Loutkář* is now in our theatre museum together with his "son" Hurvinek. The figures were presented to us by the sculptor Nosek, the originator of Hurvinek, and a nephew of Nosek senior who had made Spejbl, and who had died some years before.

The photographs had not deceived me. The puppets were certainly extremely interesting. Moreover, since that time I have met the man who put life into them—People's Artist of Czechoslovakia Josef Skupa.

Skupa and I became close friends. I found him to be not only an excellent actor and the author of the dialogue scenes between Hurvinek and Spejbl but a man who radiated hospitality and had a wonderful store of sincerity.

Professor Vesely, the editor of *Loutkář*, had died and in his place worked the historian and theoretician of the puppet theatre, Dr. Jan Malik, who met us at the frontier and at once presented me with a copy of my book *The Puppet Player* published in Prague in his translation, and then accompanied us on a tour of practically every city in Czechoslovakia.

I revisited the "V Říši Loutek" theatre. My old friend Princess Turandot came on to the stage, bowed, stretched out a hand and said that for not having forgotten her she felt herself to be my humble servant.

And now I see her every day behind the glass in a big case in our museum together with Spejbl, Hurvinek and dozens of other puppets presented to us in Czechoslovakia and Poland.

CHAPTER ELEVEN

Positives and Negatives

I showed two new numbers in the spring of 1927; a romance by Dargomyzhsky called "The Titular Counsellor" and a Gypsy romance called "Only Acquaintances."

Only a few months separated their premières but despite this the two numbers differed greatly from each other not only in plot, theme and characters, which was to be expected, but in the relation to the original.

Both numbers are still in my repertoire but belong to two quite opposite groups of work.

"The Titular Counsellor," as presented by my puppets, gives the composer no grounds whatsoever for complaint, for neither theme, content nor musical treatment are changed; the Gypsy romance, on the other hand, is turned inside out by the puppets. In "Only Acquaintances" the puppets "insult," the composer, they reverse his theme.

In "The Titular Counsellor" the attitude to the composer is positive, in "Only Acquaintances" it could be more fairly described as negative.

In writing further about my professional concert numbers I intend to deal with them not in date order but according to what they have in common with each other, or on the contrary. In this chapter I shall mention only "positives" and "negatives."

A Play in Four Lines

On my return to the Soviet Union in 1926 from our foreign tour, I made a puppet which outwardly resembled the Spejbl which had pleased me so much in Czechoslovakia though it had one difference: Spejbl was a marionette while mine was a glove puppet.

I made this puppet without any definite role in mind, but it turned out to be so comic that it quickly took over nearly all the roles of the Piccaninny and besides that the role of the doctor in "Rejuvenation."

For a long time this puppet was known as the Doctor.

I began by trying to use the Doctor in "The Titular Counsellor" too and made him a little uniform with shiny buttons.

At first the role of the general's daughter in this romance was played by the puppet that I also used for "Santuzzi."

Over twenty years have passed since I showed the public "The Titular Counsellor" for the first time, but I am still as fond of that number as ever.

I love every phrase, every word, every note and every pause in that work of Dargomyzhsky's.

What I like about it above all is the way the text and melody combine so completely, and the superb laconism of the form. Moreover, this laconism is not something artificial, it is not deliberate, it stems from the idea. It is a scheme of laconic dramatic work in which the schematism itself is its inner theme.

The formula of tragic love is employed and tragic experiences, if turned into a formula, are almost inevitably discredited and acquire an ironic character.

The entire incident, the whole play is contained in four lines of verse with the same rhythm for each line.

The first line describes the two main characters:

A titular counsellor he was, a general's daughter was she;

As the characters are at different levels in the official hierarchy we have already been made aware of a note of "danger," and so the opening line also serves the plot of the song.

Then the plot begins to unfold. In a novel it could take a chapter, in a play a whole scene, in a lyrical poem several verses but here once more a single line is enough:

He made her a modest proposal, she turned a deaf ear to his plea.

In essence this line takes us not only a further stage along the development of the plot but reaches the culmination, for in the following two lines we are already at the dénouement:

*The titular counsellor suffered: he went and got drunk as can be,
And through the delirious vapours the general's daughter did see.*

This dénouement is unexpected because of its commonplace nature. The hero does not shoot or hang himself, he simply gets drunk. High tragedy is not for officials of low rank. Drink is his way out. Only in his dreams can a man of his rank have a general's daughter for a sweetheart.

In fact this little poem is an excellent social epigram.

The composer has broken up each line into two literary-musical phrases; the fourth line in each verse repeats. We get two five-line verses:

*A titular counsellor he was,
A general's daughter was she;
He made her a modest proposal,
She turned a deaf ear to his plea.
She turned a deaf ear to his plea....*

*The titular counsellor suffered:
He went and got drunk as can be,
And through the delirious vapours
The general's daughter did see.
The general's daughter did see....*

Each phrase comprises a complete physical act so that in illustrating the phrase the puppets had no need to invent anything, to broaden or add to the text. On the contrary, all I had to do was to listen and obey the composer, to subordinate to the outline of his phrases. And it is always a pleasure to obey an author.

With the first phrase "A titular counsellor he was" the titular counsellor appears above the screen. Then there is a pause in the music. This is excellent because it emphasizes the finality and completeness of the phrase. For me this pause had even more value because it gives the spectator time to take a close look at the tiny pitifully comic creature.

The second musical phrase "A general's daughter was she" I sing a little broader. This brings out the significance of the heroine.

With this phrase the general's daughter appears at the other end of the screen.

Another pause. Again there is time for the stupidity and vain of the girl to sink in.

On the third phrase "He made her a modest proposal" "he" drops on one knee before "her" and on the next phrase "She turned a deaf ear to his plea" "she" proudly tosses her head and turns her back on her admirer.

The fifth line which is a repetition of the fourth is a musical way of emphasizing the finished idea of the whole episode and gives me the time to complete the physical action. On this phrase the general's daughter moves off and the titular counsellor droops in despair.

Thus we get to the second verse.

The first phrase takes the titular counsellor slowly along the top of the screen with heavy rhythmical steps; at the second phrase he takes a swig of vodka straight from the bottle; at the third he lets fall the bottle, sways drunkenly and falls, coming a cropper with the back of his head against the edge of the screen.

At this juncture the vision of the general's daughter ought to arise before the titular counsellor: "And through the delirious vapours the general's daughter did see." I could, of course, have made a "ghost" puppet out of voile. That is what I intended to do at first but later I realized that the turn would have ended rather pretentiously, romantically even, whereas the whole essence of the ending is its banality, its lack of the least trace of romantism.

For that reason I used no "vision." My titular counsellor lies on his back and meditates drunkenly with the aid of his feet, tracing various shapes with them in the air to the rhythm of the music. After all, the composer marked this phrase *largo*, and this makes each note come out with difficulty: "the gen-er-al's daughter." Before the word "daughter" the titular counsellor lifts up one foot, examines it attentively and, as if mistaking his own foot for his sweetheart, hugs it ardently to the strains of the last note of the romance.

In addition to the musical merits, the satirical quality, the clear-cut subject-matter, and the very precise scenario of physical action, this romance has another feature which enables the acting of the puppets to be organically linked with the song itself.

The whole romance is related in the third person. There is not one phrase that belongs to the characters themselves. After my many flops in dialogue I was happy to be able to tell the story in song without having to put my own voice into the mouths of puppets.

The Conventionalized Meets the Real

My next positive number after "The Titular Counsellor" was Korchmaryov's song "The Deacon." It is antireligious, or rather anticlerical in theme, somewhat reminiscent of Chekhov's "A Drawn-out Affair."

The content is simple. Pious old Matryona comes to see a deacon, gives him five kopeks and asks him to pray for the souls of Akulina, Marfa, Grusha, Paramon, Filimon, not forgetting Spiridon who is still in the land of the living.... The deacon is indignant at being offered so little for such a long list of names and scolds the woman. Matryona takes offence, demands her money back and in turn upbraids the deacon.

It is true that the song is not entirely in the third person, for there are phrases put into the mouths of the characters, but they are amusingly built out of repetitions and besides it is a song and not a spoken dialogue and there is no need to imitate the voices of the old woman or the deacon at all accurately. It is enough to make a slight modification of timbre.

In both these numbers—"The Titular Counsellor" and "The Deacon" —there is, in addition to their positive attitude to the authors, something else that links them with each other and with that unsuccessful number, "Firing the Samovar."

The titular counsellor drinks out of a real glass bottle, and the deacon lights a real candle which burns with a real little flame.

Had the titular counsellor exchanged his bottle for a stage property made of papier mâché and had the deacon not lighted the candle, both numbers would have lost at least one half of their expressiveness and point.

At first I gave my titular counsellor a little bottle known as a "hundred-grammer." I thought this was correct because it was puppet-like and in the right proportion to the figure. One day, however, on coming to a concert I found I had left the little bottle at home. As my repertoire consisted of only two or three numbers I could not leave out "The Titular Counsellor," so I found an ordinary half-litre vodka bottle there in the club and decided to take a risk by making my titular counsellor drink out of a bottle that was quite the wrong size for him.

And I found that while the sight of the little bottle usually drew no more than a stir from the audience the big bottle evoked a gale of laughter and applause. The audience laughed not only because the bottle was too big but mainly because its size emphasized its reality beside the unreal, imitated man. Of course after that I took that bottle every time and cursed myself for not having decided to use a big bottle from the beginning instead of waiting for an accident to correct my mistake. Of course I should have guessed it as I had already had the experience of bringing my puppets together with a "real" samovar.

The bottle incident taught me the method of bringing together the conventionalized and the real deliberately, and later on I understood that this could be done and in fact does take place not only in the puppet theatre but in all other kinds of theatre. And in literature too.

It happens usually in the form of certain undisguised digressions from the plot, theme or space, and its unexpectedness creates a specially powerful effect on the public.

In dramaturgy there is a good example of this method in Gozzi's *Turandot* when into the conventionalized plot of the fantastic fairy-tale of Truffaldino, are introduced contemporary jokes and shafts of wit dealing with real events or with people of the real life of those times.

One encounters the same thing in Shakespeare's comedies, in old Russian vaudevilles, and in those astonishingly bold and beautiful digressions by Pushkin which allow one to meet on one page Onegin, the poet himself, and the reader:

> *He came to birth, my friend Yevgeny,*
> *Upon the shores of the Neva,*
> *Of which a native (or a star)*
> *You too may be, dear reader. Many*
> *A day there I myself did see,*
> *But northern climes are bad for me.*

In offering this example of the conventionalized combining with the real I do not in any way wish to suggest that my discovery of the effectiveness of bringing a conventional puppet into contact with a "real" object has anything whatsoever in common with Pushkin's wonderful verses.

On the contrary, I mention this in order to show that I made no discovery at all.

All the same, for me it was a discovery, one that enabled me to combine in an unexpected way several phenomena of art which had previously seemed to me quite incompatible.

And in the practice of art it is usual and perhaps unavoidable to discover things that have already been discovered long, long ago.

Indeed, an understanding of the laws of this practice is often insufficient even to give you the ability to copy what other people have discovered.

You need to rediscover many of those laws for yourself as if you were the first in the field.

Man and Puppet

I brought real objects and puppets together once again in another of my "positive" numbers—"The Lullaby" from Musorgsky's *Children's Album*.

I sing this "Lullaby" not behind the screen but simply from the stage.

I wear the puppet on my right hand and keep my other hand underneath it, the way one holds a baby.

The baby to which Musorgsky gave the name of Tyapa wears a plain white vest fastened with a little button at the back. The skirt hangs loose showing the back of my hand which represents the baby's bare back.

But in referring to this as an example of the use of the "real" together with puppets I mean by "real" not only my own hand which becomes the puppet's body but the whole combination of myself and the puppet.

In this number which shows a baby being lulled to sleep there are two characters: father and baby.

The baby does not want to go to sleep. It keeps looking at the audience, it sticks its little fist into its Daddy's mouth and interferes with his singing, it uses its Daddy's finger for a dummy teat. Calming it down is no easy matter. Once it even has to be slapped to make it stop fidgeting. But, all in all, Daddy is gentle: he pats his little Tyapa, gives it the dummy, rocks it rhythmically, and when at length the baby falls off to sleep, he kisses its tow-haired little head carefully and softly so as not to waken it.

Both these characters—father and child—could be played by puppets; in that case there would be no difference of principle between them.

But in my "Lullaby" the father is performed by a man and the child by a puppet.

While playing the father my relation to Tyapa is virtually that which exists between the real vodka bottle and the puppet of the titular counsellor.

By uniting things that are usually separate something especially expressive is created. The difference in the presentation of the two characters becomes the method of the number as a whole.

That is all the more noticeable because I am myself the performer of each role.

My right hand, on which I wear the puppet, lives apart from me with a rhythm and a character of its own. The spectator realizes, the moment I step from behind the screen, that the puppet has a hand inside it. The loose gown with the back of my hand showing makes that doubly plain. At the same time, however, that right hand of mine conducts a silent dialogue with me or, ignoring me altogether, lives its independent life.

Tyapa looks at the audience with surprise. Realizing what he is looking at, I turn the same way only to notice that Tyapa has long ago turned in another direction. The more unrhythmical the puppet's behaviour is the truer it is to life and the sharper the audience's reaction.

What I liked about this number was the way that although I made no secret of the fact that the puppet was a puppet, although there always were bursts of laughter breaking all over the hall, the audience, no matter whether it was composed of grown-ups or children, and was in a large or a small place, always fell absolutely silent when Tyapa went off to sleep and I took him away carefully behind the screen.

It would seem that at the moment I slipped my hand out of the puppet, turning it back into an empty rag, the audience would have ceased to make-believe in the scene; yet they went on sitting quiet and tense as I tiptoed slowly off carrying my baby in my arms and thoroughly enjoying the taut silence that reigned in the hall.

Despite the eccentricity of the method on which the success of the whole number depends, despite the combination of real man and a puppet, I classify that number as positive, in the sense that it does not contradict the composer's purpose; for the theme of tenderness and love of children is preserved and, besides, Musorgsky himself conveyed it ironically and called the song "Lullaby with a Doll."

However, while I discovered in a good many of my numbers what sharp and interesting effects one could get from combining the conventional with the real, I came to learn that this method, as, incidentally, all methods in art, was a double-edged weapon and that it could be used on far from all occasions. In fact it can very often wreck the verisimilitude of a scene, and then the effect is neither sharp nor interesting, it is not even eccentric, it is simply unpleasant.

Hadn't that same trick of bringing a human being and a puppet together that I used with Tyapa been employed by that Czech puppet theatre where the Giant was played by a live boy and the Knight by a puppet?

Why then had that combination created an unpleasant effect? It was because the boy and the puppet were brought together "seriously," as equals in their rights as actors, in their importance. But the fact remains, they could not be equated, they were incommensurate.

In my "Lullaby" the man and the puppet are opposed to each other. The difference between them is emphasized; no attempt is made to conceal it. This emphasis is fully justified by the song itself because Musorgsky wrote it as an amusing "playing the baby." Admittedly it is lyrical but there is irony there too. Had I instead of that lullaby, taken, say, the by no means ironic "Sleep, My Lovely Baby" and sung it seriously with the puppet in my arms, it would either have seemed vulgar and sentimental or would have wrecked the composer's theme and mutilated the lovely lines.

Reinforcing the Theme

It is not my intention in this chapter to describe all the numbers I consider positive for I shall have to come back to them later when I am considering other themes. But one of the "positives" I shall mention now, because that number varies considerably from the works I have just described.

It is a romance "That summer night" written by Grechaninov to one of Heine's poems translated into Russian by Pleshcheyev. The poem runs as follows:

> *That summer night I felt like spending*
> *Alone with you an hour or two,*
> *But you pretended you were busy:*

*"I'm in a hurry," came from you.
I tried to tell you how I suffered,
How I was almost fit to die;
You made me the politest curtsey,
And laughed so cruelly in reply.
To overfil my heart with torture,
You kept as heartless till the end.
I begged a parting kiss, but even
To that you would not condescend.
And yet, for goodness' sake, don't fancy
I'll go and kill myself for you.
My love, such awkward situations
For me are not entirely new.*

While in my "Titular Counsellor" and "The Deacon" and the "Lullaby" the puppets were used illustratively, the plot and the features of the characters being preserved as in the originals, the singing of the Grechaninov song was accompanied by acting in which the puppets did not represent a man and a woman but a tomcat and a tabby.

While the introductory bars are being played, a ginger tabby with a blue ribbon at her neck and blue eyes to match appears above the screen. Almost immediately a black, yellow-eyed tomcat springs after her. He eyes the tabby briefly and with the first words of the romance starts courting her.

During nearly the whole of the first six lines the chase continues. Then the tomcat rubs his head, neck and body voluptuously against the frame of the screen while the tabby first sits haughtily at the other end of the screen without even a glance for the tomcat and then turns sharply and lays her ears back angrily. The tom's ears go back too. For a second their eyes meet in a fierce stare and then, as always happens, they break into a fast and furious fight at the end of which the tabby makes off. Her head peeps out of the middle of the screen where there is a special little concealed window for her.

Clinging to the screen the tomcat looks down at his beloved. He is petrified with anger, only his tail twitches quickly from side to side. It looks as if he is going to spring from the screen and start the fight all over again, but he suddenly sits and starts calmly washing himself. Apparently he is not the ardent lover he appeared to be. His approaches had been rebuffed. Well, what of that? It was not the first time, and after all was it really so important?

But seeing that my love scene is played by cats how can I consider it to be positive? You may be sure that Heine, Pleshcheyev and Grechaninov did not envisage the characters of this scene as cats. Of course they thought of them as human beings.

Nevertheless I felt I was right in considering that I had not misrepresented the authors of the song or destroyed their theme.

After all the music, like the words, is written ironically. The theme of this romance is mockery of a fake "tragedy of unrequited love." In no way did I distort Heine's and, consequently, Grechaninov's theme: I preserved it immaculately merely trying to reinforce its theatrical effect.

Perhaps the desire to do this arose in me as a protest against the way some singers performed this romance without noticing its ironic flavour. Some time later I convinced myself of this on hearing a well-known opera singer who performed this song frequently at concerts.

I met this singer while we were touring the Crimea in the same company.

After a concert one day I asked him to tell me candidly what he liked in my programme and what he did not.

He went through the numbers that pleased him, then ended by saying that he did not like the turn with the cats at all and could not understand why I had made such malicious fun of such a beautiful romance.

I did not argue, for I felt that if I had not been able to convince him with my art I would have even less success with my arguments.

Next day on the beach I heard myself addressed in that slightly nasalized tone which most opera singers use.

"Just a minute, Comrade Obraztsov! Don't go in yet. D'you know what? I told you yesterday that I didn't like your Grechaninov, but I went through the whole text again last night and I realize now that you are right. Just think! For thirty years I've been singing that romance as a 'classic' and it really is a song for cats, not exactly for cats, of course, but they fit it very well. It's pure mockery, full of malice, and absolutely not a love song."

So my cats were amnestied and recognized as positive even by an opera singer.

Neo-Gypsy Style

At the opening of this chapter I mentioned that at about the same time as I put on my "Titular Counsellor" I finished working on a Gypsy romance "Only Acquaintances," a song which I classified as negative.

By negative I do not mean that it was a parody. I introduced no changes in the text or the music; all the same, I completely turned the author's theme upside down.

Strictly speaking if the romance "The Tumult of the Ball" which my Piccaninny sang can be considered my first number, then I started with a negative number, because I had turned the subject of the Chaikovsky romance upside down, changing it from a lyrical song into a comic one. Vertinsky's "Just a Minute" and Borisov's "It was a happy day" were "half-negative."

To that extent, "Only Acquaintances" was a continuation along the negative path. But now I was taking that path deliberately.

The song referred to was popular at that time, belonging to a number of new pseudo-Gypsy romances which came into vogue during NEP. This vogue was quite natural as the Soviet lyrical song was only just appearing and people still remembered the Gypsy romances. Besides, NEP provided very fertile soil for sentimental trash.

I made two pug-dogs and had them perform the simple little story of the romance which consisted of a happy rendezvous and a sad, cold parting.

I do my best to sing the romance honestly, without parodying the Gypsy manner of performance, without overemphasizing the music but keeping intact all the tenderness and lyricism which the author and composer tried to put into the work. I had to do this in order to establish the theme; otherwise there would have been nothing to make fun of. The fun lay in combining the romance with two unexpected characters—dogs.

Were the listener to hear me perform this song on the radio he would not find anything funny in it; but people sitting in the hall watching it keep laughing all the time.

I remember how this surprised my godmother Auntie Kapa of whom I wrote in Chapter Three. I paid her a visit one day. She was very old by then and kept indoors, so, of course, she could not see my concerts. The first thing she asked when I entered the room was what had happened to me at my last concert. It appeared that she had heard me in a programme broadcast from the Hall of Columns in the House of the Unions. In her opinion I had sung a touching romance, and the fact that the audience laughed showed that there must have been some unpleasant misunderstanding between me and the spectators. I did my best to explain to her what the audience had been laughing at, and the next time I visited Auntie Kapa I brought my little dogs with me to give her visual proof of the way I evoked that laughter.

However, exactly the same situation would have arisen if the spectators had been deprived of their powers of hearing and only saw what my dogs were up to. Maybe they would have smiled now and again at the way the dogs licked each other's faces and sniffed each other's tails. Of course they would—for it is difficult not to smile at puppets, especially when, as in this case, they were so much like real dogs. But a deaf spectator would not be able to understand the full meaning of the number.

It is said that every actor ought to play in such a way that a deaf man should be able to follow what he is saying by the gestures alone, and a blind man guess what he is doing by hearing only the words.

This rule did not apply to my "negatives," for the whole essence of the number lay in the combination of two essentially contrasting elements—romance and dogs—and to appreciate that both sight and hearing were required.

Up to this day I go on performing this number although something of the malice and point has gone out of it as people have forgotten the romance as well as the whole "neo-Gypsy" vogue of those days. But when it was still fresh the song clearly shocked lovers of that kind of romance very deeply. I recall how the exit of my dogs, tails wagging, was once followed by a piercing whistle of disapproval from the body of the hall.

I had offended the susceptibilities of some lover of the song and he was expressing his protest at my treatment of it.

True, there was no ugly scene as the fellow was shushed down; he left the hall, and the rest of the audience applauded and encored me. All the same, I went away from that concert feeling upset. An actor does not like to hear even one whistle of protest.

Only after sober reflection did I decide there was nothing to worry about.

After all, I had "spoiled" the romance on purpose and consequently was bound to offend those for whom it was "profound" and significant. If I made fun of cheapness it meant that my mockery was aimed not only against those who produced trash but also against those who consumed it.

Fatal Passion

For the next of my negative numbers I shall have to start the story from the very beginning. This number was not so clearly and precisely conceived as the romance "Only Acquaintances." And to some extent the story of this number teaches the lesson that sometimes the character of a puppet, its anatomy and expressive qualities suggest if not the theme then the plot itself.

I began by trying to combine a Gypsy romance with the small ads about exchanging accommodation that one often read in those days. What I wanted to do was to show by these means the real meaning of the Gypsy romance and the covert meaning of the newspaper ads.

These notices were easily deciphered. If you read: "Willing exchange two small rooms in different parts of Moscow for one large one" it meant that there had been a marriage and that the married couple wanted to live together. But if you read that someone wanted to "exchange one room for two in different parts of the city" it meant there had been a divorce.

I took one of these virtual "divorce notices." It ran: "Willing to exchange large room in the centre of Moscow. All modern conveniences: telephone, central heating, bathroom. For two small rooms. Preferably in different districts."

Then I took the Gypsy romance "Do Not Leave Me." The words of this song ran: "Ah, stay with me another while. It is so quiet and lovely here! Do let me see your tender smile and kiss your eyes, and hold you near...."

I broke the newspaper ad and Gypsy romance up into separate phrases and arranged them in alternate order, giving the words of the advertisement to a man, and those of the song to a woman.

The result was a unique dialogue.

The man says: "I am willing to exchange one large room in the centre of Moscow...."

The woman sings in reply: "Ah, stay with me another while."

The man continues: "All modern conveniences: telephone, central heating, bath."

The woman sings: "It is so quiet and lovely here."

The man: "For two small rooms, preferably in different districts."

The woman: "Do let me see your tender smile and kiss your eyes, and hold you near...."

The romance comes out an easy winner. Love triumphs over newspaper prose. Husband and wife fling their arms round each other and embrace. The divorce is off.

All that seemed to me witty and contemporary.

I made two puppets: a frail bald-headed man and an enormous woman with long arms suitable for clutching her husband to her bosom.

The arms were a real success. They were made out of insulating flex. When I had my fingers inside the puppet these long arms curled snake-like at the slightest movement.

I started rehearsing but soon discovered that the number was not turning out well.

First, the whole idea seemed flat and dull, and, secondly, the long-armed woman flatly refused to sing the romance and kept trying to dance. And when she danced, her arms weaved such extraordinary patterns and were so expressive that it would have been folly not to use them.

So I got the idea of doing "Habanera."

It did not take me much time to alter the puppets. I gave my woman a red skirt, a black shawl, a tall comb and crimson lips. I drew side-whiskers on the man and dressed him in a cloak.

I doubt if I rehearsed for more than an hour. I put the number into my programme that very night.

Since that day over twenty years ago I have performed "Habanera" at nearly every concert.

What is the essence of that number? What is the theme? And if I call it a negative number, what author am I poking fun at? At Bizet and his lovely music? At Prosper Mérimée's story?

No, I am making fun neither of Bizet nor of Mérimée. In any case that is not what I want the audience to think.

Partly I am laughing at the libretto, at the situation in which Don José finds himself, thanks to the librettist of the opera. In Mérimée's story Don José and Carmen are two characters of marked individuality whose strength is equivalent though at opposite poles. The tragedy lies in the meeting of these two poles. But in the libretto of the opera that does not happen. Everything "male" is given to the Toreador. Don José has a "blue" role, he is a helpless young man, and instead of a conflict between two strong characters we have one between a strong character and a weak one.

But that is not the only theme of my number. The other theme, which is virtually the main one, is the manner in which certain singers perform the role of Carmen.

While the Don José of the opera is often presented as too lyrical and helpless, Carmen is still more often made too temperamental and passionate. And it is in the "Habanera" that you find banal performers of Carmen most possessed by passion. For "Habanera" is the very credo of inconstancy in love, of glamorous womanhood and the power of "pa-a-a-ssion."

This "pa-a-a-ssion" is the backbone of the number.

In "Habanera" my Carmen storms all over the screen, swaying at the waist, jiggling her hips, grasping Don José in her long prehensile arms, flinging him aside, only to embrace him again. She treats her "admirer" like a plaything, a mere object. She flings him to the ground, leans threatening over him and a moment later is chucking him under the chin patronizingly.

In "Habanera" I put the whole line of Carmen's treatment of Don José that runs through the opera thanks to the libretto and to that interpretation of the role that is so widespread among singers of vulgar taste.

Stanislavsky has taught us to look for the "grain" in every role.

For some singers the "essence" of Carmen is the hypertrophy of "fatal passion." This fatal passion is also the main theme of my negative "Habanera."

CHAPTER TWELVE

Parody

Every number in my concert repertoire, lyrical or satirical, is meant to make people laugh. I have divided them into positive and negative numbers, according to my attitude towards the original. But there are other numbers which will have to be placed in a special category—the parodies.

At the root of every parody lies imitation; the character of the imitation and the degree of parodying, however, depend on the attitude to the original. When the attitude towards what is being parodied is friendly the original is not "debunked" and we get a light-hearted, friendly joke. When, however, the approach is hostile, imitation remains but individual features which are considered most highly characteristic are greatly exaggerated and the parody becomes satirical.

The object of parody can be either a definite character with personal features or a generalized type.

In "portrait" parody, that is, parody of a definite character, pure imitation is the kernel of the portrait. This may take the form of a visual outer resemblance or the imitation of a manner of speech, or behaviour, or even of way of thinking.

In a "generalized" parody the original is not an individual but a group of people who have common professional, social or other distinguishing features; and in this case the character of the imitation changes, for the more individualization there is in its portraiture the less its power of generalization.

Besides these two main kinds of parody there is another which consists in parodying a given subject.

All three kinds of parody have their place in my concert programme and of these three—the "portrait" parody, the "group" parody, and the parody of a subject, or rather of a theme—I would like to tell you in this chapter.

The Portrait Parody

The present Central Art Workers' House grew out of a small theatre workers' club in Pimenovsky Lane.

Despite its cramped quarters and small auditorium, and maybe just because of that, the atmosphere of this club was most temperamental and lively.

People meeting each other at this club—actors and producers from various theatres—became close friends and looked on the place as a home from home.

The membership included writers, scientists, public figures, artists, airmen, Stakhanovites, sportsmen, etc. In the tiny auditorium took place excellent concerts, fierce arguments, interesting lectures and memorable meetings with some of the prominent people of the land. There were fairly frequent "green-room rags" consisting of short scenes, sketches and solo performances on current themes, mainly of specific interest to theatre workers.

Nearly all the numbers at these "rags" were in some degree parodies.

I took an active part in the work of the club, almost always appearing in the "rags" for which I often prepared special numbers. A frequent visitor to the club and a participant in all its work—serious as well as frivolous—was Felix Kon, an old Bolshevik. He was at the head of the Museums Department at the People's Commissariat of Education and was a close friend of literature and art.

For all his age he possessed an enormous fund of high spirits, was an orator such as one rarely found and had an inexhaustible sense of humour.

His most characteristic external features were his short stature, the sharp ironic fixed stare that came through his thick spectacles, the gay sardonic smile that was almost lost in his grey moustache, and his typical manner of speaking. Besides, the intonation and especially the rhythm of his diction were highly individual. The low notes shot up to a very high register and the drawl with which he would begin a sentence nearly always changed into a chopped, terse rhythm before he got to the end of it.

Naturally Felix Kon was an excellent original for friendly imitation.

I have, it seems, a certain knack for catching other people's manners of speech and I soon learned to speak like Felix Kon. The fact that he taught me to do it made it all the easier. Enjoying every minute of it he corrected my imitation; sometimes we held conversations between "the two Kons," in which the two of us spoke with the same musical intonation.

I began by appearing at one of our "rags" in make-up and costume as Felix Kon, but later I made a puppet to look like him and composed a script: "Report by Felix Kon on the tasks of the puppet theatre in the period of reconstruction."

Some time later I gave my Felix Kon a partner in the form of a friendly portrait of Nemirovich-Danchenko. I had no difficulty in imitating Nemirovich-Danchenko: there was not a single actor at the Art Theatre or its studio who could not do it.

At the top of my screen Felix Kon and Nemirovich-Danchenko argued about their attitude towards the Theatre Workers' Club.

I also tried to parody myself. The puppet resembled me but evidently it is not possible to parody one's own way of speaking and not only did the number turn out flat but it bore no resemblance to myself.

These three numbers, two of them relatively successful, the third one a failure, completed my "portrait" parodies.

That was natural because for this type of portraiture to be successful the audience has to know the original. Without that it is almost inconceivable. And in my main work, I had to count on having a very broad audience who could not be expected to know the personal characteristics of Felix Kon or Nemirovich-Danchenko so well.

Even imitations of very popular actors are far from successful with all audiences.

And besides, the inner idea-content of "portrait" parody is much smaller and narrower than the parody of representatives of some groups of people when the parody creates a generalized character and the audience is certain to have a much fuller knowledge of the original.

That means you can reach a much broader public.

The Public's Darling

There are some opera and concert singers of classical arias and romances for whom the performance is only a pretext for displaying their talents. They sacrifice the musical and literary idea of the works they perform to their skill, frequently with disastrous results.

They consider it necessary to display their breathing, so they drag their *fermata* for half a minute. Who can forget the way many tenors drag the last phrase of Lensky's aria in *Eugene Onegin*. "Go-o-o-o-o-o-o-olden days...."

It is remarkable how long it takes a hoary old tradition in the rendering of some arias to die.

It is quite possible that the first Cagnio to laugh in "On with the Motley" was quite sincere and his laughter suited the performance organically. But the fact that it was a success has meant that every Cagnio since then has laughed at that place. And gone on laughing for tens of years, quite independent of the fact whether it comes off or not. As a matter of fact, it generally doesn't.

Stereotyped performances of romances and arias are often carried to absurd lengths as, for instance, in certain imitations of Shalyapin in performances of "The Flea" and "Slander."

I wanted to make fun of a singer of that sort. Of his "magnificent" voice, his "immense" temperament, of his swaggering walk, his hands clutching the crumpled music, the "disobedient" lock of hair which obediently covers his bald spot, the professional grin and the exaggerated stretch of the neck for the "brilliant high notes."

I suppose I could have taken almost any aria or romance for the purpose but my choice fell on the "Song of the Toreador." It is one of the most frequently sung and most completely stereotyped numbers of those baritones—the "favourites of the public"—who are so proud of their "temperament" and their "top G."

My baritone advances very slowly to the edge of the screen. He is in tails with diamond studs in his starched shirt front. He holds a sheet of music. For a long time he stands there in silence, looking at the audience stupidly, for no other reason than that every "self-respecting baritone" has to pause while waiting for the audience to "settle down." Then he turns his head slowly towards the accompanist, gives a casual nod and goes on waiting calmly while the introductory bars are being played. That is "not his affair," after all. But suddenly, as if something had jabbed him, he flings himself at his first notes with the temperament of a bandit, which he considers to be the temperament of the Toreador. This temperament increases in intensity with each phrase; his wide mouth opens wider and wider. He tosses from side to side as he describes the fight with the enraged bull. At the words "throwing up the sand, the bull charges," he screeches "Ah" striking fear into the hearts of the audience, because that is what every banal performer of these couplets does. At last he reaches the final couplet and it is obvious what is awaiting him; nothing other than that top note, that G which is my baritone's pride and nightmare.

At this point I begin slowly to push up a thick piece of wire concealed in the puppet's neck. The head with its wide-open mouth slips off my finger and the neck, a tube of soft material, which had been concealed by a high collar, stretches higher and higher, till it is almost as long as the puppet's original height. Not without effort that high G is taken, and not only taken but held during the entire concluding bars on the piano, graphic proof of the singer's "tremendous breathing."

Deep Emotion

I reached another parody number by a devious route. It began with the idea of doing the monologue "The Miserly Knight" and conveying the idea of miserliness by the expression of the hands counting out gold coins.

I made the head of an old man. I attached to it a long flowing gown with two holes in it for the arms. I slipped the gown over my own head so that the puppet's head was above my own which served as the puppet's body. I put my own arms through the holes. The result was a very intriguing figure of an old man with a small head and enormous human arms. At the foot of the screen I placed a little stool on which I stood, thus bringing the puppet high above the top of the screen.

At first I thought I had discovered something entirely new, that no actor could be so "miserly" as my puppet, and that no one could read the Miser's monologue so expressively as it. But the monologue turned out to be not only ineffective but mystical in a decadent manner. I dislike mysticism of any sort and in puppets I consider it the most vulgar of all its manifestations.

In a word, I dropped the number. But it was difficult to drop the puppet too. After all he was an anatomical discovery.

Next I substituted the head of a singer for that of the old man. It became funny at once. Every trace of mysticism, of symbolism and decadence disappeared. Instead I got a grotesque face with disproportionately large hands.

I made a start by singing with this puppet the romance "Oh heart, quietness thou dost not need." I even made a small heart which throbbed behind the décolleté of my singer. She sang the romance and then took her own heart. This raised a laugh but it was too crude and in spite of the superficial success of the number I stopped performing it.

But the tempting possibilities of the puppet worn on my head and, moreover, having real human hands were so great that I could not get it out of my mind.

Our theatre's sculptor-mechanic Solntsev made me a new head for the singer with movable eyes and mouth. The gadgets that moved the eyes and mouth were connected with the singer's bead necklace. The slightest tug of the necklace made her open her mouth and roll the enormous pupils of her eyes.

So, as well as human hands my singer obtained another means of expression—eyes.

The hands, however, remained the principal medium, thoroughly suitable for parodying the performers of emotional or tragic romances with "deep emotion."

Singers of that category of song "convey" all their emotion with their hands: they weave and "break" their fingers, they play nervously with their beads, they fold their palms in a gesture of prayerful entreaty and once more finger their beads.

The number gradually took shape. All that was left to do was to put "diamond" rings on my fingers, so that the hands looked "feminine," and to find a suitably emotional song to parody, one that would be typical of the "intimate" singer.

While I was touring in Kiev—that was when I was still working at the Second Studio of the Moscow Art Theatre—I stayed in lodgings. My landlady had a gramophone and among her records were some Gypsy romances. Every day after dinner she played all these records through.

She was specially fond of one called "Return, and I Will Pardon All." She was quite in love with this record and when the singer reached the phrase "I love and I curse you" she would put the needle back to repeat that "marvellous phrase" which to her seemed the very limit of paradox and the utmost depths of love's ardour. I had to listen at least twenty times a day to this phrase and it was probably a feeling of revenge that made me choose this romance for my puppet to parody.

When I perform at concerts I hardly ever show my singer as the first number, because in appearance and particularly in scale this puppet is so different from my tiny dogs, the Titular Counsellor or the Baritone that it is not to her advantage to precede them. But when the spectators are already accustomed to the size of the puppets and my singer appears over the screen she looks enormous and this in itself is enough to evoke a stir of laughter.

Silently she stands waiting while the public examines her elaborately dressed red hair with the "diamond" tiara, the modestly downcast lashes and the pearl necklace against her black velvet gown.

The rustle and the laughter die down, the audience falls quiet and adjusts itself to the new scale. Only then do the singer's hands appear over the top of the screen. Yet another change of scale. The hands are at least three times as large as they ought to be. They are real, human hands, yet they are also her own. She raises them to tidy her hair, to finger her pearl necklace. "Diamond" rings flash on her fingers. More laughter from the audience. The singer waits until it has ceased, signals to the pianist and starts singing. Very softly and slowly at first, but gradually growing louder. Her eye-lashes flutter with "deep feeling." On the long-protracted high notes her mouth opens wide and her eyes roll upwards. Her hands grow agitated; she is singing with them quite as much as with her mouth, and on the words "I love and I curse you" I raise them in a tragic accursing gesture.

On presenting this number for the first time I realized that I had had my revenge on that wretched gramophone record; since then I have sung it fairly often. The only thing that annoyed me about it and that made it difficult was the fact that I could see neither the puppet, which was on my head, nor my own hands which were concealed from me by the puppet's dress.

However, quite recently I was happy to discover that I could see perfectly well through the dress which was made of very fine crêpe de

Chine. It was hard to understand why for ten years I had seen literally nothing and now suddenly saw quite clearly.

The reason turned out to be quite simple. I discovered I had been singing the whole song with my eyes shut. I shut them involuntarily and for the only reason that the puppet's eyes were most of the time closed by her "modestly lowered lashes." Had I been able to see the puppet's face during the performance I would certainly not have kept my own eyes closed. But as I could not see it I imagined how it looked. The fact that the puppet's hands were my own still further added to the sensation that I and not the puppet was performing. I was not "showing" the puppet, I was "playing" it and for that reason did not notice that I had shut my own eyes.

But even since I found out that I could see through the crêpe de Chine I rarely open my eyes, and go on singing that romance with them shut. Such is the force of ten years' habit.

The Master of Sounds

There are conductors with bad taste who like to show their authority over sound by imposing themselves not so much on their orchestras, which know them to perfection, as on their audiences. He conducts and "plays a conductor." They make every possible effort to "explain" with their arms the power and quality of each note. The left arm floats like a swan to imitate the tenderness of the violin while the right shoots out with abrupt power towards the drummer, as if hurling a stone at him.

At the *piano-pianissimo* passages both his hands are clasped somewhere in the vicinity of the stomach and on the final note when the orchestra is giving all it has to the *tutti,* those hands are being waved high over the conductor's head and are sawing the air with such incredible temperament that half a dozen orchestras would be needed to transmute it into sound.

Conductors of this sort do not realize that if they display more temperament and energy than their orchestras the public is certain to feel that the music is being played quieter than it should be.

But the conductor is pleased. He bows, he even finds it pleasant that the public should notice how disordered his hair is and how there are little beads of sweat standing out on his brow. And if his tie has slipped to one side and his shirt front has burst a stud, so much the better. Let the audience know how exhausted he feels and what a difficult business it is to be a "master of sound."

Power is literally in his hands. A conductor is primarily a pair of hands. So when I found I had made a puppet with a small almost immobile head and two huge, live hands I naturally wanted to parody a conductor.

Of course he had to be handsome. Good looks are what every conductor of this sort dreams of. And of course he had to be far from young. A venerable air is an aid to beauty.

I made a grey-haired old man with a "noble" appearance. He was in tails with a chrysanthemum in his button-hole.

I was very fond of this puppet, and still am, but I have only shown him a few times as there is rarely an orchestra to conduct at my usual concerts. By "usual" I mean the sort of concert I usually perform at, consisting of a collection of turns by artists in various genres. At concerts like this I have to show my puppets between a turn by a ballet-dancer and another by an elocutionist, between a violinist and a singer of Russian songs. I appear for some ten to fifteen minutes in all, which gives me time for only three or four numbers. But I have "unusual" concerts from time to time and these have become more frequent recently. At such concerts I am the only performer.

On those occasions I show everything I have in my repertoire and spend two hours on the stage, not counting intervals.

So sometimes I show my conductor at these solo concerts. At the very end, after everything else.

A white backcloth is hung behind the screen, at the back of the stage. The accompanist—my wife, Olga Shaganova, who has accompanied me for over eighteen years—sits behind the curtain, invisible to the audience. True, she cannot see me or my puppets either, but the puppets cast faint shadows on the backcloth and she can follow their movements that way.

These shadows gave me the idea of showing the conductor.

Having announced the final item on the programme as Bizet's *Carmen* I go behind my screen, put the puppet over my head and, grasping the conductor's baton, stand on the stool. The conductor rises above the screen. He taps the edge of the screen with his baton, as a signal to the nonexistent orchestra to be ready to start, he raises both arms, as all conductors do, and, when he has imposed silence on the audience, makes a sudden gesture; at that moment the strains of an orchestra, coming from some unknown place, burst forth in the overture to *Carmen*. It is a real orchestra with fiddles, flutes, bassoons, trumpets and drums. (The players have taken their places behind the backcloth during the preparations.)

After two hours of listening to a piano accompaniment the very sound of a full orchestra surprises the audience like a clap of thunder in January. This element of surprise is a good beginning but it cannot, of course, serve as the main element. It was my job to provide that.

It needed much rehearsal, first to learn how to conduct myself, which turned out to be far from easy, and then to teach each of the players in the orchestra to respond to every quirk of my conductor. During rehearsals I deliberately conducted at varying tempi, now holding every pause, now retarding the entry of the drums, insisting that the drummer restrain himself even if his note is in the score, and his beat has arrived. I altered the rhythm every time in different places so that the orchestra learned to be attentive to my baton. Only after all that was I able to start rehearsing with the puppet. Now the orchestra had to learn how to follow the wave of the baton from its shadow falling on the backcloth and barely visible from where they sat behind.

I had to do all this so that the audience, which realized that if it did not see the orchestra then the orchestra could not see the puppet, should definitely feel that it was not a question of the puppet trying to wave his baton in time with the orchestra but of the orchestra obeying the puppet.

Of course at concert performances I did not make those meaningless pauses but all the same I did not maintain an even rhythm during the entire overture. I overdid the *crescendos* and dragged the *ritardandos* in the manner of the kind of conductor I was parodying. And the fact that the orchestra was invisible and that only the conductor was in sight of the audience—a conductor, moreover, whom the orchestra was undoubtedly obeying—became the theme of the number and no mere trick. You see, I was parodying not the music, not the orchestra but the conductor showing off his authority over the sound. The audience saw only the "master of sound," who was producing sound from the tip of his omnipotent baton. It saw the conductor exactly as he wanted to be seen.

And when I showed this number at a concert for the first time I remembered my first childhood impression of the conductor at the opera, whose baton "played" music.

"Mortal" Danger

In this chapter I have told you about two "portrait" parodies, and three "group" parodies: the stereotyped baritone with the artificial temperament, the "Gypsy singer" with her display of "deep emotion" and the banal conductor. Now let me tell you about a parody of a subject and of a theme.

The subject I chose to parody in this number was a circus scene, the taming of wild animals; the theme was the "mortal" danger which threatens the animal-tamer and thrills the public.

This item in my repertoire differs from others in that it is not based on any literary work, romance or aria.

I do not sing at all and have very little to say. It is almost pure pantomime, the only spoken words being the animal-tamer's: "I beg your attention for a training miracle: a tiger at large"—which he says at the very beginning—and a few typical "Ap's" which he utters at particular moments in the turn.

When the animal-tamer announces his number the usual circus march is played and the tiger appears. It is a huge, striped beast with shining yellow eyes and a red mouth.

The tamer advances boldly to the tiger and strokes its head. The tiger bares its fangs in a lazy, peaceable snarl. It doesn't feel like snarling but that is what is expected of it. After all if it did not snarl there would be no "danger" for the tamer and that is the whole point of the number.

The "training miracle" begins. The tamer lays a chunk of meat on the tiger's nose. The tiger flings it into the air and catches it as it comes down.

And then the "most terrifying" moment comes: the pianist imitates the roll of the drums; the tiger opens its jaws as wide as possible to display its "bloodthirstiness." Several times the trainer sticks his hand

and then his head between these jaws. For at least ten seconds his head is exposed to "mortal danger." Then the jaws open, the animal-tamer bows and the tiger spits. He found having a hairy human head in his mouth somewhat repulsive.

Had this taken place in the circus ring the public would have rewarded the "fearlessness" of the trainer with a round of applause; but my parody aroused only laughter.

The tamer however is not satisfied. He wants to make the tiger repeat the whole number. Again the fearful jaws part, again the tamer places his hand between them. But when he wants to place his head in the tiger's mouth the tiger clamps his jaws tight and turns away. He has obviously had quite enough of behaving in so untigerly a way.

The trainer gets angry, he tugs the tiger's ear and forces him to open his mouth. But the tiger turns away once more and even goes to one end of the screen. The trainer is furious. For the third time he forces the tiger to open its jaws; then he quickly pops his head in.

The drums beat their "alarm call" once more; the tense seconds pass.

And now the tiger loses control. Uttering a short growl it draws the tamer into its jaws like a piece of macaroni; the legs kick in helpless despair, then disappear into the belly of the "bloodthirsty beast of prey." In the circus there would have been shrieks of horror at this moment but people rock with laughter at the parody.

The tiger spits again and calmly wipes its mouth with a paw.

Of course this is not a parody of the tiger. Nor of the tamer. It is a parody of that commercialized "danger," it mocks at the part of the circus public which would not pay to watch a tame tiger if it knew for certain that the tiger would never and in no circumstances gobble up its trainer.

CHAPTER THIRTEEN

Theme and Form

The distance between the birth of an idea and its realization is so great, so much time is involved, that there can be no certainty about the straightness of the line that process will take.

If you take the analogous case of the writer, from the first sketchy outline through all the rough copies to the book in its final form, you will find that during the lengthy process of work not only do characters crop up or drop out but that the nature and fate of those characters who survive till the manuscript goes to the print-shop change in quite remarkable ways.

These changes depend on many things. Among others on mere chance. It is just as important to be able to make good use of accidental features as it is to free oneself from them, for chance findings can be either treasure or rubbish.

That is why in describing my search for the form most apt for a given theme—that is, for expressing its idea—and the evolution of a form—that is the evolution of the means of expression—I shall often refer in this chapter to "chance occurrences" which in one way or another have influenced my work.

Meeting Friends

For many months four men lived on an ice-floe in the Arctic Ocean and during that time became the darlings of every Soviet man, woman and child. When the ice-floe split the whole country took the fate of those four men to its heart. Ice-breakers were sent to intercept the drifting ice-floe. Excitement rose. Would they be rescued or not? What if the ice should crack again? At last the wireless told us that the Arctic explorers had been rescued and that they were sailing for the mainland. Everyone rejoiced, there was general happiness. Leningrad and Moscow prepared to give the men a heroes' welcome.

I was on a tour in Leningrad at that time and the city authorities asked me to participate in a concert to be given on the day of the arrival of the expedition in Leningrad. And though time was very short I wanted to put on a number specially dedicated to this welcome given to Papanin and his companions.

The theme was clear enough but I had no subject. What ought my number to consist in? What puppets should I make for the occasion? How could I best greet the explorers from my little screen? I decided that a polar bear would serve the purpose best.

But how should I make that polar bear?

A small bear manipulated with three fingers could hardly deliver a monologue or sing a romance. Puppets of that sort are really at their best when they act in pairs, which gives them an opportunity of personal contact with each other. I decided that if I were going to use a bear it ought to be a big one, like the one I had used for my singer.

I bought two ermine capes second-hand and from these a polar bear's head and its front paws were made. As my own head had to go into the bear's neck all that was needed was to make the back of the neck out of ermine and to have a piece of thin gauze with white buffalo hair sown on to it for the front. This gave me an opportunity, albeit very limited, of seeing something, of breathing freely and, above all, of avoiding the muffled effect that ermine would have had on my voice.

The bear's mouth was made to move. The lower jaw was connected by strings with my chin so that as I sang the bear opened and shut its mouth in absolute synchronization with mine.

In spite of the fact that only the bear's head and forepaws appeared above the screen the effect was created that a real live full-size polar bear was standing there. But not a savage angry bear. A touchingly lyrical bear. That is, I suppose, a feature of a polar bear's appearance.

Next, what ought that bear to sing or say? How could he greet Papanin's men, himself being a "polar" bear, that is to say a denizen of the very place they had come from? On the contrary, he would have to take his leave of them, and, moreover, do it sadly because everything about him made him a "positive" bear. Happiness was not for him, for his human friends were leaving him.

At first sight all this seemed to be a contradiction of the theme—that of meeting friends—which I had chosen for my number. In searching for a means of expression suitable for the theme—a form—I had, it seemed, run into a blind alley and would either have to drop the polar bear puppet or reverse the theme to suit the puppet—the form. But that was only at first sight.

I was not in the least alarmed by the prospect of having to make the bear deliver a valedictory rather than a welcoming monologue. Far from it. I welcomed the prospect as a discovery that made my further work on the form of the number easier. After all it had to be a comic turn; in other words the bear's grief at parting had to be taken as imaginary, overtly contradicting the real joy of meeting. And thus the theme of the meeting would stand out all the stronger.

With the help of the writer Vladimir Polyakov I paraphrased the words of an old Petersburg romance, the first four lines of which run·

Beside the river's tranquil stream
We watched the sunset's purple beam.
You pressed my hand; fast as a kiss,
It passed, that moment of pure bliss.

Translated into the language of the polar bear—it was a she-bear, by the way—these lines ran:

Upon an ice-floe white as cream
We watched the polar sunset's beam.
You squeezed my paw; swift as a kiss,
They passed away, those hours of bliss.

Now as the bear had firmly established its sex, and as she was addressing one and not all four members of the expedition, it followed, first, that this member had to be its leader, Papanin, and second, that the song would have to proceed in lyrical style. The continuation went this way:

The sun went down, the shadows gathered faster,
The polar night reigned silently above.
Ah, that long night! A full six months it lasted,
But what, indeed, is half a year for love?

> *The end drew near, so cruel, so uncanny...*
> *Why have you left me here to weep and moan?*
> *Return, I'll pardon all, my sweet Pa-pa-pa-papanin;*
> *The ice without you seems so cold and lone!*

I soon realized that the whole process of thinking up the number, writing the text, buying the fur and making the paws was taking so much time that I could not hope to have everything ready by the time the expedition reached Leningrad. To be in Leningrad and not to take part in the celebrations however would have been a disgrace. Nor did I want to put on one of my old turns. I decided to curtail my season and leave for Moscow. In that way I would win a little time. Papanin and his men would be sure to spend one day at least in Leningrad, and during that time I would manage to finish the bear and perhaps be able to show it in Moscow.

In that way I presented my polar bear to the heroes of the Arctic.

I worried more than usual about that performance because it had to be done without a try-out anywhere else. Besides, I was afraid it would seem a bit flippant and tactless for so solemn an occasion.

But my polar bear had not been above the screen for more than a few seconds and had said no more than a few words before I realized that there was nothing to worry about. The actor's "radar set" brought back a reflection of the first lines from the audience and after that every word and every gesture became easy and amusing.

The bear had finished and I came out smiling to take the applause. I folded my screen and left the stage. But at the end of the concert I was asked to show the bear again and once more she sang: "The sun went down, the shadows gathered faster" and wiped away her tears with her shaggy paw.

The Fable

In summer 1947 I was invited to take part in one of the variety concerts given in the Hermitage Gardens in Moscow. I had nothing new to show and did not want to show anything from my old repertoire, especially as I had performed in Moscow very often during the previous winter season. So I either had to turn down the offer or somehow get something new ready in a very short time.

To save time I took out some of my puppets who had nothing to perform. I had plenty of these. The drawers of my writing-desk and two suit-cases were packed full of them. Some of them were very nice and interesting. In the past I had made them with some definite and—I thought—interesting purpose in mind, but had not managed to work out the themes. So there they lay jostling one another, frogs and geese, a raven, an old woman in a knitted jumper, a cow, a donkey with a big ribbon round its neck, a bewhiskered Polish officer, the head of a goggle-eyed feldsher, the head of a "high-brow" with spectacles but no eyes behind them. Puppets in abundance. I spread them about the room and telephoned to Sergei Mikhalkov, the poet, and invited him to come to see me. I demonstrated to him nearly every puppet in action, attempting to stir in him the desire to write a fable which would provide work for some at least of my unemployed puppets.

The geese and the crow had the greatest effect on him. Actually, they did have the best chances of finding employment. The crow was enormous. Its huge wings opened and it could "fly." It could clack its beak and was quite capable of speaking. It hopped beautifully about the top of the screen, it perched with its feathers ruffled and looked winning and peaceful but it could also stretch its neck and become fierce and angry. I had made it on some occasion; it was to sing a song complaining that Soviet airmen had robbed the crow of its reputation in the air. The number did not come off, although it got as far as my concert repertoire. But the verdict of the audience, expressed by silence or coughing, is for the actor one against which there is no appeal. The crow found its way into a suit-case; now it flew out to gaze at the fabulist with hope in its yellow eyes.

The geese too were as well equipped as the crow for stage appearance. To tell the truth, they were only the heads of geese with long necks made out of stockings. I put my arms up the stockings as far as the elbows and stuck them out of holes in the screen in a quite lifelike way. Ten years before they had tried to sing the romance "We have never loved each other." But the public rejected that number too. True, not as firmly as it did the crow's song but enough to make me stop showing it.

Now, with Mikhalkov's arrival, the geese too put an end to that spell of idleness that no actor enjoys, especially when he knows he has talent. And those geese certainly had that.

So I slipped a gander on to one arm and a crow on the other. Mikhalkov took a clean sheet of paper and a fountain-pen and we began creating a fable, trying out each line in turn with the puppets. Sometimes the gestures of the puppets originated in the poet's lines, sometimes a new line arose out of a successful gesture of the puppet.

We sat up all night on it. Dozens of sheets of paper were flung into the waste-paper basket, we smoked every cigarette in the house, and at five in the morning we got a fine political fable called "The Crow and the Goose." You can read it in one of Mikhalkov's collections of fables.

I went to sleep a happy man. All that was left to do was to perfect the actor's side of the number.

I worked the two following days on this, only to find that the number was decidedly not working out. When read, the fable sounded sharp and caustic. The puppets made it sound flat, forced and not at all funny. Why that was so, it is difficult to explain in words but if I were to read the fable to you now and then act it with puppets you would agree with me. In short, the crow, the geese and with them all the rest of my "unemployed" puppets went back to the drawers and the suit-cases.

I thumbed through a collection of Mikhalkov's fables that had already appeared in print. Of course, I had read them before but however hard I had explored the possibility of using them for my concert programme I could not imagine them being acted by puppets.

If the characters of a fable literally "begged" to be portrayed by puppets it seemed simply impossible to act the subject of any fable.

In the first place, in some fables three or four characters appeared simultaneously, sometimes even more, and I had only two hands; and secondly, the very structure of the subject-matter was difficult, even impossible, to turn into physical action. This was all the more regrettable because the fable's place in literature is in principle very much like that of puppetry in the theatre, and because the themes of many of Mikhalkov's fables were important and necessary.

But one day as I read each fable for the tenth or twentieth time I saw, greatly to my own surprise, exactly how puppets could play the fable "The Tipsy Hare." It was as clear as if the fable had been written for me.

The theme of this fable is toadying, that wretched survival of pre-revolutionary days. A very tenacious vice. Mikhalkov's merit in dealing with this theme is, in my opinion, the fact that the fable condemns not only toadies but all those who like toadies. In other words, it criticizes the producer as well as the consumer.

Here is the fable:

> *One night, to mark his birthday as was meet,*
> *The Hedgehog called the Rabbit for a treat.*
> *It went along till dawn, the celebration,*
> *In noisy mirth and generous libation.*
> *When parting time came on*
> *Our friend the Rabbit was already so far gone,*
> *That, hardly sane enough to leave the table,*
> *Said: "L-let's go home..."*
> *"But do you think you're able?"*
> *His worthy host replied;*
> *"You've much too much inside.*
> *Just go and take a nap until you've quite come to,*
> *To be on the safe side.*
> *They say a Lion's been here somewhere, too."*
> *Much good persuading Bunny when he's drunk!*
> *"What do I care?" he cried. "What's that to me?*
> *It won't be I—he'll be the one to funk.*
> *Go bring him here and just you see!*
> *I'll beat your Lion black and blue:*
> *Look out if I don't eat him, too!"*
> *Those drunken boastings woke the forest lord,*
> *Who spied the braggart scrambling through the brush,*
> *And, grabbing Bunny, roared:*
> *"Stop, little beggar, what's the rush?*
> *So it was you, sir, making all this din!*
> *Why, sir, as I perceive, you stink of gin!*
> *My goodness, how can folk lap up such slush?"*
> *From Bunny's brain at once the spirits fled,*
> *And for a remedy he racked his head.*
> *"B-but I... B-but we... B-but you... Oh, let me please explain,*
> *You see, I've just been at a birthday party,*
> *And, I'm afraid, the drinking was too hearty,*
> *But all to you, sir, and your family—it's plain*

Why I'm so drunk—you've no cause to complain!"
Here Leo sheathed his claws and let our Cross-Eyes go,
And even squeezed his paw and called him clever.
A strict teetotaller, the drunkard's deadly foe,
He favoured flatterers, however.

I give the text of this fable as I perform it. It is a little shorter than the published version: I have cut slightly the Hare's "tipsy" monologue and changed two rhyming lines at the end.

As you see, this fable has three characters. But, luckily for me, never more than two appear at the same time—first the Hedgehog and the Hare, then the Hare and the Lion. The climax of the fable is in the second meeting. The theme of the fable lies in the "contrast of scale." The "small" character always toadies to the "big" one. That is always the case.

So, we see, the Lion is not only zoologically bigger than the Hare but bigger because of his "social position."

I had the immediate desire to exaggerate the contrast in sizes and to make the Lion as big, the Hare as small, as possible.

The number begins with the appearance of two small puppets—the Hedgehog and his visitor the Hare. Their duet is very short. I made the line "Much good persuading Bunny when he's drunk!" into a kind of "aside" by the Hedgehog, addressed to the audience. At that line the Hedgehog goes off and the Hare, left alone, goes on boasting: "'What do I care?' he cried. 'What's that to me?'" etc. But at the words: "Those drunken boastings woke the forest lord," the Lion sticks a huge paw from behind the curtain (I manage to get my hand into this paw once it has been freed from the Hedgehog). This paw, which is about the same size as the Hare, grasps the Hare by the scruff of the neck. Its size and "fearsomeness" come as a shock of surprise to the audience. But the paw is followed by the lion's head that comes up from behind the screen. It consists simply of my own head wearing a mask with a mane sweeping down to my shoulders.

The Lion takes up the entire width of the screen and looks tremendous. Beside him the Hare is a mere mite. The Hare's life may be reckoned in seconds. He quivers like an autumn leaf: "B-but I... B-but we... B-but you..." and then suddenly finds a means of salvation—toadyism.

He has chosen the right path. That huge paw which had just been holding him by the scruff of the neck is now patting him indulgently on the cheek; when the Hare leaves, the Lion gives his tiny "hand" a hearty paw-shake.

The Hare goes off, and the Lion complacently combs his noble mane with his two paws (my second hand is free by then).

I tried out this number on my friends, then at a few concerts, and, finally, agreed to take part in the concert programme at the Hermitage Gardens.

The birth of a new number is always a pleasant event; for me this number was specially agreeable because in it I had managed to dramatize not a vocal but a literary, spoken work, that is to say I had done something which, you will recall, I had dismally failed to do in my "home theatricals." And I was the more delighted because the literary work was a fable in which the story is told in turn by a third party (the author), one or other of the characters, and finally in dialogue. And dialogue had once been my greatest stumbling-block.

What helped me to get over that difficulty this time was the fact that I did not attempt to make a clear break between the voices of the characters and speak for the Hare in a "hare's voice" and for the Lion in a "leonine" voice. Throughout I preserved the effect of a fable being recited, that is to say, the effect of a third person, even in those places where the fable went over to straight dialogue. And this unique feeling of being the narrator constituted an extra pleasure in performance.

Hands as Actors

Long ago when I was just beginning to work with puppets I prepared a number called "Santuzzi." I mentioned it in passing in the chapter "Home Theatricals."

"Santuzzi" was a puppet version of a rather cheap little song to words by Agnivtsev. The number was short-lived and would not be worth mentioning were it not for one small "discovery" that it contained. Of that discovery I must tell now.

According to the subject of this ditty the heroine comes out of the bath in the costume of Monna Vanna (the song I admit was of a somewhat frivolous nature). I dressed my heroine in a bath-robe which revealed a good deal in front. What was "revealed" by this frankly risqué décolleté was the palm of my hand. This live human palm looked like the bare flesh of the puppet. And for once it really was bare flesh.

The number disappeared into limbo but, it seemed, 1 did not forget what can only be called my "trick." And when I was working on Musorgsky's "Lullaby" I made, you will recall, a dress open at the back for my Tyapa. Santuzzi's bosom became, in a way, Tyapa's back. Through the gaps in the baby's night-dress the back of my hand could be seen. It looked quite like a baby's back. I sing my "Lullaby" very often at concerts and every time the audience laughs delightedly at the sight of the child's little body which has got nothing at all indecent in it because it is a baby's.

After the "Lullaby" I had a number which I have not mentioned at all because it was not interesting either as a failure or a success; but now the time has come to say a few words about it.

It was a "negative" version of a little song of Vertinsky's called "Your fingers smell of incense." The song is mystical and decadent in spirit, about a woman who has died and whom "God is leading up the white staircase into shining Heaven."

I intended to make fun of this song. I made a very stout "God" with a halo and a "dead" girl, or rather, the "soul" of a dead girl.

What is a soul? Something with little wings.

I cut a pair of little wings out of paper, stuck them to my hand and fixed the girl's head on the tip of my forefinger. The result was a nude, bony, winged creature. When the "soul" flew off to "God" the slow and heavy "funeral" motive of the song switched to the syncopated rhythm of a fox-trot and a dance between "God" and the "soul" began.

This number was a rather sharp antireligious, antimystical one, but it did not stay in my repertoire for long. The original of the song was little known and consequently there was nothing to parody in my "negative" rendering.

I was not particularly sorry to see it go as I was conscious of its faults, but I did regret that the "soul" had to go with it. It was a highly expressive puppet, if you can call a human hand with a head on one finger a puppet.

All the same it was a puppet. For the same reason that the Russian Petrushka, the French Polichinelle, the English Punch and other sorts of glove puppets are puppets; for the principle of this sort of puppet consists of two elements only: the human hand and a puppet's head. No body. Only a costume. Remove your hand and it ceases to be a puppet. But strip a hand puppet of its costume and leave your hand exposed with the puppet's head on your finger and the puppet remains a puppet.

Not only does it keep all the acting properties of the puppet but even somewhat enhances them. I am aware of that every time when, modelling a puppet's head in clay or plasticine and trying it for size, type and expressiveness, I slip the half-made figure on my forefinger without any costume or gown.

You get a creature that is astonishingly alive. And if a puppet becomes alive it means it is fulfilling the most important, the primary demand that is made of it.

The theatrical expressiveness and acting possibilities of hands are so interesting that I felt the desire to put on a number in which a puppet of this kind appeared not as a trick, like my "soul" was, but as a form in its own full right. But the conventionalized nature of this form requires complete consistency in all details. That is a law of art. Because the hand only hints at the human body, without attempting to portray its anatomical structure, the head too must only hint at a human head and not show it in anatomical detail. Were I to make a "lifelike" head with nostrils, modelled ears, wrinkles, hair and so on, it would look unpleasantly naturalistic on my bare hand and, apart from that, it would fail to combine with my hand to form a unity. So I had to make a head without anatomical details and find that degree of laconism which would enable the audience to recognize the thing as a human head. Children's drawings show us where the limits of that laconism lie. Two dots for the eyes—a comma for the nose—a minus sign for the curved mouth—and a circle round the lot.

Made in the solid, with a round ball instead of the circle, the same laconic treatment proves effective. And as I had to make two puppets I took two wooden balls, one a little smaller than the other, for I needed a woman and a man. In each ball I fitted a little perpendicular wooden rectangle for the nose, or rather, for the main feature of a nose—the way it protrudes. That completed the sculptor's job. All that remained was to draw the eyes (black for the man, blue for the woman), the mouths (a straight line for the man, a little circle for the woman), and the hair (black with a side-parting for the man, red with a middle-parting for the woman).

But if the hand and the head provide only a hint and not a portrait of a human being, how can the puppet become an actor? After all, the art of an actor, more than any other form of art, is representational.

Actually, if you saw a puppet of that kind in its static form you might think it was absolutely incapable of representing a human being. To begin with, it had four arms, one (the thumb) on one side and three (the third, fourth and little fingers) on the other.

However, this impression vanishes the moment the "puppet-hand" starts moving. Its movements reproduce not the mechanics of human movements but their emotional content.

If the movements of an inanimate being lack emotion, the movements of any kind of animate being are distinguished precisely by the fact that they are governed by emotion. For that reason the emotional expressiveness of gesture is the decisive feature in the representation of a human being by a puppet. And as the hand possesses these properties it follows that, despite the apparent dissimilarity and its conventionalized character, it can attain an excellent likeness of a human being in motion.

Further, because the expressiveness of the human hand in the movements of each of its fingers is very great and highly precise, the "puppet-hand" is capable of conveying not only powerful emotional human gestures but also the psychological shades of various emotions. That, probably, was why I chose for my "puppet-hand" the psychological subject of Chaikovsky's romance "We were sitting alone by a murmuring brook."

The theme of this romance is the tragedy of love arising out of a situation when "he," in spite of the favourable circumstances, does not dare to declare his affections at the right time ("... not a word of my love did I say") and later on, in his old age, regrets his timidity ("the secret of love still was locked in my breast").

In some measure, of course, the "puppet-hands" make fun of the theme and mock its "psychological" character. But the irony is gentle. The result is not a complete "negative" and the general lyrical note is preserved.

When I showed that number for the first time I feared it would flop. I was afraid that it was only to me that the expressiveness of my hands seemed interesting and that the audience would take it as a silly trick. However, the audience on the first night welcomed the new number unreservedly, tempestuously, in fact. This pleased me but did not entirely set my anxieties at rest as that audience was composed of actors, writers and artists, members of the Theatre Workers' Club where I was appearing in a concert. I was afraid that the "puppet-hands" had appealed to this audience only because they recognized a certain audacity in the conventionalized method and the novelty of the form. In short, I was afraid that the number had proved a success "for connoisseurs." But I did not want to work "for connoisseurs," although their opinion was important and very valuable for me.

The work of an actor, like that of a writer, is good only when it appeals to factory workers as well as to academicians. That is an immutable law especially for a Soviet concert performer, a Soviet variety actor. For that reason I did not feel sure about the number until I had shown it to the broad public. The occasion arose at a concert for Moscow youth in the Hall of Columns at the House of the Unions. However, that audience accepted my work too. My fears vanished and since then I have performed the number fairly often. It is also sure of a place in my solo concerts, and I always derive a special satisfaction in performing it.

I can no more explain to you exactly where that satisfaction comes from than I can describe the behaviour of the puppet. Perhaps the illustrations will to some extent show you what I cannot put in words. But I am certain I am not wrong in speaking of the number's expressiveness. And my confidence is the greater because many of the people whose criticism I am most afraid of and whose opinions I value, also took my work well. They included Nemirovich-Danchenko, Stanislavsky and Maxim Gorky. They were connoisseurs, true, but they were not gourmands. I was also glad to note that my treatment of Chaikovsky did not offend musicians and composers like Ippolitov-Ivanov, Igumnov, Gliére, Shostakovich, Prokofyev and Gnesin. Indeed, whenever I had occasion to perform to composers and musicians they always asked me to show "We were sitting alone."

At first I thought this number with the "puppet-hands" to be a mere episode in my work. A very interesting episode for me, but, all the same, only an episode. I did not think I would ever again find a theme for which I could use this form of puppets.

However, very soon afterwards a theme occurred to me, which literally demanded to be interpreted in that and no other way, a theme, moreover, of which the "puppet-hands" were a much more organic part than in the Chaikovsky romance.

I wanted to play Mayakovsky's poem "Attitude to a Lady" with puppets.

> *Were we two to be lovers*
> *Would be fixed that evening:*
> *'Twas dark,*
> *And no one could possibly see*
> *And I did lean over,*
> *And I did say, leaning,*
> *As good*
>   *as any good parent might be:*
> *"Passion's slopes are steep.*
> *You know it, too.*
> *The farther you keep,*
> *The better for you."*

This poem can be read in no longer than half a minute. Its brevity is its theme. It is only a step to the "slopes" and for that reason no time must be wasted. The poem is a joke, an anecdote.

An anecdote nearly always consists of verbs and nouns. Anyway, it does not like a lot of adjectives. In this poem, for example, it is not at all important what sort of people "he" and "she" are. "Passion's slopes are steep" means the same to everyone.

I wanted to keep in this number only the verbs, that is, the actions, and to strip the characters of any individual, descriptive features they may have possessed. I simply took two wooden balls of different sizes. I did not give them noses or draw eyes and mouths; I kept the figures as laconic as Mayakovsky's drawings for the "ROSTA Windows."

I do not know in what measure this, the shortest of the numbers in my repertoire, corresponded to the theme which the author embodied in his poem, but I am sure that its spirit corresponded to Mayakovsky's artistic method.

The puppet, consisting of a bare hand with a ball on the forefinger, is a sort of formula for the anatomical structure of any glove puppet.

When in 1936 the artist Andrei Goncharov, with whom I had studied at the art school, designed my book *The Puppet Master*, he drew for the cover the white silhouette of a hand with a ball. It became a kind of emblem. It was so apt graphically that it imperceptibly became the emblem of the Central Puppet Theatre. And recently I discovered that it had found its way to the cover of the Czechoslovak magazine *Loutkár* and had become a part of its emblem.

However, this laconism did not prove to be a limit to the evolution of the "puppet-hands."

During that evening Mikhalkov and I worked together on that unsuccessful rendering of the fable "The Crow and the Goose," Mikhalkov told me he was writing a fable entitled "Hands," consisting of a dialogue between the left hand and the right hand.

A few days later, I telephoned to him and he read to me the following short fable:

> *"I am the Right Hand. All the power's in me.*
> *I write out signatures," the right hand proudly said.*
> *"That's fine," the left rejoined offendedly,*
> *"But what, sir, would you be without my aid?"*
> *"I'm more in view, I'm used in voting* For.
> *I shake the Seniors' hands," the right said, looking big.*
> *"But being seen too much is apt to bore,"*
> *The left replied and showed the right a fig.*
>
> *But, we must say, the quarrel was in vain,*
> *For being a commercial director,*
> *Their owner used them both when out for gain,*
> *And each, if need be, served the other as protector.*

I did not have to spend much time on the first, the main part of the fable. The text itself dictated the movements of each hand. The second part was much more difficult. At first I tried coming out in front of the screen and speaking the moral—the last four lines—as from myself. But that turned out to be uninteresting and unconvincing, and, what was worse, far less expressive than the fable itself. That was no good at all. It is bad enough if something within the number itself fails to come off. One can work on that however. But a number without a real ending is no number at all. At first I thought I had run into a blind alley, and that I would either have to drop the idea or ask Mikhalkov to rewrite the dialogue in such a way that it would end with the subject itself.

But later I found there was a solution. I made myself a mask, consisting of a pair of spectacles and a rather fleshy papier mâché nose with a moustache below it to match my own fair hair. At the end of the number, from behind the screen appears the owner of the hands, a sleepy, half-tipsy fellow—the commercial director. And then I whip off the mask and bow.

In this number my hands are no longer "puppets" for they imitate nothing. They bear no resemblance to human beings. They are simply hands, but their gesticulations have to be different so that the audience will see at once that they have different psychologies. The right hand is "ruder," more "orthodox," and probably more stupid than the left. Its gestures are sharper, more precise. The left hand is more cunning, its gestures more finicking.

The differences of the characters have to be stressed primarily because it is there that lies not only the sense of the dialogue but the unexpectedness of the dénouement, which reveals the theme. And this unexpectedness consists of the fact that both hands belong to one man and have no face of their own.

To conclude my story of the evolution of the "puppet-hands" I should like to make one important thing quite clear.

It sometimes happens that after a concert where I have performed "We were sitting alone" or "Attitude to a Lady" or "Hands" some member of the audience who has enjoyed that number particularly comes up to me and asks me to show him my hands, without any screen or play-acting. Usually this person has the impression that my hands are more mobile than "ordinary" hands and is somewhat disappointed to find that they are the most ordinary pair of hands and that I cannot move each joint of each finger separately or bend my fingers backwards and so on.

On such occasions I have to explain that the essence of the number does not lie in the physical properties of my hands but in the fact that any pair of human hands has an extraordinary power of expressiveness. All that is required is that one should be responsive to this expressiveness and see in the human hand its independent acting potential. The important thing is to feel one's hands to be "independent," in the same way that any puppeteer feels his puppet to be "independent," although in fact he himself is directing the movements of that puppet.

The Living Face

I wanted to make fun of a bad public speaker. The kind of speaker who ruins any subject by a stereotyped speech.

How was I to find a form of puppet which would make anybody say at once: "Ah yes, that's a public speaker"? What is it that is most characteristic of a bad speaker?

I think it is to be found in the way he usually expresses all his ardent temperament by flourishing his right arm. To see him at the rostrum with the top coming up to his chest, you would think he had no left arm at all. Only the right one: that horribly irritating right arm that lays down the law, threatens, denies, affirms....

I decided to build my whole number on the exaggerations of the right arm. I would make a head very large in proportion to a usual puppet's head, one that I could hold with my left hand, and use my own natural arm, just as it was, for the puppet's single arm.

The puppet turned out to be convincing and amusing. It was unquestionably a public speaker. All that remained was to find the theme of his speech. Of the speech, not of the number, for the theme of the number was clear: stereotype.

But for all my efforts—what I wrote myself and what others wrote for me—the text of the speech was shamefully inadequate. The puppet had to be relegated to the "suit-case of the unemployed." Summer came round. I left for the country and in my spare time started working on the number again. I did not have the puppet with me. I sewed together a shirt with one sleeve for the right arm and stuck my left fist through the neck to serve as the puppet's head; round my fist I tied some rags and drew a woman's stocking over the lot to keep the rags in place.

This stump had to represent the speaker's head, and it did so quite well. True, it had no face but by bending my fist at the wrist I could make the head turn in different directions much better than a papier mâché head could do.

In this way I realized that I would have to make the head for that puppet in such a way that I could get my fist in it.

But a few days were enough to show me that there was absolutely no need to make a head. I had one already: a splendid head with a face that was literally alive.

I only discovered this when to save time one day I slipped the stocking over my fist without bothering to bind it with rags. I pulled the slack of the stocking tight and at once saw that I had only to move my forefinger against the inside of the stocking to get a nose. And if I stretched my fourth finger and pressed it on the stocking a little lower down I got the chin. And if then I began to move the rest of my fingers the whole face became alive and the folds of the stocking became the folds of skin on a human face, creating an effect of facial expression.

All that was left to do was to sew a couple of buttons to the stocking for eyes, put on the spectacles and a little moustache suggesting a mouth. The face became so alive and expressive that it almost became the centre of expressiveness of my public speaker. In any case it was no less expressive than his arm.

In short, the puppet was a great success but I was still without the text of the speech.

So the second speaker went into the suit-case too.

Then one day the post brought me an envelope. Inside it was a cutting from *Pravda*, on the back of which was written in pencil: "This is what Obraztsov needs." The sender was Aduyev, the writer, and the cutting was an article by Ilf and Petrov called "The Happy Element." The article was funny and sharp-edged. It poked fun at the pseudo-methodical work of certain organizers of community outings. Aduyev probably thought I could make use of the article and portray the "happy elements" on their outing with the help of my puppets.

But the article included a speech by the representative of a recreation park on the theme "How to take a stroll in the park, with whom to take a stroll in the park, and how to take fresh air."

The speech began like this:

"Comrades! We must, once and for all, put an end to those foolish and harmful theories according to which strolling is just a matter of walking. That, comrades, is what cows, dogs and cats do—they walk. We must, I insist, give an assignment to every strolling element so that this element, comrades, would not merely be strolling but accomplishing a serious piece of work at it...."

This speech was, indeed, just "what Obraztsov needed."

I only had to shorten it a little and rearrange the order of the phrases so that each one gave the puppet an opportunity to gesticulate.

I spent little more than two days rehearsing the number. It was a roaring success. The audience rose to it at the first performance and since then my "Public Speaker" has for many years occupied a central place in my concert repertoire. I have never left him out. And for that, of course, I must thank Aduyev. But for that good turn of his my Public Speaker might still be lying in the suit-case alongside the other "unemployed" puppets.

This new, very interesting and expressive method of using a miming puppet naturally could not be restricted to one number.

Yelena Gvozdeva, the artist who worked at the Central Puppet Theatre, found this method very attractive and made miming puppets on the principle of my Speaker; but not simply out of stockings—she combined various materials and jersey cloth.

At my request she made me a "Hitler." That was before the war. I wanted to show Hitler yelling about nazism in German or broken Russian. But the speech did not come off. Probably because it was a mechanical transfer of the method of one number to another. And that is never successful. Or very rarely.

Hitler had been in the suit-case for at least a year. I would take him out occasionally and look at him with the idea of making something out of him. But as I did not find looking at Hitler a particularly pleasant pastime I tore off his small moustache and fixed a big ginger one in its place.

For some reason the puppet's face immediately assumed a drunken look. Drunkenness—there was a theme. That would be something worth working on. I stuck a rubber tube in the puppet's neck, with the lower end leading to a small tank, and made my Drunk drink "vodka."

The result was so effective that the physical behaviour of the puppet solved the theme without a single word having to be spoken.

The Drunk looks round.

He fills his glass carefully, trying to fill it to the brim.

He raises the glass and looks at it lovingly.

He sniffs it.

His moustache and even the tip of his nose twitch slightly.

He drinks. He sits petrified for a moment. Then his face creases into a thousand wrinkles.

He pours himself another glass. He drinks again. The tempo quickens.

Finally, shaking the bottle so that the vodka whirls—all real drinkers do that—he flings his head back and pours the rest of his "half-litre" straight down his throat.

The number was a success. But the idea could be strengthened and the joke turned not only against the process of getting drunk but against, so to say, the motive for drinking. For that I had to make up my mind who this Drunk was and find a psychological and not simply a physical subject.

Through force of habit I started looking for the subject in a song. The first one that came to mind was Beethoven's "Drinking Song."

Its first verse runs:

> *Come on,*
> *Let's have another*
> *Like that!*
> *More grog—for my brother*
> *And me*
> *Are leaving each other!*
> *Let everyone join in the toast!*
> *Who says we're drunk, by golly?*
> *It's true, we both feel jolly,*
> *But who dares suppose we are drunk?*

There are several verses, each one being a kind of toast. This makes the song very suitable as an illustration of someone constantly refilling his glass, drinking and growing tipsy.

I started rehearsing. All the physical movements of the puppet fitted the text most aptly; nevertheless I was left with the feeling that I had done something not quite honest. I was sacrificing the inner meaning of the song for the sake of a subject that was superficially suitable. This song is the drinking song of a traveller, of someone who, maybe, is setting out on a long sea voyage. It has a certain grandeur. The words are gay and amusing, the melody simple and manly with a faint touch of sadness.

It always pained me to see the way certain basses try hard to act the drunk in a naturalistic manner when they perform this song on the concert stage. They put on a dazed look, chew their lips and even sway from side to side.

What right had I, then, to do the very thing I disliked so much in others, and to do it, moreover, in an even more exaggerated way?

The puppet was wrecking a fine song.

I felt sorry about the music as well as the words. Moreover, the idea of the number too was diminished: for that puppet was capable of making much sharper fun of drunkenness, given another target for its humour.

I put aside Beethoven's "Drinking Song" and getting some of my friends together showed them my Drunk singing every simple song or romance that touched on the subject of drinking that I could remember.

I sang comic songs: Ippolitov-Ivanov's "Seated in a cool cellar beside a barrel of wine," Khrennikov's "The buds are cracking with the noise." I even tried out "Chizhik-Pyzhik, where art thou?" And all of them succeeded more or less.

My Drunk played every one of them quite aptly. But the puppet was only underlining the point of these songs, he was not revealing any new or additional quality in them.

It was only when I turned from comic songs to a "tragic" romance that the puppet justified its existence. The song in question was a Gypsy romance which ran:

> *Fill up that glass, it has no wine.*
> *No wine—no song, as goes the saying.*
> *'Tis wine that makes life seem so fine:*
> *Drink deep—then life's a game worth playing.*
>
> *But if you play and lose the game,*
> *And if you drain the wine of joy,*
> *Then break your glass—it's all the same,*
> *Your life is but a broken toy.*
>
> *Fill up the glass—your love has gone*
> *And never will return again.*
> *Another holds her in his arms.*
> *So one more glass to drown your pain!*

Both the author of the verses and the composer were quite serious about this song. And singers used to render it seriously too. And those who liked the tragic declaration about drowning one's sorrows in wine listened seriously to the song. This cheap sentiment is in fact often the motive for getting drunk. In other words, I had found just what I needed.

In "tragic" drunkenness all the physical behaviour of the puppet acquires an enhanced expressiveness. Now he raises his glass in sentimental happiness: "No wine—no song, as goes the saying." Now in sentimental grief: "Your love has gone and never will return again." But in either case the conclusion is the same: drink, drink, there's nothing for it but drink.

The satirical theme took on precision. The number became sharp and malicious. My friends "passed" it, and ever since then—more than eight years ago—I have shown my Drunk at almost every concert.

The Enemies

Laughter takes various forms. It can be friendly and it can be angry. When we laugh at the funny things a child says or does we are only expressing a greater tenderness towards that child. That is friendly laughter.

And we laugh in a friendly affectionate way at grown-ups too if they have some amusing and quite harmless idiosyncrasy.

The things that Vasily Tyorkin* does and thinks about often make the reader laugh and yet Vasily Tyorkin is one of our favourite characters in literature.

But there are times when people's behaviour reveals their bad qualities—stupidity, meanness, boastfulness. And when this happens the very fact of revealing their vices makes us laugh.

And that laughter is angry, scornful, destructive.

The artist who aims at arousing laughter in the reader or spectator always senses, or, at any rate, ought to sense, the kind of laughter he wants.

He must know whether he wants the reader or spectator to laugh in

---

* Vasily Tyorkın—central character of Alexander Tvardovsky's well-known war poem.—*Tr.*

a friendly way or whether that laughter should expose something that has not seemed funny previously.

Most of my concert numbers arouse laughter of one sort or the other.

Some of them arouse friendly laughter. But not many. Far more often I try to make fun of something which I find bad or harmful. In doing so I am prompted by feelings of derision, hostility, anger.

But there are two numbers in my repertoire which I must place in a special category, numbers which had their origin in something more than anger. In hate.

They were satires on Hitler and Mussolini, conceived during the war.

Every one of my compatriots shared this unbounded hatred of the mortal enemies of their country.

My task, then, like that of any satirist whose theme is the enemy, consisted in giving that hatred a concrete form.

In solving this problem I had to shun all nuances and half-tones, all personal, little individual characteristics in the objects of my satire.

That was why I had not succeeded in my first attempt to make a satire on Hitler with the help of the miming puppet that later became my Drunk. That puppet was too amusing, and how can amusement express hatred?

At the beginning of the war our theatre organized a concert party to send to the front; it took us but a few weeks to mount a special anti-fascist programme consisting of several satirical numbers.

Hitler, of course, figured in that programme. He took the form of an enormous dog which had only two external—and quite local—signs of Hitler—the black tooth-brush moustache on the upper lip and the characteristic lock of hair.

The theme of the number was the enemy, or, rather, the enemies. The subject was a conference in the Reich Chancellery. The form of expressing the theme was a pack of dogs.

Four dogs came to Hitler's conference: a bulldog—Mussolini, a poodle—Petain, a spaniel—Tiso, and a black mongrel—Horthy. Hitler made a speech. Not one word was spoken; it was all done with barks and growls.

During the "discussion" the other dogs barked and uttered servile whines.

This item proved to be the most popular of all in the programme.

One day while we were performing at the edge of the forest one of Soviet aircraft flew over. It happened just at the moment when "Hitler" was starting his speech. The roar of the engines drowned his barks. The actor, S. Samodur, who was playing Hitler was not put out. Hitler raised his muzzle, followed the flight of the plane until it disappeared beyond the tree-tops and then scratched the back of his neck with one paw. One of the soldiers present shouted: "Ah-ha, don't like it, eh?" and a gale of laughter swept the glade.

In this book I am not dealing with the work of our theatre but I could not resist the temptation of describing that incident because it is typical of the feelings of both actor and audience when it is a question of a satire on an enemy, which has been inspired by a hatred that all share.

Hitler was the enemy of our country, the enemy of everything in the world that was alive, clean, and good. The enemy of mankind. A nonentity who imagined himself to be a Napoleon. A man with a hypertrophic mania of his own greatness and invincibility.

In thinking about a satire on Hitler for my own solo performances I decided to pour derision on Hitler as a nonentity—or, rather, to formulate that aspect of him in a concrete manner.

I cannot remember why for this number I chose a monologue of Death but the inner motive for that choice is understandable. In those days—autumn 1942—it was but a step from life to death. Heavy fighting was in progress everywhere. The fascists were taking hard knocks one after the other, but they were still at the gates of Leningrad and in the Northern Caucasus, they held the whole of Ukraine and the Baltic states.

Anguish and hatred were the dominant emotions of every Soviet man and woman in those days. And these were the emotions that prompted me in my work.

I wanted the number to be an angry one, I wanted it to be a satire on Hitler, but I had no intention of making it "funny."

Death's monologue, addressed to Hitler, was written for me by Yevgeny Speransky, an actor and playwright of our theatre.

It began by praising Hitler for enabling Death to reap so rich a harvest, but it finished with a malicious warning that the last victim of Death's scythe would be Hitler himself. The theme of the number was the dialectics of death, the idea was that Hitler's "greatness" was a sham and that in reality he was a nonentity.

As the idea was inherent in the monologue I had to find a clear-cut and convincing visual way of expressing the number. One visual way of conveying the idea of nonentity is by scale, so I had the Hitler-puppet made small. But as a puppet looks small only in comparison with another, the Death-puppet had to be big. So naturally I decided to use a head-puppet—the same kind as I had used for my Bear and my Concert Singer.

There are various ways of expressing Death in art. Sometimes Death is an angry figure, sometimes it is friendly; sometimes tragi-comic, sometimes quite commonplace. Remember, for instance, the surprisingly commonplace portrayal of Death as an old woman in Russian fairy-tales.

But a commonplace Death could not serve as the prototype of my puppet. That would have been a contradiction of the literary image created by the text.

The monologue was satirical but in style it was declarative and emotional, even rather solemn. This combination of the satiric with the lofty gave the monologue its particular sharpness. So the Death-puppet also had to be tragic and satirical at the same time.

Boris Tuzlukov, the artist of our theatre, made a Death in the form of a skeleton in a black cloak and a red hat with a feather in it. My head fitted into the puppet's chest and I looked out through black voile hung between the ribs. My arms were concealed by the cloak but I wore white kid gloves on my hands. These gloves were painted black along the bones to create the effect of a loose-jointed skeleton. The shoulder bones and the forearms were cut out of wood, linked at the joints and running along the cloak from the puppet's shoulders to my wrists where the gloves began. The general effect was solemn and terrifying, a Lady Death of the days of medieval chivalry.

Death held the tiny Hitler-puppet in its left hand. This puppet could not move independently. It was a puppet in the full sense of the word. It appeared to come alive only when Death shook it and made it dance to the words:

> *Make haste, my friend, make haste, the hours are flying fast,*
> *And so your soldiers, too, shall soon be flying.*
> *Then I myself shall bring you to your last,*
> *Most awful trial before your day of dying.*

At the end of the monologue Death took Hitler by the head and the legs and simply tugged with both hands. Then Death disappeared and I came out from behind the screen and spoke the final lines myself:

The hour is near—the trial will be cruel;
For all your doings you shall pay in full:
For deadly shrieking bombs, for blood-smeared knives,
For slaughtered children, trampled flowers and lives.

Many years have passed since then.

The Death puppet has for long stood in our theatre's collection as a ine example of Tuzlukov's work; the two halves of Hitler as wrenched apart at the last performance of this number I simply threw away. However, I have not forgotten the emotional content of the number. I well remember the sense of excitement I felt on account of the seriousness of the theme. Every word of both those monologues was associated with the events at the front, with the announcements of the Soviet Information Bureau, with the newspaper reports heard over the radio, with thoughts for the safety of one's own dear ones. And when I spoke the words "For all your doings you shall pay in full" concrete experiences of real life and the names of real people swam before my mind's eye.

I made my Mussolini in 1944. There was something theatrical in all the repulsive activities of this man, beginning with the first *fasci* in 1919. The theatricality was carried out with demagogic methods, with the methods of political agitation—the salutes, the elaborately staged parades, the histrionic emotion and hysteria of the public speeches.

The *Duce* was the best "actor" or, rather, the best clown of fascist Italy. At the time he was at the zenith of his career, playing the buffoon after the conquest of Abyssinia, and, later on, together with Hitler, of France, his clowning was something to be detested, and nothing more. In 1944, however, an element of the comic had come into it. The end of the war was in sight. The fate of the *Duce* was clear to all. The clown's situation was tragi-comic.

So I decided to make my Mussolini sing Cagnio's famous arioso from *Pagliacci*, without changing a single word. If you will recall the words of that song and imagine Mussolini singing them towards the end of the war every phrase will acquire a new and quite unexpected sense and sound like an allegory in a political lampoon.

To act! When my mind is in a turmoil! My words, my actions I do not understand. And yet I have to act. Am I a man? No, I am Pagliacci. On with the motley, the paint and the powder. The people pay thee and want their laugh.

The Mussolini puppet was made with movable jaws but it was not a miming puppet like the Drunk and its grimaces were limited to two or three fixed expressions.

Mussolini wore the traditional clown's loose costume, not white, though; I made it black with white pompons. As my Cagnio-Benito had to make "tragic" gestures and strike theatrical poses I gave the puppet long arms which could be moved by means of what are known in the profession as "canes"—thin rods concealed by the costume. The costume also hid two little tubes which led to the eyes. These tubes joined below, and on the end of the single tube I fixed a rubber scent-spray bulb to hold water. And at the phrase "eating thy heart" where the opera singer usually leaves the stage with a hysterical sound between a laugh and a sob, my Mussolini sobs too and tears spurt from his eyes to a distance of two metres.

This number remained in my repertoire up to the very day when its original was hanged, an event which robbed it of any sense and made it, so to speak, "historical." Until then, however, Mussolini enjoyed a very active life among my puppets. It went round a whole chain of concert halls in Moscow but I doubt whether it was ever as successful as it was in the Balkans: in Sofia and especially in Bucharest. Rumanian audiences insisted that I show my Mussolini at every concert and made me encore the number, and when members of the audience met me on the street they would call "Mussolini," come up and shake my hand and roar with laughter.

Rehearsals

In dealing here with the evolution of the means of expression in relation to the demands of the theme on the form, I have spoken essentially of the creative process of the producer, who in most cases was also the author of the subject and the theme.

But besides the work of the producer and the author each number requires rehearsal. And that is a purely actor's process.

True, these processes are closely linked: ideas about how to act the role-to-be unavoidably rise in my mind the moment I start thinking about how to write and produce it.

And when you start to think about a role it means you have started to work on it.

That is the sole reason why there were times when pure rehearsal was short and I was able to appear at a concert with a new number literally the next day after running through the number for the first time at home.

However, such occasions were rare, much rarer than those when on the contrary I had to spend a long time on rehearsals. And by rehearsals I mean strictly acting rehearsals when no further changes are made in the appearance of the puppet, or in the theme or structure of the number and when I, now the actor, had to find the inner character, and learn to express it in the behaviour, the intonations and movements of the puppet.

In short, I had to go through that whole process of building up a role that every actor has to go through when he is working on a new role.

Usually, however, the actor rehearses in the presence of the producer who sits in at rehearsals and tells the actor what is right and what is wrong, and directs the role accordingly.

But as no one ever produced my numbers for me and I was always the producer and stage-manager I had to rehearse and at the same time watch my work, comment on it and correct whatever did not please me in it.

Naturally, you will be quite justified in asking what practical steps I took to do that.

For some reasons many people who ask me that have already made up their minds that I rehearse in front of a mirror.

That is not so.

In rehearsing any role, including a puppet role, before the mirror there is always a danger of becoming stereotyped. You can use the mirror to test the general outer effect but nothing else.

However, you would be even further from the truth if you supposed that I worked alone for days, weeks and months in rehearsing a number in every detail and then went straight on to the stage and performed it. I have never rehearsed that way, and never could.

Imagine a man who wants to learn to swim mastering all the movements of a swimmer, lying on the floor of his bedroom, and then going straight to a swimming contest. He would not have the slightest chance of winning; he would be lucky if he did not drown in shallow water.

And I would have drowned with my new number, as surely as if I had worn a millstone round my neck, had I rehearsed it thinking only of the sea I had to swim in, relying only on that "radar" process which I could use at the concert.

Of course there are some concert performers who can and do work on themselves alone. That is particularly true of musicians. When you play the piano you do it to some extent for yourself, you get some pleasure out of it as a listener; but it is quite impossible to perform one's puppets to oneself.

And besides to perform any serious musical work on no matter what instrument you need to spend a great many hours mastering the purely technical difficulties, while there are no technical difficulties at all in working my puppets, nothing that requires practice.

For this reason I only occasionally rehearse alone.

Having made my puppets I put them over my hands and, without a word, running over the lines in my mind, try out the puppets' movements for the whole scene.

This does not take more than fifteen or twenty minutes. There would be no sense in going on any longer as I simply would not know what more to do.

Then I call my wife. She sits down on a sofa opposite the screen and watches the result of my work.

Only now can I speak the lines aloud because now it is really necessary to do so. They are no longer being thrown to the wind. Someone can hear them. And as in this first performance of my future number I must explain my intentions, there inevitably arises in me a certain degree of emotion.

But only a very little. First, because my audience consists of one, and only one, secondly, because I am working in a room and not in a theatre, and, thirdly, because I am only trying out my future emotion.

Of course, on those occasions I do not rationalize as I am doing now. Not at all. I do not restrain my temperament, my emotions, according to some theoretical methodological conceptions; I rehearse as actively as I feel like, as actively as is convenient. The only thing I do not consciously permit myself to do is to force my emotions.

On these occasions my wife is not only necessary to me as a spectator, thanks to whom my activity as an actor is stirred; I need her as a critic of what I am trying to do.

Her criticism is professional because my wife's main profession is dramatic acting, because, as the result of countless performances in which we have appeared together at concerts, she has a sense of the powers of expression of puppets, and finally, because I share with her all my thoughts in the initial process of a number, which means that she knows all that the author and the producer demand of the number and can thus judge the actor, me, according to my own laws.

If the number I am preparing needs musical accompaniment, I arrange the screen so that my wife can see the puppets while playing the piano. Then off we go.

Usually, I do not rehearse like this for very long. As soon as the general plan of the puppets' behaviour becomes clear and I see that each successive rehearsal is adding nothing new and is merely a mechanical repetition of the preceding one, I stop rehearsing. Sheer repetition is not only pointless, it is dangerous. It does not strengthen what has already been established, it only exhausts it.

At that stage I summon everybody else in the family circle—my son and daughter and the "help"—seat them on the sofa and show them my work.

And only because I have a new audience my emotions involuntarily quicken again.

Now too it is still far from being a fully-felt emotion but all the same its scope has broadened. That has happened because by now I to some extent understand the general composition of the number and, consequently, feel capable of that sense of improvisation which arises in me only when the general emotional path has become more or less clear, when I have set up the first sign-posts at the turning points and when I know the logic of the separate parts of the puppets' physical behaviour.

By presenting my number to my family circle and squeezing out of them every criticism I can, I get fresh material to work on and can resume rehearsal, polishing up what is good or changing everything and starting afresh.

However, that spell of rehearsal reaches a point where I do not know what to do next and again have need of an audience.

Preferably an audience which knows nothing about the number: one which will look at everything with fresh eyes and fresh feelings, without prejudice one way or another. From that my emotions are again certain to expand somewhat.

I ring up one of my friends and invite him over. I show him my number, sense his reactions to it and ask him for his impressions. That throws some more light on the number.

After several of these rehearsal cycles the moment comes when I feel the need of showing my work to a larger audience. Then I invite a number of friends in, collect all the chairs in the flat and arrange them in rows in my study so that my dress rehearsal and the ensuing discussion take place "in public."

This is necessary not only because the opinion and advice of many—not only one or two—can be highly useful but chiefly because the reaction of a large audience is always more precise. One spectator may laugh but that does not mean that ten will laugh at that place. The silence of one may be no more than a polite silence. The silence of ten is a sign of attention.

And so this increased reaction of a larger public unavoidably raises my emotions.

If with my emotions at their higher pitch I do not detect any false or strained note in my inner feelings, but, on the contrary, enjoy a sense of freedom, I know that the period of rehearsal has not been wasted and that I can introduce my new number at a concert before very much more time has passed.

Far from every new work leads safely to the concert hall. I often stop rehearsing at one stage or other as I realize that something is at fault with the author-producer's side of the work and that it would be futile for the actor to struggle to overcome those faults. Either the whole conception of the number has to be revised, or the composition has to be reconstructed, or new puppets are needed, or the whole number has to be dropped despite some of the good things in it.

But even when the number has successfully passed through the whole period of rehearsal and been "passed" by my friends, there is no sure guarantee that it will be a success.

That will be decided by its first real performance before an auditorium. And it requires several performances to polish and complete the work. Coming back from one of those early performances my wife and I set about rehearsing straight away, not waiting for the morning, to correct and strengthen the number in places prompted by the reaction of the audience.

I have described the entire process of rehearsal as it actually takes place. In all its stages it is the result not of a theoretical method but simply of practice.

But now in describing those stages in their logical order and recalling not only cases of satisfactory results from rehearsal but also failures, I have come to certain conclusions applicable to work of any kind on a role, and not only to rehearsing without a producer. These conclusions concern the process of imparting emotion to the performance of a role.

Emotion is the very life-blood of a role.

And if that blood is to course warmly and to pulse normally it must flow through the blood vessels and along the arteries of the role.

Rehearsal is primarily a process of shaping and preparing those arteries, in other words the direction in which the actor's emotion flows. If the arteries are not prepared, if their walls are too thin, the blood will break them and spill out. The actor's emotion will fail to remain within the confines of the role and will become a personal emotion, not that of the character; it will turn to hysteria or to something stereotyped.

Ksenia Kotlubai had told me that one can only act before an audience and that it was wrong to act at rehearsal. But it took many years for me to understand that this law is the law of emotion.

Only the auditorium permits an actor to open the sluice-gates of this emotion, and even then all the channels have to be ready.

The rehearsal period is that in which the channels are gradually strengthened and broadened simultaneously with an equally gradual strengthening and broadening of the emotions. And the flow of the emotions can be strengthened only in so far as the channels are ready to take it.

Never less and never more.

Only in that event can there be a sense of truth in the rehearsal, and it is precisely true emotion that an actor has to get used to during rehearsal.

Twenty Years Later

The idea of some new theme or new means of expression is not always realized, for it is not always an easy matter to find the form to clothe it in.

I have had many failures in my work, and I have written of them. There were various reasons for these failures, but the one thing that I have noticed and which may be the result of a personal trait (I don't mean quality, not at all) is the vitality of an idea once it has been aroused.

You have probably noticed that if by chance you do not manage to complete some trivial thing, or finish a sentence—because the coffee pot comes to the boil—or eat a piece of bread—because you are called to the phone—you are left with a gnawing feeling of something left undone when you have taken off the coffee pot or laid down the receiver. And until you have remembered that unfinished sentence or that half-eaten piece of bread nothing can set your mind at rest. And if you do not succeed in remembering you are left with a feeling of vexation.

I feel somewhat the same way when I fail at something in my work and do not fulfil my intention. This feeling of not having finished my piece of bread remains with me for years. Even if I stop thinking of it and remembering it, sooner or later it will pop up. I could mention dozens of examples but will mention only one, the latest.

Twenty years ago I tried without success to make a number of "Rejuvenation." I told you about it in the chapter on Home Theatricals where I explained the cause of the failure and tried to analyse what ought to have been done to put the number on its feet.

Perhaps just because I described this number in such detail the memory of an unfinished piece of bread rose afresh and once more I felt a hunger to eat the uneaten.

And so while I was writing the subsequent chapters I could not stop thinking about this number.

I got Mikhalkov to come round again, told him the outline of the physical treatment of the number and even illustrated it with whatever puppets were at hand. Again Mikhalkov and I sat up late into the night and the result was a new Mikhalkov fable, the text and scenario for the number-to-be. The same doctor, the same patient, the same head-changing act as before. This time, though, the doctor substitutes a jackal's head for the man's.

The result was a caustic political satire. The puppets were soon made and I started fitting them into the text.

Whether that number will be a success or not is hard to say. Only the audience can decide that for certain, if I risk submitting the new work to its judgement.

CHAPTER FOURTEEN

Contact with my Audiences

I have told you about all my numbers, the way they were created and the way they looked when completed.

My ultimate aim in working on every one of them was to present them to an audience.

And that means that I must tell you about my contacts with the audience; otherwise I would be giving you a distorted, incomplete idea of my profession.

Within the Limit of Time

I shall begin my account of meeting my audiences by describing the emotions that contacts of this nature arouse in the actor, emotions that in the end distinguish the actor's profession from other professions in the world of art: from that of the writer, the architect, the painter.

When an author writes a book he writes it for "the future." He knows that the book will outlive him. Even in the physical sense. He knows that in scores or hundreds of years' time someone may be reading his book, as he now reads Tolstoi, Pushkin, Lermontov, Shakespeare, Dante, Aristophanes, Homer.

He knows that a particle of his own life will live in his book, as I know now that someone, somewhere, when I am no longer alive, will read this book and, maybe, find something of interest in it. I know that the phrase I have just written will live longer than the hand that wrote it.

When the architect, equipped with a drawing-pen, a pair of dividers and a T-square, draws on a sheet of cartridge-paper pillars, architraves, balconies and staircases, he is thinking of the house which is going to stand on the street of a town, of a house which will last longer than its architect. He has the right to hope that the proportions he has established will please people in scores and hundreds of years' time, as we are today pleased by the buildings of Rastrelli, Bazhenov and Kazakov, the carved stone of the Novgorod cathedrals, the brick towers of the Kremlin, the multitopped wooden steeples of the churches of North Russia.

The writer, the architect, the painter, and the sculptor outlive themselves in their work.

The theatrical or variety actor has none of this. He cannot live into "the future," he lives for the present, for this very second.

The works of art created by such actors are not cast in durable material. They are immaterial. They are action—movement which arises the moment the actor appears on the stage and ceases to exist as soon as the curtain falls. From that moment the work of art—be it a role, a song or a dance—ceases to have any existence. It remains only in the memory of those who saw it.

Sometimes this memory is reinforced on paper in the form of a review or an article, or even in books on the actor's work. Yet however gifted the review, article or book may be it cannot replace the real actor or re-create his art any more than the description of a feast can replace even the most modest meal at home.

But apart from this basic distinguishing feature of the actor's profession, besides the fact that it creates works of art which consist of definite movements within strict time limits, the profession as a whole is limited by time. An actor rarely goes on acting to the end of his days. Many of those whom the average person thinks of as having died long ago are in fact still alive. They are to be met in trams and trolleybuses and in the Underground. They are still alive but they are no longer actors. Old age has affected their hands, their legs, their voices, their eyes—in other words the whole equipment with which they created their works of art no longer functions.

The first to quit the stage are ballet-dancers. For them the age of thirty-five to forty is old age professionally, and sometimes professional death. In this profession the years of study are sometimes longer than the years of work.

After the ballet-dancers come the singers, especially tenors and sopranos, and after the singers the dramatic actors, among whom the first to go are those whose particular talents do not allow of their playing character old men and women.

The professional power of the writer, the sculptor, the architect, the painter may mature with age, as it did with Tolstoi, Gorky, Repin, Rembrandt and Leonardo da Vinci.

But can one imagine an eighty-year-old tenor singing Lensky in *Yevgeny Onegin* or a sixty-year-old actress playing *en travestie*?

Professional death is no easy thing. It is hard to die before one's own death. You will draw no comfort from the old theatre-bills, from the carefully clipped newspaper cuttings, or the illuminated addresses in leather covers with silver inscription plates presented to one by "grateful audiences." Far from giving you enjoyment such things only sadden you.

I don't know how many years longer I shall perform. I don't know how soon my acting qualities will deteriorate, when I shall die professionally. But I know that sooner or later this will happen. And though I have not the least intention of taking my leave of the stage or of writing my own obituary I want to use this occasion, while my profession still lives, to say how happy I am that I adopted the profession of puppeteer and that I have served it so long. I am not distressed at the oncoming of this professional death. It does not distress me not only because I already have a second profession as producer and director of my theatre, but because there is simply no reason to draw pessimistic conclusions from the special particular features of the actor's profession.

On the contrary, these features are bound up with creative professional feelings belonging to the actor's profession alone and to no other. When a painter works there may be minutes, hours, weeks, months even, between the drawing of each line, between one brush stroke and another. He can take his own time about it. When an author writes a book minutes, hours, weeks, months may pass between one word and another, between each sentence, each chapter. He too can take his own time. A book which the reader can read in a few hours may have taken several years to write, since the writing and the reading of a book are measured differently in time. An actor's appearance on the stage, however, and the reception of his acting by the audience take place simultaneously and at the same pace from the first moment to the last. It is precisely because the actor's art is not embodied in anything material, and exists only in the very process of its creation, that is, only in time, that this time is concentrated and condensed in a way known in no other artistic profession.

This property of concentration is comparable with the time spent by an athlete on the running track or, more aptly, with that spent by a surgeon performing an operation.

An actor's time is not divided into hours, minutes and seconds, but into fractions of a second, each of which is of value even when there are pauses, which are as precious as a milligramme of radium.

The means of expression of the actor—what we call gesture and intonation—can become means of the creation of a role only when their exactness in time is so perfect that they cannot be measured, that any chronometer would be too crude for them. A half-hour spent by a painter at his easel or a writer at his desk bears no comparison with the thirty minutes a ballerina dances or with a scene between Iago and Othello. They are different in compactness, in energy and for this reason in duration.

For a writer three minutes mean nothing. They do not suffice even to think out the short phrase I have just written. But for an actor three minutes constitute a lifetime. Twice as long as it takes to sing the Grechaninov romance which I illustrated with my cats. So you can see into what tiny fractions of seconds the actor's three minutes have to be divided, seeing how much can be packed into that time.

There is so high a degree of activity in the professional life of an actor that however short it may be it cannot be measured by the usual time-scale. And it is in that activity that the true nature of the actor's happiness is to be found.

An actor's life on the stage is determined by a precise scale of time. He cannot divide word from word, sentence from sentence just as it pleases him, since he is subordinate to the law of that sentence, its theme, its temperament and its "partners"—movement and action.

The actor is within the power of time, and yet he feels himself to be its master. He feels in no way cramped within his three minutes of action; on the contrary he feels as free and easy as if time did not exist.

This specific feature of time, common to all actors, since it is characteristic of the creative process of acting, is in some measure exaggerated on the concert stage. In the legitimate theatre, after all, the actor has helpers—other actors, lighting, decorations and so on—while on the concert stage, the artist is usually alone. The ten or fifteen minutes allotted to him are his own. He alone is responsible for each fraction of a second. The eyes of the entire audience, however large it is, are on him alone, their ears hear only his voice. He can rely only on himself. He has no partners, there is no scenery. Thus time becomes even more condensed and feelings are greatly heightened. That inevitable "dialogue" with the spectator of which I have written in "Lessons of the Human Theatre" becomes even more tangible and carries greater responsibility.

I feel this responsibility from the first moment of contact with the audience, when I first appear on the brightly lighted stage. A thousand eyes meet mine. It is a more powerful, a sharper, a more awesome feeling than the similar one felt in the legitimate theatre.

Another thing. To the actor in the theatre even the hundredth performance is like a first night because the audience is always different. That is even more true for the actor on the concert stage because for him the halls as well as his audiences are constantly changing. This heightens his feeling that he is never repeating himself. After all, the very size of the auditorium is bound to have some relation to the nature of the performance. It would be impossible to stage my "Habanera" in the Large Hall of the Moscow Conservatoire with the same intonations and with the same nuances of gesture as in a club room seating two or three hundred.

Not all the thousands of concert performances I have given have been on the stages adapted to puppet performance. I have used a ship's deck as my stage, a forest clearing at the front, even the back of a lorry.

That is not all. Not only do the types of hall change but the type of audiences varies enormously. At holiday times, such as the October Revolution celebrations, or for May Day or Soviet Army Day—I may perform several times in a single evening. And the composition of the audience differs from one concert to another. From the university students I may go to the cadets of the Zhukovsky Air Force Academy, from them to women textile-workers of the Tryokhgornaya Mill, from them again to an audience of professors and academicians at the House of the Scientist, and finally, late at night, perform for actors in Cinema

House or artists holding their celebrations at the Central House of Art Workers.

Were I to take sound-recording equipment with me and record a given item at each of these shows, it would be found that all the recordings differed. There would be differences in the power of the voice, in the length of a given phrase or pause in a given intonation, and in the reactions of the spectators, even if the item had been successful at each show.

These differences do not arise because I consciously alter the manner of performance according to the composition of the audience, whether elderly professors or young students, all men, as happens when I am performing to military units, or all only women as at the textile mill. No. These differences arise spontaneously and unconsciously out of the different kinds of contacts.

It is true that I find it almost impossible to detect any fluctuations in the character of the performance. But when I watch other actors I can always see the measure of this fluctuation. I am not speaking of fluctuations in quality, which are also possible and often depend on the spectators' reaction. I am speaking of inner differences in execution when qualitative evaluations do not differ at all. I would suppose that the more talented an actor, the fewer fluctuations he has and at the same time the greater the range of difference between his performances.

I often heard Vasily Kachalov in concert performances. He was excellent every time but always in a different way.

That matchless voice of his sounded different each time. Different too was that amazing process of creating a phrase, and every visual image evoked by the word. One had the impression that Kachalov was not merely speaking but thinking aloud and that the words one heard were only a part of what he was seeing with his inner eye. For that reason people did not merely listen to Kachalov, they watched what he was talking about.

When he read Tolstoi's *Resurrection* they saw quite plainly the train which bore Nekhlyudov away and the wooden platform, and Katyusha Maslova running along that wooden platform.

I often appear at concerts where many other actors are on the bill. Usually I know them all pretty well as I have appeared with them dozens, indeed hundreds of times over a period of many years. All the same, I am often to be found in the wings watching and listening and that not only when some "novice" turns up in the programme but when someone I specially like puts on a regular, familiar number.

I love to hear the precise and sensitive way Valeria Barsova tries her remarkable voice.

I have heard her sing Alyabyev's "Nightingale" at a workers' club, in the Hall of Columns at the House of the Unions, and on the stage of Sofia's Opera House. She never repeated herself. She sounded altogether unique at the benefit performance in honour of Ivan Moskvin when she went up to the old actor, laid her hands on his shoulders and sang "The Nightingale," addressing every note and every word to Moskvin alone, though every note and every word was audible to the whole audience too.

Rina Zelyonaya, the child impersonator, performs short tales and poems. The point is not that she impersonates children excellently, catching every intonation. Many people can do that, but I have never seen anybody so good at showing child psychology, at revealing the soul of a child, anybody who can show the child theme with so much tenderness and nobleness that the whole auditorium falls in love with that child.

Although Rina Zelyonaya's performances always arouse laughter they demand great concentration and attention from the public, for each of her stories is a mosaic of very delicately observed intonations and mimicry.

However, it is not always easy to hold the attention of the spectator, for the actor often has to overcome a mood created by the preceding number.

At concerts for some special occasion or celebration there are often performances by large troupes like the Soviet Army Song and Dance Troupe, the Pyatnitsky Russian Choir, or the Moiseyev Folk Dance Troupe.

Picture the finale of a number figuring a troupe of dancers. A Ukrainian folk dance. Moiseyev's inexhaustible imagination as a producer creates a new choreographic combination every moment, a new mise en scene, new rhythms. Brilliant costumes, the swirl of skirts and ribbons, red-hot temperament, the drumming of heels, the shrill music of the accordions, excited applause in the auditorium, shouts of "bravo" and "encore"—and every encore more inventive and temperamental than the one that preceded it.

The dance ends. The curtain falls. And while the stage is being made ready for another number the compère announces Rina Zelyonaya.

The actress comes out in front of the curtain. She looks small and lost after all those things that are still alive in the eyes and ears of the audience.

It does not seem possible that the audience will listen to her, let alone understand what she has to say.

I stand in the wings and, moving the edge of the curtain back a little, watch that astonishing and complicated process by which the actress fights for the audience's attention. She has the whole auditorium against her. One against a thousand. At first sight it looks an unequal, a hopeless contest but the actress has at her disposal not only the audience's affection for her but also her mastery of her art.

She speaks her first lines very carefully. Quieter than usual, perhaps. Her gestures are equally careful, more so than usually.

The audience begins to listen and watch, and gradually silence is restored. Attention is focussed on this small woman who is no longer a lost figure, but the only one. It is almost as though you can see the big hall shrinking in size. Her quiet voice sounds loud, although in fact she has not raised it. Now not only every word but every sigh is audible.

After Rina Zelyonaya comes Vladimir Khenkin. Again I find it hard to leave my observation post. I know all Khenkin's repertoire practically by heart, but I always like to see the way he modifies the stories he tells.

The strength of Khenkin's talent lies in the completeness with which he identifies himself with the audience.

You cannot say that Khenkin recites any more than you can say he performs. He "relates," making himself at once the hero and the author of his stories, whoever's stories they may actually be.

You feel that not only the words but the content and even the theme have only just occurred to him as he walks on.

And though he rarely improvises he always seems to be doing so, because his intonation always depends on the reaction of the audience to his previous line, as if he were replying to it. Moreover, he addresses himself not to the auditorium as a whole but to individual people in it. Sometimes to a married couple in the front row of the stalls, sometimes to a group of students in the balcony, sometimes to a box and sometimes into the wings where the firemen stand spluttering with laughter.

Khenkin's enormously lively temperament, his extraordinary sensitivity to the audience's reactions, and his faultlessy efficient "radar" set impart a special character to his performances.

Imagine a tennis player who could take on single-handed a hundred opponents at once.

Imagine that for every ball he sends over the net dozens come flying back into his court from all over the place, and imagine him returning every one of them without fail.

That is what a Khenkin performance looks like.

He flings a phrase across the footlights and immediately catches the reaction of each member of the audience to it.

He never misses a single one. He takes every ball. He does not even miss a creaking door. He catches it with his voice or by a turn of the head or by a surprised arch of the brow.

Khenkin is never taken unawares; he turns every response from the audience into dialogue and weaves it into his own story. I once saw Khenkin perform at a concert for the company of the Theatre of Satire where he himself worked.

With that slightly hurried gait of his he walked to the middle of the stage and took in the whole auditorium with a rapid glance I knew what that glance meant. He had a "hard-boiled" audience before him. People who knew him well. His friends, companions in many a play and concert. It was going to be difficult to "play tennis" with them. It might not come off. He might get an indirect reaction and that would introduce a false note.

But before I had time to reflect Khenkin smiled faintly at somebody in the third row. That was enough for people sitting in the first two rows to look round to see whom he was greeting. By then Khenkin would be looking at someone else, at the side. And again a few people would involuntarily look that way. The "tennis match," in fact, had begun and after Khenkin's first few lines I knew he had nothing to fear from that "hard-boiled" audience because they were fully extended in this extraordinarily exciting championship match in which he was always the winner and the vanquished were always happy.

Even when the actor is subordinated to a strict melody or musical pattern, to a precise rhythm or movement, he finds various ways of performing. I always find it very interesting and instructive to see how the dancers Anna Redel and Mikhail Khrustalyov broaden their movements when dancing on the wide stage of the Chaikovsky Hall and how compact the same movements become when they gain a fresh charm on the small stage of the House of the Actor.

I have spoken of these matters not because I wanted to assess the value of my comrades' performances but merely to use them as examples in order to explain that sense of variety and uniqueness which an actor experiences every time he performs. Thanks to that alone he is able to sing the same song, act the same role or dance the same dance over and over again.

I have no idea for I have never counted them how many people I have shown my puppets to in thousands of concerts during all those years; but, it must long since have passed the million mark, without including those who have seen me in the cinema.

But however many times I have performed a given item I have never been bored, for each time I performed it afresh.

As long as the audience finds that item interesting it cannot bore me. That would be a contradiction of the very nature of the actor's feelings.

The joy of making contact with one's audiences is a great one, and I am happy to have experienced that joy so often.

First Concerts

However, if I say that I am happy because I have so often felt the joy of performance it does not at all mean that I have not experienced the misery of failure. I have already said something about that.

For every actor, however great his experience and skill, even a little failure is a wound that does not heal easily or quickly. And when the failure is a big one, a flop, the actor simply gets ill.

I too have had to drink this bitter cup. I too have been wounded by my failures and have suffered grievously as the result of flops, yet that has never succeeded in diminishing the sense of joy I have derived from most of my contacts with audiences; I have known happiness throughout the twenty-five years of my professional work on the concert stage. It is a happiness comparable, perhaps, to that of a successful marriage when the love one feels on the first day lasts for a quarter of a century.

But what should I consider the first day of this "marriage" of mine? That is very hard to decide.

I have told you that my "love affair" with the puppet began imperceptibly. That often happens with real love affairs too. At first two people find it pleasant merely to chat. Then they want to meet more often, and idle chatter turns into serious talk about work and life. And then meetings become indispensable and absence becomes unbearable. That is love. And then there is no more separation and meetings merge into an unbroken life line. That is marriage.

That is what happened to me. At first I was content to "chat" with my puppets, then the theme of our "conversations" became broader and periods of separation grew shorter till, finally, it was clear that I was in love. Then we parted no more and I was married—I had found my profession. I suppose I ought to consider December 31, 1923, as the day I registered my marriage, for that was the day of my first performance. In that case the registration was unsuccessful. I almost flopped. All I got from that concert was some money and a sense of shame. And shame always weighs more than any amount of money. I think the reason why I got over that sense of shame fairly easily was, first, because I did not seriously consider my first concert for money to be the beginning of my profession and, secondly, because the failure was not the puppets' fault. I was performing at a New Year's Eve party. My screen stood in the corner of a small hall without a single chair or bench in it. A few people stood in front of the screen and the rest of the people walked about behind them talking at the top of their voices without being able to see anything over the heads of the others.

My "home theatricals" cured me completely from the effects of this failure.

But beginning from 1926-27 professional concerts became more and more frequent with every month, every week that passed.

In September 1927, I gave one concert only. In October two, in November seven. By April the next year the number had increased to twenty-two, in December to thirty-nine and in April 1929 to forty-six, that is, about three concerts every two days.

At first, the appearance on the concert stage of a man carrying a screen, who for some reason intended showing puppets to grown-ups, evoked a stir of incredulity among the audience; sometimes I even heard sarcastic remarks; but nearly always the scepticism vanished after the first number, and when I emerged from behind my screen I would be met with friendly looks; it was obvious that the ice was broken.

Gradually Moscow audiences grew used to this new concert genre, and to my name; now I could count on being greeted with applause, not only on being rewarded with it at the end of my turn. All the professional signs of a "hit" were apparent. On the bills I was transferred from the category of "And Others" to name-bearing actors, and later went into what is known as the "red line." Compères stopped announcing me early in the programme and moved me into the middle, not being afraid even of letting my turn come right before the interval. More and more were the days when I had more offers than I could accept and had to turn them down.

The whole thing happened so quickly that I took it as something quite strange and elemental, though terribly exciting and jolly. I simply could not get used at once to this profession that had dropped on me out of the blue, and at first I was terribly afraid of appearing in large halls. I remember very well how I went on turning down offers to appear in the Hall of Columns because I thought it was absurd to appear there with my tiny puppets. Now, after having performed hundreds of times there, I consider it one of the easiest of places to show them in.

I remember how terrified I felt when I was invited to appear daily for six weeks at the Music Hall (now the Operetta Theatre), though I must say that it was those concerts which established me, for immediately after that season I was approached by a manager from Leningrad with a contract for a summer season at the variety theatre in the Leningrad Recreation Park. The terms were more attractive than anything I had ever dreamed of. They were so good that they not only delighted me, they worried me. I was afraid that after my very first appearance in a new city, where absolutely no one had ever heard of me, it would be quite clear that I was not worth the money I was being paid.

These anxieties became greater when, on arriving in Leningrad, I saw, stretching across the entire width of the Nevsky Prospekt, near the park, a banner bearing my name in enormous letters, and up against the iron railings of the park itself huge plywood cut-outs, at least three times life-size, representing two of my puppets.

Never before—nor after—did I have such a brash advertisement.

However, the first performance went well, and since then I have often appeared for summer seasons at the Leningrad Park. I know nearly all the Leningrad clubs too, quite as well as the Moscow ones, and though in recent years I have been appearing in considerably more important solo concerts, the memories of my first impressions of my Leningrad debut are still fresh. They belong to the memories of the exciting days of my professional youth when anxiety, joy and surprise at the unexpected growth of my profession were tightly knit together.

Memory's Diary

Nothing is of more fundamental importance to an artist than his visual capacity, the power of seeing life around in all its manifestations, of seeing both what is significant in it and what at first sight seems insignificant and accidental, and of "registering" what he sees so that he can grasp and understand the links between the great and the small and realize that the small often contains something very large, and vice versa.

Before one can learn to make a work of art one has to learn to see life. And the more sides of life the artist sees the broader his power of generalization, the richer the content of his images.

In this respect the profession of variety-artist has one noteworthy advantage. The very fact that he is always touring provides him with the opportunity of seeing much. Every concert at a factory, every performance to a military unit or to students or academicians, every visit to a new town, to a new republic, to a new country is significant for the actor, not only because he is meeting a new audience, but also because of the life that is going on all round. He meets life everywhere: in his travelling companions in the train or aircraft, on the rivers and in the clouds, in the steppes and in the mountains, in the streets of cities, in the rhythm of everyday events, in the noise of factories, in meeting people of various professions, feelings, ages, and nationalities.

It is no easy task to follow how and when what one sees will later on become material for one's work; the melting down of experience into artistic images is in many respects a subconscious process.

Everyone's memory has its unwritten diary—a diary thousands of pages long. Some of those pages are mixed up, some have been torn out of the diary. Many entries are hard to decipher, many are blurred. Where confusion is greatest is over dates, names of people and places, and addresses.

The memory is sometimes careless about documents and facts, but it preserves images with the thoroughness of a collector. Images of whole decades, images of particular days and hours of our lives, images of feelings, of events, of people. It records them in amazing detail, preserving colours, scents and sounds. If you work in art you need not regret the missing pages in memory's diary. In any case they would not have been usable. But when you read through the pages that have survived, read them carefully. Do not rewrite them, do not change a word or a line, for they are precious pages. The memory can make factual mistakes but it never lies. It is an accurate register of the emotions and it is highly doubtful whether you can improve on it.

Besides, our memories do a great deal of work for us, not only in discarding what is useless but in sorting our perceptions. They unite things that are of the same family, they separate things that have nothing in common, and, reminding us of some event or person, they supply all the necessary footnotes, and always in the form of concrete images.

My memory's diary preserves a record of many concerts, cities, clubs, theatres and audiences, but each record is different. In one case I remember my sensations at the very moment of performance, in another I remember nothing of the performance but recall very clearly the place where it was given and that place itself has become an image, whether it be a factory shop, the deck of a warship or an improvised stage made out of office desks in some club.

Some concerts I recall in the image of the whole auditorium and its reaction as a whole to my performance, others linger in my memory in the shape of a single person, but when that is so that person has left no less of an impression on me than meeting thousands of people.

I cannot write down every page in my concert diary but I want to tell you about a few concerts, which I shall describe as I remember them. For that reason the performance itself may take a quite insignificant place in some of these descriptions.

There is one group of concerts which can be described simply as "student concerts."

It is a large group. Student concerts usually come in big batches, several in one evening; they take place either in the autumn at the beginning of term, or during the winter vacation or in spring when the new-fledged graduates are celebrating. They are wonderful concerts. Of all the images that my memory preserves they are the happiest and loveliest. They leave in my memory an integral image of youth, of health, of happiness. And of the future, I ought to add. That is true, no matter what the name of the college or institute I have come to perform at, no matter what profession my audience is going to take up in the future—chemistry or teaching, power-engineering or medicine, history or agronomy. I have only to list those professions to see in my mind's eye the streets, the buildings, the halls: the spacious club of Moscow University with the little spiral staircase up to the stage, the square auditorium of the Teachers' Training College on Devichye Polye Street, the high amphitheatre and gallery in the Higher Party School on Miusskaya Square. The image of the audience, however, which fills these halls and auditoriums is a single one, and the word "future" is the most significant one in describing it. These people are preparing themselves for life. And not only for their own private lives, but for the life of their country. Their eyes glow with a happy dream. Not an abstract dream but one that can be fulfilled, because the future they dream of is their own.

There is always something festive and gay about performing to students. However often you do it you never grow tired of it. I always want to prolong such concerts, to show every puppet I have lying in my suit-case behind the screen.

This sense of happiness is made up of many elements.

First there is the audience's sensitiveness and devoted attention. Not only do they applaud hard enough to bring the house down, shout themselves hoarse and laugh so heartily that you feel a smile coming to your lips as you sing. The main thing is that they watch you and listen to you so attentively, that a gale of laughter will be followed immediately by a hush as tense as if the hall were utterly empty.

On these occasions every word you sing spells happiness and every gesture of the puppets means joy. And you sing the better for it and you act more subtly, more sensitively.

But the joyful nature of these concerts lies not only in the actor's emotions during performance. You have a feeling towards the audience as if they were your own children, your own pupils. And this feeling is all the stronger when the concert is part of the celebrations of students who have just taken their finals.

Then the faces of your audience are inspired by a great event—the road to life has been opened to them. I see boys and girls strolling during the interval in the foyer and corridors, people who that very day have become doctors, agronomists or architects; they write down each other's addresses, and walk together excitedly in groups or pairs, perhaps for the last time.

Tomorrow they will be setting out for places all over the country. They will take with them their formulae of chemical reactions, their knowledge about the resistance of materials or of the integral calculus. And they will take a little of me with them too. I too have been a part of their lives during these years. I know that from the way they receive me and by the way they take their leave of me. In their applause, in their shouts, in the little notes they pass up with requests to sing the Chaikovsky number or "Return," in their insistence that I encore the "Tiger Tamer," I feel their "encores" to be words of farewell too.

So now memories of my Tiger or my "Habanera" are about to scatter all over the country. To Tomsk and Kuibyshev, to Arkhangelsk and Chita and Astrakhan. And it seems to me that I too have made my contribution to these young people's knowledge. True, my contribution is not in the form of formulae or numbers but of images and themes, of perceptions of certain aspects of life, which will also be of some use to them among those images they have formed from the books they have read and the plays and films they have seen. Of course they will be of use to them, provided they remain in their memories' diaries as these splendid Soviet students have remained in mine.

Some concerts, however, stick in my memory in the form of a single person who appears to combine in himself the image of the whole audience. Perhaps that is because memory has discarded all the rest.

I do not recall what year it was before the war when I flew with a group of Moscow actors to take part in some concerts connected with the opening of a new factory in the Ukraine. I have clean forgotten what I performed, but I brought back from that trip the image of a man whom I first noticed sitting in the front row of the stalls. He had a very infectious laugh. On the following day I went to the rolling mill. A man in stained trousers, stripped to the waist, was swiftly wielding his black iron hook and guiding the brightly glowing strip of white-hot steel. The muscles in his naked torso bulged as they do only in books on anatomy. His face wore a look of such intense concentration that I would never have recognized him as that man in the stalls had he not flashed a smile at me. "Flashed" is the word, for he had no time for more.

The next day I was his guest in a room with a well-scrubbed floor, clean rugs and a dining-table covered by a starched white cloth. He wore a suit which concealed his muscles; only his eyes and his powerful hands spoke of his love for that newly opened steel mill.

I was pleased to have had this man in my audience. I liked hearing the amusing and serious things he had to say about my performance. I was glad he and others like him needed me at their celebrations and that I had taken part in the events.

The image of a whole profession, summed up in one person, is often stronger than the sum of observations of separate people. I have given many performances for doctors—at hospitals, at medical colleges, in conference halls during congresses.

I do not remember at what concert it happened, and I do not know why that surgeon in the audience thought I ought to watch him conduct an operation. I turned up at his hospital and before I knew it I was wearing a white smock, a little cap and a mask, and was standing in the operating theatre with the professor and his students, all dressed the same way, like a lot of conspirators in a detective film. All I could see of my companions was their eyes glittering through the slits in their masks.

On the operating table an unknown person lay under a sheet; my former spectator, his long rubber-gloved fingers moving with calm efficiency, rapidly moved aside his patient's intestines, clipped something, sewed something, put the stomach back in place and, turning to his assistants, said: "You can sew him up now."

Then he took me round the wards and I saw the people who owed him their lives, people who might have died but who were now alive. Little children, young boys and girls, old men and women. He addressed every one of them familiarly, he knew their names, he loved them and they loved him for it. There was hope or gratitude in every eye that met his; they were the eyes of children. And I began to understand the reason for the love a child has for its mother, and a mother has for her child. I understood the reason for a mother's pride.

And now, whenever I come out on to the concert stage before an audience of doctors, I always remember that surgeon and the patients in his wards.

Every time I take the stage at a concert I always feel some anticipatory nervousness. Every actor feels this. It takes different forms and it varies in intensity, but it is almost always a healthy, creative nervousness.

Sometimes it is coloured by the events of the day, by the celebration in honour of which the concert is being held. It may be a national holiday or the local celebration of a town, a factory, or some institution or other. Then the sense of excitement in the auditorium affects us actors too. It may be the anniversary of the establishment of Soviet government in Byelorussia, or of the defeat of Hitler's armies at Stalingrad; it may be the arrival of a foreign youth delegation or the finals of an international chess tournament, or the end of a national athletic contest. Taking the stage I meet all kinds of people, all kinds of eyes and temperaments. Members of the government of Union Republic; generals and officers of the armed forces in parade dress wearing all their medals; foreigners, who every few minutes ask something of their interpreters, who have no time to reply because they too are interested in watching the stage; chess-players who talk in the intervals about time-troubles and gambits I understand little about; athletes of many nationalities, who have not yet cooled down from their leaping and running and hurling the discus and who hold cups and prizes and diplomas they have been presented with just before the concert.

Sometimes creative nervousness is crowded out by a sense of impending danger. The danger of failure. You may fear that the auditorium is too deep, or that the lighting is inadequate or that it is too late and that people will have to hurry away for the last tram or train on the Underground.

Generally speaking, all these "technical dangers" have a harmful effect on the performance, for they are hard to master. You cannot bring people sitting far from the stage any closer to you by performing well, nor can you increase the power of the lighting or stop the clock.

But there are "dangers" which mobilize and reinforce your creative emotions.

One is the "danger" of severe criticism. To some degree that exists at every concert. But it is all the greater if the audience is made up of people who are themselves employed in some branch of art—musicians, artists, writers, or actors.

I have to give many concerts of that sort. I am constantly performing at the Central House of Art Workers, the House of Architects, the House of Writers, the House of the Actor.

I have mixed feelings about these concerts. You cannot help feeling a special sense of responsibility when on coming out before the footlights you meet the searching look of familiar eyes, and recognize Goldenveizer, Shostakovich, Ulanova, Maretskaya, Birman, Zavadsky, Marshak, Ilya Ehrenburg or such severe critics and reliable friends as Moskvin, Tarkhanov or Alexei Tolstoi were for me.

I set up my screen, slip the puppets over my hands and realize that every false note, every scrap of bad taste, every trace of showing-off would be noticed by these critics, and that I should feel quite ashamed even if they failed to mention it to me. And, of course, they will most certainly mention it—immediately after the concert, or, it may be, later, when we meet at a party, or at another evening like this.

This sense of responsibility enhances my pleasure in the performance and my satisfaction if it turns out to be a success.

But the danger and the responsibility are even greater if the performance is addressed to a single man and if that man happens to be a really serious judge of quality, a really "dangerous" critic. Dangerous, because you will believe absolutely in his verdict.

Naturally I was very alarmed, though I was also very pleased, when during the winter of 1935 Afinogenov, the dramatist, handed me an invitation from Maxim Gorky to visit him at Sosny and show him my puppets.

Sosny lies outside Moscow. Gorky's country house was situated amidst pine woods on the steep bank of the Moskva River.

As our car rocked along the snow-clad road I remembered the time Gorky came to a concert at the Music Hall. I do not recall who told me the story and I cannot vouch for its accuracy, but what I had heard both amused and alarmed me.

Among other numbers in the programme was one called "The Girls" in which several girls appeared together. They were all the same height, the same build, wore the same make-up and the same clothes, and they all danced the same rhythmical steps.

They were "trained girls," and the whole idea of the number lay in the precise timing of every movement and in the lack of individuality of each dancer.

During the interval Gorky went back stage. The dancers crowded round him. They asked him how he had liked their number. Gorky thought for a while and then said with some embarrassment: "You've done a lot of hard, difficult and quite useless work." I don't know whether those were his actual words, but I know it is the sort of thing he could have said, for Gorky had a serious, earnest attitude to art.

So I was afraid that after I had shown him all my puppets Gorky would get up and say exactly the same to me.

However, when I had performed for him the number with the balls on my "naked" hands and coming out from behind the screen saw Gorky wiping tears of laughter from his merry eyes, my anxieties vanished.

Gorky did not tell me that my work was of no use to anybody; on the contrary, my puppets went down very well with him and when he came to give me advice it was more in the order of thinking aloud about the possibility of making the puppets' acting more telling and pointed. But, he added, "I cannot give you any advice on concrete examples or a concrete repertoire: you are working organically, you are on the right inner lines. No too concrete advice coming from an outsider can be of any use to you."

I have written in my first book about this meeting with Gorky; but the sense of joy and pride it gave me arises in me again whenever I think of that house at Sosny.

Everything about that house seemed marvellous to me at that time; it had such a warm, cosy, family spirit. And there was Gorky himself telling me merrily over the tea-table how he was afraid of tea with "tadpoles" in it (that was his name for the tea-leaves), and going to bed obediently at eleven o'clock, the moment he was reminded that "Doctor didn't allow him to stay up later"; and there were his grandchildren—two little girls, Darya and Marfa, and the other members of his family sitting round the table.

That visit to Gorky's place was frightening enough in anticipation; but I was just as anxious and alarmed when I had to perform for Stanislavsky.

That was as long ago as 1927. I was asked to take part in a concert arranged by the Association of Friends of the Stanislavsky Studio.

I knew that there was a possibility of Stanislavsky turning up at this concert and for that reason did not accept the invitation at once. In those days I respected Stanislavsky's pre-eminence in the theatre world no less than I do now. If his verdict on my puppets were to be unfavourable I would take it as a severe blow. On the other hand, if he liked my performance, his "visa" would make me feel enormously happy. In the end my wish to show Stanislavsky my puppets overcame my fear and I accepted.

I showed "Just a Minute," "The Titular Counsellor" and "The Deacon." In short, practically all my repertoire at that time.

After the concert Stanislavsky came up to me and congratulated me on my work. I was happy.

However, when, eight years later, in 1935, I had to perform once more before Stanislavsky I was, if anything, even more alarmed at the prospect. That was understandable. In 1927, after all, I was only twenty-six, an age at which one takes risks lightly. Besides, at that time I did not feel that puppeteering was the one and only thing in my life. It was a side-line, an interesting one, of course, but definitely a side-line; whereas now in 1935 it was my work in the legitimate theatre that I considered a side-line and the puppets the main thing. So I was risking very much in submitting my puppets to Stanislavsky's judgement once more.

I had the more reason to feel alarmed because my second appearance before Stanislavsky was not a regular concert one. It took place in Stanislavsky's house in Leontievsky Street. A group of actors, members of the Theatre Club, were going to see Stanislavsky in order to have a talk with him about the theatre and to tell him what we were doing; afterwards, as a mark of gratitude, we were going to stage a short concert.

That is what made me feel more anxious than anything else. We knew each other's repertoires off by heart. I was afraid that my comrades would not react to my puppets, that they would watch them without a single laugh. In the absence of reaction from the audience I might act badly, and then Stanislavsky would think I was never any good.

And that is what would have happened if Stanislavsky had not possessed that quality—rare among producers—of being absolutely direct in his reactions as a spectator.

He laughed as sincerely, as loud and merrily as I could have hoped for from the best audience, though, really, my audience on this occasion consisted of Stanislavsky alone.

It was a wonderful occasion from beginning to end.

All of us entered the house in a mood of solemn exaltation.

We gathered in the big room which was fitted up for rehearsals, as Stanislavsky's state of health confined him to his house where he used to hold his classes.

We took our seats quietly and spoke in whispers: we felt moved at the thought that we were going to see Stanislavsky in the flesh.

Stanislavsky came into the room. We rose to our feet to greet him, feeling even more excited. And, indeed, he did look extraordinary. His frame was enormous, very gaunt but well-proportioned, and somehow he seemed to glitter. His white hair glittered, the skin of his face glittered, his eyes glittered under the white brows.

We greeted him and sat round a big table. The conversation started. The oldest of us was young enough to have been Stanislavsky's son, yet Stanislavsky was the youngest of us all.

Every phrase, every thought was young. Though he had dozens of years of professional work behind him, Stanislavsky spoke about the theatre as if he had only just started working in it and the most important and significant work lay ahead, with all that he had done being mere preparation for it.

One cannot learn to be a genius. One cannot learn to be a Stanislavsky. All the same one must learn from him. But not only how to "work with actors." Of that nothing will come though you master all the rules of the "grain," and the "subtext." Nothing will come out unless the student possesses the main thing that Stanislavsky possessed: youthfulness in the perception of life, a keen sense of the truth, the will to struggle uncompromisingly for it, and an absolute faith in one's cause. Those things, of course, are not easily learned, but on coming back from Stanislavsky's house that day I could think of nothing else. I thought how necessary it was for every artist to see the world with open eyes, without fear or prejudice, and to believe in his cause, in the path he has chosen, not because it is his but because it is the only right one for him.

You can have this kind of faith only if you feel that your work is necessary—necessary not for yourself but for others.

The joy of personal success is real and complete only when a man sees his success as a confirmation of the fact that he is needed; the greatest tragedy for anyone is not failure or lack of recognition on the part of others but the loss of his faith that what he is doing is needed.

This desire to be needed was enhanced and sharpened in everyone during the war. It was especially frightening to think that at this very time everything you had grown accustomed to doing and had learned to do might suddenly seem unnecessary.

At the outbreak of war I started working with the company of our theatre on a special anti-fascist programme for a group to take to the front. However, I did not feel quite certain that it would really meet the needs of the country and the army. I felt all the time that I was only trying to justify the work of our theatre to other people. And I began to lose my respect for the work and for myself.

It was only when we performed to a new, military public and saw the reaction that my sense of being useful returned.

We had to perform many times. At recruiting stations, in barracks, on station platforms, in munitions works, at pit-heads, hospitals and at the front itself.

It would be difficult to list all these concerts and quite impossible to describe them. So I will tell you only about those which live most clearly and vividly in my memory's diary.

1941. A war hospital. Doctors and nurses in white smocks. The blue-lapelled grey dressing-gowns of the wounded men. A concert is in progress for those who can get to the hospital club-room.

Several are wheeled there.

The concert goes well, in a jolly atmosphere. True, not everyone can applaud. Some have both hands bandaged, but if one hand is sound they applaud by slapping it on their knee. Two bright fellows co-operate in the applause each providing one hand which they clap like children playing a game. It is not easy to see such things. One has to get used to them.

One young fellow, little more than a boy, is sitting in a wheel-chair, laughing as he watches the puppets. He has neither legs nor arms.

When I make my bow I try to look away, then I realize that I mustn't. That would be cowardly and wrong. And when among other numbers I show my Tyapa I take up my stance right in front of this young man so that he can see better; he rocks with laughter at the way Tyapa sucks his dummy.

In the wards lie many wounded men who cannot come to the club and who are too ill to be brought in wheel-chairs.

They hear that a concert is going on in the club and send a "delegation" asking us to perform in the wards.

The doctor tells us it is very necessary we should—more necessary than we imagine—and that for many patients our performance would be more important than medicine, that it will make them eat better and sleep sounder.

And from the look in his eyes we realize that he is not merely paying us a compliment but that he knows what he is talking about, knows it from his own professional observations.

So we go from ward to ward, giving a performance every time. I performed eleven times that day. Those who could, sat up in bed to watch me. Those who could not lift their heads from the pillow were able to see when their beds were tilted.

In one ward a patient who had just been operated on lay groaning in his bed. I said to the doctor: "Perhaps it would be better if I don't perform here. I'd rather the rest missed the concert than upset a seriously wounded man." But the doctor said: "No, you must perform. It's just what he needs." And I did not hear a single groan during my performance, and when I came from behind the screen I saw the man's eyes looking at me searchingly, seriously. Then he suddenly smiled, turned his head to the man in the next bed and said with a laugh: "Clap for me."

In another ward lay two men. They were mortally injured. The doctor had told me that, and added that I must not fail to perform for them.

I did so. And afterwards I saw two faces full of life. Two happy faces.

Never in my life have I given a concert to an audience of only two, but never have I felt my profession and my work to be more useful than it was on that occasion.

I felt these worries about my usefulness again when our group of actors left Moscow in a military lorry to give a concert at the front.

That was in the summer of 1942. The lorry took us through country I remembered well from my childhood days. I knew every river, every village road and the main roads with big lime-trees dating back to Catherine II's time, the little towns with churches on the hill-tops. I knew every village.

How strange it was to be driving through these places, so dear and familiar, and yet not to recognize them. Iron tank-obstacles stood piled up at the cross-roads, little wooden bridges spanned the broad ravines, damaged tanks rusted beside the roads and in the wet, muddy ditches. Houses became rarer as we drove on. Entire villages had been reduced to remnants of villages and farther on the road was lined by nothing but Russian stoves with long chimneys looking surprisingly white because the snow and the rain had washed off the charred traces of the fires. Thirty chimneys on the right of the road, thirty chimneys on the left. That had been a village. We dropped to the river. The iron bridge lay toppled over like a damaged model in a museum. Beside it stood a clean new wooden bridge smelling of resin.

Beyond the river stretched a field of yellow, full-eared rye dotted with peaceful-looking corn-flowers. The driver told us we had reached the front. Hard to believe. Surely this was not the front! What were corn-flowers doing there?

And as if to settle our doubts something unexpected happened: a fascist aircraft darted like a small dragon-fly out of the clouds and the field is momentarily split with the roar of anti-aircraft fire. There were many guns there. They projected from among the rye like sticks.

The aircraft circles and flies back into the clouds.

Now it is clear that this is the front and that the corn-flowers really are out of place.

We drive into the woods. They are tranquil woods with birch-trees and firs and aspens with leaves atremble. There are wild strawberries in the glades, red and ripe and probably very sweet.

The driver brakes and sings out gaily: "Here we are." "Where?" "Where we were told to come: the tank corps."

Odd. There's not a tank to be seen. Where is the corps? I can see nothing but wild strawberries.

We walk along a path. A sentry pops out from behind a tree but the lieutenant who is leading our party says something to him and the sentry disappears.

We walk on and gradually realize that the strawberries like the cornflowers are quite out of place too.

We pass a shelter screened with branches of odorous fir and some camouflaged tanks. Ahead of us we see a little house built out of thin aspen trunks. You would have to look at the pictures in children's fairytale books to find houses as small as that. Rightly speaking there ought to be a cock, a cat and a fox living in it but it turns out to have been built for us. There are gauze curtains at the windows. On the table a bunch of wild flowers sticks out of a shellcase. The nurse gathered them for us. Daisies and round yellow marsh bells.

We have to report our arrival to the chief of staff. I go farther on down the path. I know the password. The sentry lets me through, with a smile for my civilian dress.

I had been told the route to take: "Go along the Kreshchatik, carry on till you reach the corner of Nevsky, turn left and you'll find headquarters"

And, believe it or not, the winding paths have their names. I see little notices nailed to the trees and, written on them, words like Kreshchatik, Nevsky, Sadovaya, Naberezhnaya and the names of other famous city streets. There has to be some way of marking the ways through the woods so the paths have to be named.

The people who live in those woods have come from all over the country, from many cities, and they have named the paths after their favourite streets. They are defending the whole land, every one of its cities, and so there is nothing surprising in the fact that the streets of various cities they hold dear should cross and recross in these woods.

Leningrad is still besieged, Kiev still in German hands, but we hold our concert on the corner of the Kreshchatik and the Nevsky, their main streets.

Dusk was falling when we finished, and late that night the whole wood became alive with the sound of cracking timber, the clanking of iron and cries of voices raised in command. The tank corps was going up into the line. We could hear the roar of artillery, the explosions of shells.

And then I understood why the corps commander and his chief of staff had been so glad to see us and why, while watching the concert, they had kept on glancing at their men and why they thanked us so warmly when we had finished.

It was a great honour to perform to a tank corps on the eve of battle. A year later I visited Iran.

From battle-girt Moscow, so austere, so united and purposeful, a group of Soviet artists flew over forest and steppe, over the Caspian and the snow-crested mountains to Teheran. We landed in a city that was half-Europe, half-Asia, where dirty ditches ran at the edge of asphalted streets with plate-glass shop-windows, where Fiats and Buicks overtook donkeys so heavily laden that one expected their fragile legs to break at any moment, where the reckless motor-cyclist is met by the swaying, bell-hung camel looking something like a cross between a bear and a swan.

People of all nationalities, of all colours and all types of dress mingled like illustrations to an ethnographic atlas. Men wearing fezzes or turbans, in service caps with or without cockades, in sun helmets, in silk hats, felt hats, caps. Women in silk, their eyebrows plucked in the latest European style, and women wearing veils or cotton shawls, their frightened eyes looking out. Old men like Magi or apostles out of the Bible.

Our first concert was for the Soviet colony.

We got a wonderful reception. Indeed, the stock phrase is scarcely applicable to the warmth that flowed to us from the audience. We were received as people from Moscow, people who had just been walking on the streets of Moscow, on the soil of Moscow. People who had come from "over there."

It was not merely a concert, that joyful, tender, boisterous meeting with friends on the festive eve of May Day.

After giving several concerts in Teheran we flew south. Over more mountains, still higher, looking from above like drawings by Gustave Doré for Dante's *Inferno*. Then desert. A river to the right, a river to the left. The Tigris and the Euphrates. I thought they flowed only in crossword puzzles and in the Old Testament, but here they were as large as life. Frozen blue serpents. And around them stood feather besoms. Whole woods of besoms growing in neat lines. Plantations of fig. We circle. A great river. Ocean-going ships. Factory chimneys. Another circle. Abadan tilts up, then slips away sideways. We land. It is a bit chilly in the aircraft, for we have been flying high. As the door opens the dense, sultry air bursts in. Bare-legged, sunburned foreigners in tropical uniform click Leicas at us. Then they put their cameras back into their cases, stretch their hands to us and say in the purest of Russian: "Hallo, Comrade Yakhontov! Hallo, Comrade Obraztsov! We expected you yesterday." They turned out to be Soviet airmen, men from Moscow, Leningrad and Kharkov. But how could we know that from their unusual rig-out? We were driven off in bouncy Jeeps to quarters that had been allotted to us—half-cylindrical little houses like tin cans cut in two and laid on their sides. And there we lived, dashing for the showers every few minutes and drinking ten litres of water a day. The temperature rose to 50° C. To console us our friends said: "This is nothing. In summer it rises to over 70°."

We had visitors for our first concert. Several lorry-loads of British and noisy Americans who expressed their appreciation by whistling and shouting.

A few days later at the request of our allies we drove by lorry to some remote military camp. The territory of the camp was fenced with separate sections for British, Americans and "Coloured."

We gave our concert at eight in the evening, in the open air, if one can call that hot boiled milk air. There were between four and five thousand in the audience. Arabs, Persians, Indians, Americans, British, Poles—we counted twelve nationalities. The searchlights brought clouds of mosquitoes and huge beetles down dead on to the stage. We had to sweep it clean after each turn. Bathed in sweat we gulped down water and thought tenderly of the Moscow winter.

During fifty days, inclusive of travel on land and by air, we gave sixty-six concerts. We covered the whole coast of Iranian Azerbaijan. We were in Tabriz and even in that narrow wedge of Iranian territory between Soviet Armenia and Turkey where the towns cling to the mountains like swallows' nests.

Our final concert took place in Teheran again, at the officers' club on the eve of our departure.

There were fountains playing in the garden. Green lawns. Ladies with trains to their dresses, ambassadors and military attachés, supper with all kinds of pilaff to eat, rows of cars in the street outside. Above, the southern sky with its slow sunrise. Then back to the hotel, off with our starched shirts, a hurried packing of our bags.

At five that morning we took off from Teheran and at six in the same evening we saw below us the streets of Moscow, the bridges, the Kremlin, the runways of the airfield.

We were at home for supper. Then I went to my desk. Outside the windows reigned the darkness of Moscow at war. I sat there till the sun began to rise again. The balloon barrage was slowly lowered. The silent silver sentries would spend the day sleeping under the foliage on the boulevards.

But performances abroad are linked in my mind not only with impressions of foreign lands, towns and people, not only with an actor's emotions before a new kind of public.

Strange as it may seem, foreign tours and performances are linked with special feelings about one's own country.

First, absence makes one's love for one's homeland stronger, more tangible; and secondly, one finds a reflection of one's own country in foreign lands. Differently in each case, of course, but there is no mistaking the recognition of its strength and importance that one sees in every look turned on us, in the guarded looks of enemies and the joyful looks of friends.

And if I had felt that more than twenty years before in Germany, Czechoslovakia and America, I experienced a particular sense of happiness when, during the war in which so much depended on the Soviet Union, and everyone—friend and foe alike—realized the vital importance of Moscow, I saw the Soviet Union from afar and felt proud to be a Soviet citizen. This sense of pride was something we all felt when in the spring of 1945 we made a big concert tour of the Balkans.

In Sofia our concerts became a part of a tremendous national celebration—that of the reunion of Slav brothers.

A Slav Congress was taking place. There were street processions with banners, decorated cars, orderly columns of trade unionists, dances in traditional costumes. Our concerts became something much more than mere performances. Artists and writers of Sofia before whom I appeared in a solo concert overwhelmed me with so many questions that I talked about the Soviet Union for over an hour. I told them about Moscow, about our theatres, our schools, about the discussions and concerts that take place in the House of the Actor, or the House of the Cinema, about the way we live and work and even about the way the buildings on Gorky Street were moved back on rails. What pleasant and joyful a feeling it gave me to be there, thousands of kilometres from Moscow, telling these eager listeners about my own country; how proud I felt to have the right to call it my own!

This feeling of being first and foremost a citizen of the Soviet Union and only after that an actor came to me perhaps even more strongly in Rumania where we happened to be during a period of transition in its political regime.

We could sense the internal struggle that was going on and sometimes it took external forms that were quite astonishing in their contrasts. It was highly interesting to look out of one's window in a Bucharest hotel and see a detachment of the royal guard marching to music in gold and silver uniforms laced with braid, and gleaming helmets surmounted with horse-tails; and close by, in the yard of a neighbouring building, a hurdy-gurdy playing our Russian Katyusha (when could the man possibly have made the new cylinder?).

The big cinema where we performed was always full to overflowing. People stood in the aisles, shouting and clapping. The moment the curtain fell the people sitting in the front rows sprang up and climbed on to the stage. They thrust fountain-pens at us like stilettos. They handed us open note-books, programmes, sheets of paper. There was no escaping their demand for autographs.

Though it is a long time ago since that Balkans tour I can see and feel every incident in it as though it were but yesterday. I remember the graves of our soldiers in the streets of Belgrade with the flowers and the little lamps that never go out on them. The flowers are changed every day by people who live in the neighbourhood, and the old women of Belgrade tend the lamps. The people of Belgrade greeted their Soviet visitors with embraces and looked at us with tears in their eyes. I felt that I had been in Yugoslavia and met these people before and that I was now coming back to them after a long absence.

On the main square at Skoplje the bank had been destroyed by a bomb. Long dark curtains fluttered from the windows and waved over the square like funeral drapes. On the opposite side of the square people had gathered to meet us—men, women and children carrying red apples and little bowls of home-made sweetmeats. These people begged us not to stay at the hotel. They took us by the arms and led us to their houses and gave us their best rooms, their best beds, and the best their kitchens could provide.

In my postscript to the chapter "In Foreign Lands" I wrote that not long ago the State Central Puppet Theatre made a tour of Poland and Czechoslovakia and that in two and a half months we gave 95 performances there. But besides the shows the theatre put on I gave over 50 solo concerts during that period. In Warsaw, Cracow, Lodz, Katowice, Bielsk, Wrocław; in Prague, Plzeň, Bratislava, Brno, Gottwaldov, Olomouc, Malaya Ostrava.

Sometimes these concerts were given in very large halls, sometimes in small club-rooms; some were in the shops of factories and some in university auditoria. There was not one concert where I did not feel myself to be first and foremost a Soviet citizen. And this complex emotion in which were mingled joy, pride and a vast sense of responsibility towards my own land could not be otherwise, for the audience too greeted me as a *Soviet* actor.

After a concert at Plzeň, workers of the engineering works that used to belong to Škoda came back stage and begged us to visit the works. On the next day we walked through kilometres of shops and factory yards passing furnaces, foundries and forges.

It was not because we were actors that the engineers and workers were so proud to show us their works but because we were Soviet people, representatives of the Soviet Union; and when they saw us off they asked us to convey their greetings to Soviet workers.

At concerts in Warsaw and Cracow, at Prague and Bratislava the big concert halls were packed.

The audiences laughed at my Dog and my Cats, they applauded "Habanera," "Tyapa" and "The Drunk," they encored me time without end, but it was not only to my own and my puppets' performance that I owed the success of my concerts but to that great love for the Soviet Union that flowed to me from the public.

So many people wanted to see the actor who had come from Moscow and I had so little time at my disposal that almost every day I had to perform late in the night for writers, architects, artists, teachers or actors, and every time those performances would end with dozens of questions about the Soviet Union, about Moscow, about our schools and factories, about our theatres and painting, about every aspect of Soviet life.

And telegrams and letters poured in on us from those towns we did not visit.

Sometimes it was quite painful to have to decline the invitation to perform extended either to the theatre as a whole or to me personally.

Here is an extract from a letter written by schoolboys from the small town of Chrudim, members of a Russian language group:

"Dear Sergei Vladimirovich,

"We, members of a Russian language group at the agricultural school at Chrudim, invite you very warmly to visit us before you leave for the Soviet Union. Our group is a very old one, it has formed three years ago. Since last autumn we have our own recital group. We know the poems of Pushkin, Mayakovsky, Surkov, Yanka Kupala, the fables of Krylov and Mikhalkov. We read Russian authors and are very interested in your theatre....

"We have just read that you are giving your last concert in Prague on Jan. 11 and then leaving. What about our country district? It isn't fair that only the big towns see your theatre. Why, at home you go right up into the Arctic Circle. Isn't that true? Please fulfil this request of Czech country boys.

"Come just for their sake. It will give us very great pleasure. And we will pass on our impressions to all our villages...."

Knowing that our theatre has its own museum all the puppet theatres of Poland and Czechoslovakia presented us with puppets, but I think the most precious and most symbolic of these gifts was one of six little marionettes made of bread.

These fragile puppets, carefully wrapped in cotton wool, reached me with a letter from a student named Georgi Tichy. I received them after a conference of puppeteers which was held in the auditorium of Josef Skupa's theatre. Puppeteers gathered there from various towns of Czechoslovakia.

The letter ran:

"Dear Comrade,

"My wife and I attended the conference at Skupa's theatre on December 26, 1948. That was a day that will ever remain in my memory because you fortified our determination to create a new, realistic art, and because it was the last day I spent with my wife.

"On the following day she died tragically."

The letter continued with the sad story of how his twenty-two-year-old wife Iola Potažniková had died as the result of an accident. Among her things her husband found several puppets made out of black bread in a nazi concentration camp in 1939, where at the age of thirteen the girl had been imprisoned with her father who was killed there.

The letter closed with the words:

"I am sending you these puppets so that you, comrades from the Soviet Union, should see that we too have fought and are still fighting for a better life so that our children can live better and breathe more freely."

These precious little puppets were sent not to me and not to our theatre, but to the Soviet people, to the Soviet Union.

And it was to the Soviet people, to Soviet actors that were addressed the bouquets and the laurel garlands with ribbons in the colours of national flags, interwoven with the crimson ribbon of my own land.

And it was to the Soviet people that the happy smiles were addressed, and the joyful looks and the merry sound of applause.

And if the "memory's diary" has a table of contents (as of course it has, for we use it to seek our reminiscences), then over everything my memory retains of concerts in foreign lands must be written: "I am a Soviet actor."

When I am in Moscow I do not think about that. Here the only difference between me and my audiences is that I am an actor and they are workers or students. But abroad I am first and foremost a Soviet citizen, and that is the most important thing.

CHAPTER FIFTEEN
On Rereading the Book

And so I have reached the end of my book. I have described every step I took to my present profession, I have told how I worked on individual concert numbers, and, finally, I have given you an account of the concerts I appeared at.

I have just reread my manuscript and I realize that it is very difficult to transform myself into an objective reader, difficult to judge whether what I have written is serious and interesting.

That perhaps is why before dotting the i's and crossing the t's, before taking my leave of the reader, I felt the need to draw some general conclusions and return once more to the things I consider most important for myself.

* * *

For a long time the first chapter seemed to me to contain too many reminiscences and to be out of place in a book devoted to my profession, but after rereading the manuscript as a whole I realize that this chapter is necessary and that this is the right place to tell you why.

I was born in Moscow, in 1901. In other words, the first stage in the formation of my aesthetic taste—and the first stage is a very important one for every artist—took place before 1917, that is, in the years when symbolism and stylization were rampant, the years of *Mir Iskusstva,* of Leonid Andreyev, Balmont, Sollogub, Maeterlinck, Böcklin, Churlianis.

These were dangerous years. Not only the Petersburgers were almost completely infected by mysticism and stylization; far from all the much more stable Moscovites resisted the temptations of the fashionable aesthetics.

True, Levitan and Korovin stood firm, but Vrubel was severely affected, and Serov in the last period of his painting threw overboard all his talent and painted such stylized and artificial works as the portrait of Ida Rubinstein and the "Rape of Europa." There is no need for me to dwell on the Moscow magazine *Vesy* which held aloft the banner of the symbolists.

Even the Moscow Art Theatre, so young, sound and truly original, was somewhat infected by decadence. Luckily, it was not very serious, and productions like *The Blind, The Life of Man* and *The Drama of Life* did not succeed in spoiling *The Cherry Orchard, The Lower Depths, The Powers of Darkness* or *Uncle Vanya*.

Thanks to the fact that I belonged to an engineer's family which had absolutely no connection with the art world and thus did not feel the slightest influence of the aesthetic philosophy of those years, I remained immune to the infection

It was not my merit but my luck to which I owe that, but lucky I really was, for the puppet theatre offers particularly fertile ground for symbolism and stylization.

* * *

The fact that I did not take up my present profession at once and started with painting and drawing was also nothing to my credit, for I did not deliberately choose that way as a preparation for puppets. But that was lucky too and I ought to thank fate for it since without a love of representational art and without some professional knowledge of it I would have found my profession much more difficult. In fact, I doubt whether I would ever have taken it up.

Lucky for me too that I went on to the stage without any, not even amateur, training. Thanks to that, I did not bring with me to the stage any style of acting, any stereotype methods—for the simple reason that there was nowhere I could have picked them up. True, I was completely inexperienced and began in the theatre from scratch, but my teachers were experienced, sensitive and exacting. People of highly developed taste and of great integrity.

And the older I grow the more I feel how immensely valuable for me were the fourteen years I spent on the stage, first of a musical and then of the "legitimate" theatre.

* * *

In describing how I first became interested in puppets while engaging in "home theatricals" and in further describing my period of professional work, I have explained how I always tried out my work, as I still do, on different people—friends and acquaintances—inviting their opinions and advice. And here I should like once more to say how very important I believe this to be.

I am convinced that the most important condition for the growth of any artist is the ability to listen to other people and—above all—not to lose the taste for doing so as the years go by, a thing that often happens to those on whom fortune smiles.

One must always look for criticism and advice and find teachers everywhere; one must never take offence at the sharpest criticism; one must learn to look for the basic reason of every reproach, even when that reproach at first seems unfair.

That is why I am glad I have always worked in a team. Had it been otherwise, had I been only a concert artist during those long years, it would have been much more difficult for me to find advisers and teachers.

Working in two theatres has never interfered with my concert work; on the contrary, it has helped it, for I have continued to learn from many of my fellow-workers. Although today I head this theatrical group, I consider many of its members, whether they know it or not, my teachers, each in his own way. I am not afraid to submit my work —both as producer and as performer—to their judgement, and often I find their judgement final and binding on me.

Is this a deliberate giving up of individuality? An absence of personal convictions? No. It is putting them to the proof, defining them more precisely, and, in the final count, intensifying belief in them. Belief in the correctness of the path chosen is vital. Without it nothing can be accomplished.

If I try to learn from the many, this is far from meaning that I am prepared to agree with anything and everything, with any standpoint, any taste, any interpretation of art. On the contrary, there is a good deal I actively dislike and I do not hide this.

* * *

I have faithfully described the birth of my various show numbers. That birth sometimes appears accidental and even confused; I feel it is time to make clear whether or not I consider that those creative processes follow a tortuous path in accordance with certain laws, or whether this tortuosity simply comes from my personal shortcomings and my own inability to organize the process.

From what I have written the first step in the creation of a number may seem to be quite fortuitous.

I conceived a number from a newspaper and a so-called Gypsy ballad, and made a puppet with long arms. The number did not get across; but the puppet's arms moved wonderfully in dance rhythm, so the idea of "Habanera" came into my head and I got an item making fun of overdone Carmens.

It occurred to me to do the monologue of Pushkin's Miserly Knight. I made a special puppet for it, with a small head and no arms at all, using my own arms and my own unconcealed "living" hands instead. After the first try-out with Pushkin's text it was clear that my number was decadent, that is, contrary to Pushkin's idea, so I dropped it at once; but from the new form of that puppet I had invented stemmed the "Gypsy singer."

Further work on both numbers—on "Habanera" and on the "Singer," went more or less smoothly, but the birth of the theme itself appears accidental. Nevertheless I consider such "accidents" quite normal. Moreover, I do not think that the numbers themselves in their final theme, their final idea and final form are by any means accidental.

To make my point clearer I would cite the following well-known example.

Pushkin suggested the subject-matter of *Dead Souls* to Gogol.

Does that mean that Gogol chose the first theme of an interesting subject-matter that came to hand and that *Dead Souls* was only written thanks to a casual conversation which might never have taken place? Of course not. The theme of which the subject-matter was suggested was not at all accidental. It was precisely a Gogol theme and not a Pushkin theme. If Dostoyevsky had used that subject-matter we would have had quite a different work of art, with a different theme than Gogol's.

The theme lives in the artist's mind long before any thoughts of the form it shall take. It lives as a reflection of his environment and his own individuality. It lives, but it has not as yet been expressed in words or images. For it to take on its first tangible expression, the theme must encounter some kind of reality.

This encounter only appears accidental; it is in fact inevitable. Gogol bore in his mind the theme of the Russia of his times, which was his own conception of Russia. Pushkin's subject-matter gave Gogol the opportunity of embodying his theme, and so we got Korobochka and Plyushkin, Sobakevich and Manilov. But Pushkin's suggestion did no more than prompt the creation of these characters, it was not the reason for it.

Surikov, the painter, said that the image of the boyaryna Morozova suddenly came to him when he saw a black crow against white snow. This seems accidental enough, but that crow was only making concrete for Surikov the theme of the image which had been growing in his mind before then.

Newton grasped the law of gravity when he saw an apple fall from a tree. But the fall of an apple was not the *reason* for the discovery of that law, it only prompted the discovery.

The first concretization of a theme in an image often appears to happen unexpectedly, by accident, but that is a false impression, for no theme can take concrete shape which has not had long inner preparation before that moment of concretization, its first "materialization," one might say.

In chemistry there is a term "catalyst"; a catalyst is a substance which, while taking no part itself in a reaction, produces reactions between other substances by its presence.

Surikov's crow and Newton's apple served as catalysts. My puppet's "dancing" arms were like catalysts for the theme of second-rate opera; but that theme was my own, had been alive in me long before the appearance of those "dancing arms," and partially realized by me already in my number about a baritone singing "Toreador."

* * *

But however accidental the origin of a character may at first sight seem to be, the work on it must be controlled and directed by normal, merciless logic.

I suppose there is no declaration of creative method so harmful as the so-called "inspiration," in other words, counting on thoughtless illogical intuition.

While working on my show numbers and as a producer I try as hard as possible to test everything with the measure of logic.

And the unit of measurement can only be the ultimate aim of the theme—its idea. One must never deceive oneself, never try to justify one form or another unless it is justified by the theme and stands up to the test of the idea. Almost all my failures I have described were the result of my being inattentive to that truth.

But measuring one's work constantly by the idea means searching and persevering for the exact, the only form, since that form is the means of expressing the theme. An inexact form confuses the theme, destroys the idea and often replaces it, quite against the author's will, with another idea that is sometimes in direct contradiction to the first.

Lermontov's *Masquerade* is a completely realistic drama. The poison is mixed into an ordinary ice-cream, and when poisoned Nina feels unwell she asks her maid to loosen her corsets. The action takes place in the 19th century set in a number of private houses in St. Petersburg. Only in one scene do we see a masquerade; the other scenes are in the apartments of Arbenin, Nina, or Baroness Stral.

How then could Golovin have thought of designing the scenery for *Masquerade* at the Alexandrinsky Theatre in the same style that he used for Molière's *Don Juan,* with all that drapery and a heavy atmosphere of masquerade throughout?

He was influenced by the title, considering that it summed up the idea of the play and that the life of the society described by Lermontov was a masquerade where, behind masks of high-society convention, lay cynicism, evil and futility.

But Lermontov was writing about the concealed masquerade of the mind. Concealed and therefore tragic. And in this masquerade the masks are torn off by actions of the characters of the play and not by cascades of stylized drapery and symbolic backcloths and costumes.

The title of Ostrovsky's play *Don't Sit in Someone Else's Sledge* also sums up the idea, but it does not follow that this play ought to be put on with a proscenium arch decorated with a shaft-bow hung with little bells.

For all their beauty, theatricality and interest, Golovin's designs are wrong for the reason that Golovin did not measure them with Lermontov's real idea; instead of that he replaced that idea, destroyed everything that Lermontov had done in writing the drama of Arbenin and Nina in a setting of his own times, not stylized in a different epoch.

In describing my failure in putting on the Petrushka show and comparing my work on it with Zaitsev's organic work I said that in the long run I welcomed that sharp lesson, for it implanted in me an active distaste for any kind of stylization and imitativeness that has remained with me all my life.

In the second volume of this book, where I shall have to speak of the stylistic problems solved in my productions, I shall return to this question; now I want only to reiterate that I consider a work of art to be organic only when no intermediaries come between the artist and life, only when the artist sees life with his own eyes and not through the eyes of another artist or another period and when he speaks of what he sees in his own words and not in the translated language of stylization.

That organic perception of life is the only thing that I want to learn from the great figures of art; I wish to imitate only one of their gifts, the gift of imitating nobody. And that, in its turn, is possible only if everything you do in art is done not in a general sense but for something particular. In other words if you know the theme of your work, know its ultimate aim, its idea.

Antokolsky, one of the best 19th century Russian sculptors, made an excellent observation about the art of Ancient Greece when he said that "it teaches us to understand how highly important it is in art not to do nothing for the sake of nothing."

* * *

I have written about the themes of each of my numbers in what seems to me sufficient detail but I have not summed up those themes.

Now the time has come to do that, because it is only the sum-total of those themes that determines the general theme of my concert life, that is, the main thing I want to convey to my audience.

The violinist who plays the "Valse Sentimentale" answers to the audience for his choice and for his skill in conveying the theme to it, but Chaikovsky is responsible for the theme itself.

The actor too who at a concert recites "Mtsiri" or "Lovers of Meetings" answers for his choice of poems and for his ability in reciting them and putting across their content, their themes, but it is the authors, Lermontov and Mayakovsky, who are responsible for the themes.

But surely the author of the Gypsy romance I sing cannot be held responsible for what my little dogs make of that song which, after all, is only the material I am using to work out an altogether different, quite contrary theme.

So that means I am responsible to my audience not only as executant, as actor, but also as author, for in most cases I am the author of my numbers. And it follows that more than any other kind of actor I am responsible above all for *what* I am performing, for the theme, in fact, and only in the second place, like any other concert performer, for *how* I perform it, that is, how convincingly I unravel the theme.

What, in fact, have I performed on the concert stage? Has my work been of the slightest use to anyone?

Everybody works according to his ability, some doing more, some doing less, but everyone ought to know whether he is doing good or harm. Artists are not released from that obligation, especially as there are no works of art which do neither harm nor good. If a book, a picture or a melody is accepted by a reader, a spectator or a listener, it means that the reader, spectator or listener has had his emotions stirred; and emotions must be either harmful or useful. They cannot be neutral.

It is very easy to do harm with art, to arouse bad emotions, far easier than some artists, actors or writers think, because the action of a work of art is often stronger than the author himself, and the result of this action broader and more significant than may have been expected.

And just because a work of art has this power of arousing emotion, that is of getting to some extent out of control, any silly little cheap joke told on the stage may do much real harm. A banal description of the hero of a novel, a falsely acted love scene on the stage, a sentimentally sung ballad or aria at a concert can create a false and, therefore, harmful idea of authentic heroism, real love, real and not petty lyricism.

I should like to feel that the laughter with which the audience responds to my performances is something different from the laughter aroused by a vulgar joke. I should like to feel I have never aroused one bad emotion among my audience, that I have not done any harm.

On the contrary, I believe that, leaving aside the question of the scale of my usefulness, what I am doing is right, useful and good. I cannot but believe this, for otherwise I could not have worked and could not have been happy in that work.

Naturally, it is harder for me to define how my work has been useful than it is for another to do so; but, all the same, I shall try to define the main theme of my work.

If a man perceives life around him actively, then his theme will be the struggle to fulfil his desire, that is, to change that life. That is his dream, his love.

The greater the artist the more exactly will this theme be reflected in his works. And if we recall the names of really great artists it is this aspect of their work that we are most conscious of. The theme. Not always easy to define in words but an emotional perception of individual differences—expressed in images—arises in us the moment we mention the names of Pushkin, Tolstoi, Gorky.

However, with all their differences of themes there is something they have in common. An assertion of life.

It is precisely for the way they assert life, for their deep humanity, that I am so fond of Pushkin, Tolstoi and Gorky, although as an actor I was least successful in roles whose theme was their human quality, and found it much easier to play satirical, sharp character parts such as that of the intriguing Terapot in *La Périchole,* the crazed Strymodorus in *Lysistrata,* and the cold-blooded, complacent cynic, Professor Dossa in *Prayer for Life.*

When I had to act real grief or great love I immediately grew afraid of doing it falsely. I began to feel I was immodest or sentimental, and then, naturally, I closed up and felt constrained, and the creative spirit either disappeared altogether or came in jerks. But as soon as I had to make fun of sentimentality or artificiality, of stupidity or evil, the task became clear and those creative forces arose, without which it is impossible to play any role.

This preference for satirical and sharp character roles which I felt both in the musical and the legitimate theatre was much more marked in my work with puppets.

But there is nothing at all contradictory in the fact that I love Pierre Bezukhov but would find it much easier to act the part of little Napoleon "with a cold in the nose," or in the fact that I love the film

Chapayev but prefer to act my "Public Speaker" and my Pagliacci-Mussolini.

Are not Krylov, Saltykov-Shchedrin, Gogol, Ilf and Petrov, the Kukryniksy just as active fighters "for a better life" as Pushkin, Tolstoi and Gorky? The only difference lies in the means they use. They use laughter, irony, satire. And if they are not "the ploughers and the sowers" they are at least those who "root up the tree-stumps and burn the rubbish."

And I like to think that my life on the stage has in its small way been devoted to rooting up the tree-stumps and burning the rubbish.

I love the broad, tranquil, Russian character of Natasha Rostova with her real womanly and maternal love that asserts belief in a happiness full of vitality, not a hypocritical or sentimental one.

I love the wonderfully tender figure of the Jewish girl Golda, daughter of Tevye the milkman, created by Sholom-Aleikhem. I love the strength, boldness and modesty of her love.

And I want people who listen to "intimate" little songs and pseudo-Gypsy romances to stop thinking that those who sing them and the songs they sing are telling them about love.

I want to destroy the harm done by false language and false feelings, which hinder people seeing love.

I want to see girls in love envying Natasha Rostova and Golda and not the singer in the "fashionable" décolleté dress who sings "I Love and I Curse."

That is why I show this singer fiddling nervously with her necklace.

I love Sholokhov's Aksinya in *Quiet Flows the Don* with her strong physical passions and, hence, her purity. I love Gorky's Malva.

I do not want banal, vulgar performers of Carmen to deceive people, tricking them into thinking that their artificial passions are beautiful.

That is why I show my "Habanera."

I do not think that my number gives the slightest offence to those who love Mérimée and Bizet, or to those singers who resist the temptation of vulgarizing the role.

If the romance of literary work I perform is itself satirical then I follow the author and show Dargomyzhsky's "Titular Counsellor," "The Public Speaker" of Ilf and Petrov, Grechaninov's "That Summer Night," or Mikhalkov's fables. And if the author looks rubbish to me

I try to debunk him with laughter and sing "Fill up the Glass" or "Only Acquaintances."

My theme is the theme of the satire: the theme of struggle against false feelings, against false emotions, against banality, against wrong, against lies. Only a few of my numbers have a lyrical element: Musorgsky's "Lullaby," "Papanin's Polar Bear," and, to some extent, Chaikovsky's romance "We Were Sitting Alone." But in this category, too, there is a line of irony running parallel with the lyrical line.

However, in defining the theme of my work in art as satirical I am referring only to my work on the concert stage.

In my work as a producer, I try my hand at "positive" themes as well as satirical ones; these include the romantic-heroic genre, and I should add that themes of that category are not in any way "alien" to me as most of the plays I have produced at our theatre were written specially for us or were even born in the theatre itself, and in those births I have always played a direct part.

Now all that remains is to draw the conclusions from the chapter "Contact with my Audiences."

I wrote that chapter because my work in entirety—like the work of any actor, indeed—would be inconceivable, impossible in fact without audiences.

The actor is the man who plays. "Plays" is an inexact and, in my opinion, wrong expression. For the actor does not play, as a child plays, by himself and for himself.

The word "actor" derives from the word "to act," that is, it is connected with the idea of action. Though more exact this does not define the profession of actor either, because every living person acts. The engineer, the miner, the doctor, the soldier, the athlete—they all act.

What distinguishes the actor is the fact that he shows his action. And the words "he shows" are the important words in the definition of an actor.

If he shows it means he must be showing to somebody. You can't make a show of anything to nobody.

And there can be no idea of "creative processes" in the making of a role, a number or a production without thought being paid to the audience that has to be faced.

Those who say they work "for themselves" are either not telling the truth or are simply incapable of analysing the motives of their work.

"To show" one's work, to act before an audience is shameful and bad only when it is exhibitionism, which is a prostitution of one's qualities.

But if the actor has a real aim, if he feels his "show" to be something necessary, then he is doing something real.

He is creating art.

To show life on the stage, to show with vivid, graphic conviction what real heroism and real love are, to unbare falseness, lies and vulgarity, is to do what the writer is doing when he describes life in words and forces the reader to *imagine* everything the spectator can *see*.

And if you have to have someone to show it to, this someone—the audience, in fact—becomes a source of energy to the actor, not only in the moment of performance but during preparation for that performance. You cannot think about *what* you are doing without thinking about *whom* you are doing it for.

It is impossible to work "in general," to work without addressing yourself to some audience.

That is why in describing my methods of work I felt obliged to describe those for whom I work.

I do not know how far I have succeeded but I beg you not to consider what I have written about my meetings with the audience as mere reminiscence.

My memory's "diary" is not finished. Every day I add to it new pages.

This book is not an account of a former profession but of my present profession. My "contacts with my audiences" continue.

My audiences are citizens of the Soviet Union, my fellow-citizens.

And as making contact with them is the ultimate aim of my work my book had to end with an account of those meetings.

* * *

Rereading my manuscript I realized that many of my readers are justified in complaining that I have left many highly important problems unsolved and that the book gives an impression of being unfinished.

I am aware of that, but, nevertheless, I deliberately have not raised those questions which belong more properly to an account of my work as producer at the State Central Puppet Theatre.

I have said little about the puppet as actor, about the puppet's expressive powers because in my book about the theatre I shall have all the puppets of the theatre at my disposal and they sometimes number more than two hundred for a single production. Besides, different productions employ an enormous variety of systems of puppets and each of them possesses its own expressiveness.

I have said practically nothing about the qualities an actor requires to play with puppets as I shall be able later to introduce examples not only from my own work as a concert performer but from the work of many actors playing a great number of roles at our theatre.

I shall be able to write about a collective and about the remarkable process by which a play is born, being a product of the imagination and talent of every single person who takes part in that production.

I shall be able to tell about the hard and crooked path of searching for a repertoire suitable for puppets.

And only then shall I be able to reply to the question that is most important to a man of my profession. It is the question of the place of the puppet theatre among other varieties and forms of the theatrical art, of the art of the puppeteer as a special, very powerful and active arm of the theatre.

Moscow 1950

www.ingramcontent.com/pod-product-compliance
Lightning Source LLC
Chambersburg PA
CBHW020647230426
43665CB00008B/344